Research and Practice in Applied Linguistics

General Editors: **Christopher N. Candlin** and **David R. Hall**, Linguistics Department, Macquarie University, Australia.

All books in this series are written by leading researchers and teachers in Applied Linguistics, with broad international experience. They are designed for the MA or PhD student in Applied Linguistics, TESOL or similar subject areas and for the language professional keen to extend their research experience.

D1522084

Marilyn Martin-Jones
BILINGUALISM

Martha Pennington
PRONUNCIATION

Norbert Schmitt
VOCABULARY

Helen Spencer-Oatey and Peter Franklin
INTERCULTURAL INTERACTION

Devon Woods and Emese Bukor
INSTRUCTIONAL STRATEGIES AND PROCESSES IN LANGUAGE EDUCATION

Research and Practice in Applied Linguistics
Series Standing Order ISBN 1–4039–1184–3 hardcover
Series Standing Order ISBN 1–4039–1185–1 paperback
(*outside North America only*)

You can receive future titles in this series as they are published by placing a standing order. Please contact your bookseller or, in case of difficulty, write to us at the address below with your name and address, the title of the series and one of the ISBNs quoted above.

Customer Services Department, Macmillan Distribution Ltd, Houndmills, Basingstoke, Hampshire RG21 6XS, England

Tasks in Second Language Learning

Virginia Samuda and Martin Bygate

Lancaster University

First published 2008 by
PALGRAVE MACMILLAN
Houndmills, Basingstoke, Hampshire RG21 6XS and
175 Fifth Avenue, New York, N.Y. 10010
Companies and representatives throughout the world

PALGRAVE MACMILLAN is the global academic imprint of the Palgrave Macmillan division of St. Martin's Press, LLC and of Palgrave Macmillan Ltd. Macmillan® is a registered trademark in the United States, United Kingdom and other countries. Palgrave is a registered trademark in the European Union and other countries.

ISBN-13: 978-1-4039-1186-5 hardback
ISBN-10: 1-4039-1186-X hardback
ISBN-13: 978-1-4039-1187-2 paperback
ISBN-10: 1-4039-1187-8 paperback

This book is printed on paper suitable for recycling and made from fully managed and sustained forest sources.

A catalogue record for this book is available from the British Library.

A catalogue record for this book is available from the Library of Congress.

10   9   8   7   6   5   4   3   2   1
17   16   15   14   13   12   11   10   09   08

Printed and bound in Great Britain by
Antony Rowe Ltd, Chippenham and Eastbourne

To the memory of Chris Brumfit

Contents

Acknowledgements

Our most central acknowledgments should be apparent through the references in these pages. We owe particular debts of gratitude to tutors, colleagues and students, through the years at Lancaster, Leeds, London, Manchester, Michigan, Oregon, Reading and Sonoma; to our patient and constructive editors; and to our enduringly supportive families, including Dave, for never forgetting to ask whether we'd finished writing this book.

Lauzerte
Summer 2007

Introduction

Quote 1.1   Dewey on educative, uneducative and miseducative tasks

If one means by a 'task' simply an undertaking involving difficulties that have to be overcome, then children, youth, and adults alike require tasks in order that there may be continued development. But if one means by a task something that has no interest, makes no appeal, that is wholly alien and hence uncongenial, the matter is quite different. Tasks in the former sense are educative because they supply an indispensable stimulus to thinking, to reflective inquiry. Tasks in the latter sense signify nothing but sheer strain, constraint, and the need of some external motivation for keeping at them. They are *un*educative because they fail to introduce a clearer consciousness of ends and a search for proper means of realization. They are *mis*educative, because they deaden and stupefy; they lead to that confused and dulled state of mind that always attends an action carried on without a realizing sense of what it is all about. They are also miseducative because they lead to dependence upon external ends; the child works simply because of the pressure of the taskmaster, and diverts his energies just in the degree in which this pressure is relaxed; or he works because of some alien inducement – to get some reward that has no intrinsic connection with what he is doing.
(1913/1975: 54–6)

This book explores the 'educative', 'uneducative' and 'miseducative' properties of tasks in second language education. As part of the raw material that second language teachers, learners and researchers work with in different ways, tasks have been an element in second language teaching and research for over 30 years, and yet their use continues to invite controversy and debate. One of the aims of this book is to explore why this should be so, and to consider what people do to make tasks educative or uneducative, why this can happen and what the alternatives might be.

Part 1
Background

Introduction

Part 1 offers a broad overview of the historical and conceptual background from which 'tasks' have emerged as a significant force in second language education and research. The use of holistic activities for learning is not unique to language education, and has been one of the major focuses of educational debate over the last century. Nor indeed are tasks exclusive to education: they are a key research construct throughout the social sciences. Hence in Part 1 we review the construct of 'task' from a broad perspective, before narrowing the discussion to the use of tasks within language education.

1
Language Use, Holistic Activity and Second Language Learning

1.1 Holistic activity

In talking about the role of tasks in second language learning, our starting point is the assumption that the aim of second/foreign language teaching is to develop the ability to use the target language. By 'use' we mean that the language is used not only to practise or show mastery, but also for information (personal and professional), for social, political and artistic purposes, as well as for aesthetic pleasure. One way of engaging language use is through holistic activity.

Concept 1.1   Holistic activity

Use is 'holistic' in the sense that it involves the learners' knowledge of the different sub-areas of language – phonology, grammar, vocabulary and discourse – to make meanings. Holistic activities contrast with analytical activities, in which phonology, grammar, vocabulary and discourse are each taught and studied separately, and not used together. Analytical activities are designed to reduce the number of aspects of language which the learners have to attend to, so they can concentrate more narrowly on a selected target feature, as in a pronunciation exercise focusing on a selected phonological contrast, for example. Holistic activities involve the learner in dealing with the different aspects of language together, in the way language is normally used. Much first language learning occurs through holistic activities, and it seems likely that holistic activities can also play a significant role in second language learning, teaching and testing.

Tasks are one kind of holistic activity. The holistic nature of tasks can be represented schematically in a diagram such as the following:

In Figure 1.1, the words *in italics* are points where the learner is required to make a choice. The overall purpose is broadly set between teacher and

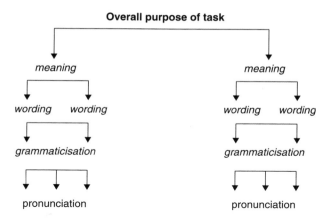

Figure 1.1   Schematic structure of a task

learners. The italics indicate that to achieve this purpose the learner must choose and sequence relevant meanings, words and grammar, with the pronunciation following in the light of that choice. By involving learners in making purposeful, on-line choices of meaning and form, a task engages holistic language use: through engaging with the task, learners are led to work with and integrate the different aspects of language for a larger purpose.

In contrast, analytical language activities have been traditionally used in language teaching to focus attention on a pre-selected language item or items, as in a drill involving the production of a particular vowel sound or a minimal pair contrast without attention to meaning.

Concept 1.2   Analytical activity

An exclusively analytical activity, like an exercise focusing on a single verb form, would predetermine the meaning, or the meaning and word, or the meaning, word and grammatical structure, or even the meaning, word, grammatical structure and pronunciation, with the learner being required to work with the target forms at some point of focus isolated by the exercise.

The argument of this book is that it is in holistic language work that key language learning processes take place, and that tasks are invaluable in achieving this purpose. Yet, although tasks seem to offer a key resource for language learning, the very fact that they are holistic creates a fresh series of educational challenges. For, like any teaching activity, tasks need to be seen to serve a learning goal in the eyes of the learners and teachers who use them. This raises important central questions, in particular:

- What goals can different tasks serve for different students?
- How can tasks be exploited by teachers and learners to meet those goals?
- What are the strengths and weaknesses of different tasks, and of different ways of using them?
- What could learners and teachers usefully know about tasks that the tasks are made to serve learners' and teachers' ends?

An enduring pedagogical challenge – and a recurring theme in this book – is how to balance a focus on aspects of the target language in ways that enhance learning, without losing the overall holistic quality of normal language use.

1.2   A sample task: Things in Pockets (TIP)

Example 1.1 illustrates what we mean by 'task' and the weight of some of these questions. In this task, participants are given a bag of objects, allegedly the contents of a person's pockets, and are invited to work in small groups to speculate on the identity of that person. Each group needs to reach a consensus on their ideas concerning the person's identity, presenting and justifying their conclusions to the rest of the class, first as an informal oral presentation and finally in written form as a poster or report.[1] In this version, the groups use a chart to record their initial hypotheses about the person's identity under categories such as age, gender, occupation, etc. The chart also requires groups to register the degree of probability/possibility of each initial hypothesis:

Example 1.1   A sample task

Things in Pockets

An overcoat was found on a plane after a flight from San Francisco to London. The objects that you have in front of you were all found in the pockets of that overcoat. Can they tell us anything about the owner?

As a group, look at everything carefully and share your ideas about the identity of the owner of the overcoat. Be ready to present your group's ideas about the person to the rest of the class and to explain how certain you are about your ideas.

---

[1] A different version of this task appears in H. Riggenbach and V. Samuda (2000) *Grammar Dimensions: Form, Meaning, Use: Book 2*, Boston, MA: Heinle & Heinle.

Example 1.1   (Continued)

You can use the chart to organise your ideas and to show how certain you are about each one. For example, if you are 100% certain that you know the person's name, write it in column 3 (100% certain). But if you are not at all certain about the person's name, use Column 1 (less than 50% certain). If you are almost certain that you know this person's name, use Column 2 (90% certain).

	Less than 50% certain (it's possible)	90% certain (it's probable)	100% certain (it's certain)
Name			
Sex			
Age			
Marital status			
Occupation			
Likes and interests			
Recent activities			
Any other ideas			

In the rest of this book, we will be drawing on this task (henceforth TIP) as a reference point for highlighting issues involved in task use, design and research.

In Example 1.1 we see what the task looks like as it appears on the page, as set out by a materials writer or task designer. While this reflects how the designer envisages the task unfolding when enacted, it does not in itself say anything about what actually *will* happen or about the different ways that learners and teachers might redefine and reinterpret the designer's intentions. To highlight areas of potential difference between the task on paper and what happens when it is enacted, Breen (1987) distinguishes between 'task-as-workplan' and 'task-in-process':

Quote 1.2   Breen on task-as-workplan and task-in-process

Any language learning task will be reinterpreted by a learner in his or her own terms. This implies that a pre-designed task – the task-as-workplan – will be changed the moment the learner acts upon it. The task-as-workplan will be redrawn so that the learner can relate to it in the first place and, thereby, make it manageable. ... When considering what happens during language learning tasks, we can initially distinguish between the original task-as-workplan and the actual *task-in-process*. It is the latter which generates typically diverse learning outcomes and the quality and efficacy of any task must be traced directly to its use during teaching and learning. (Breen, 1987: 24–5)

Example 1.1 then is an illustration of the TIP task-as-workplan. Example
1.2 is an illustration of the same task-in-process. It shows students engaging with the TIP task as part of their normal classroom coursework in
a 'low intermediate/high beginner' intensive English pre-academic programme in a North American university. The extract in Example 2.1 is
taken from an early phase of the task: the teacher has divided the class
into groups and invited them to brainstorm their initial thoughts about
the identity of the person. The learners in this example are four young
women – three Japanese and one Swiss-French – in their early twenties
who were familiar with each other as classmates, and who also associated
with each other as friends outside the classroom. Here they are looking
at the objects, and having established the owner as male, are trying to
figure out his likely marital status on the basis of a diary and other
personal items:

Example 1.2   Sample task-in-process: Things in Pockets

Group 1: Marital status episode

```
1    A:      Maybe he divorced
     C:      Why?
     A:      Because Paula Paula maybe Paula his girlfriend
     N:      Divorced?
5    C:              Can I see?
     Y:              Yeah at lunchtime (indicating diary)
     C:      Or, or
     N:      Yes, but
     C:              he married but he has girlfriend
10   A:      Not divorced?
     C:      Not divorced but he has another girlfriend
     A:      Ahh, it's possible
     Y:      If, if he married and he has girlfriend why write down in schedule
     A:      [noooo]
     C:      [noooo]
     (laughter)
15   A:      Ohhh
     C:      Divorced
     N:      (reading from diary) Wice presi vice president lunch vice president
     Y:      His company?
     N:      Or
     Y:      (reading from diary) Anniversary
20   C:      What's this thing?
     Y:      Anniversary, wedding anniversary (.) He's married
     C:      {huh?
     A:      {huh?
     Y:      Wedding anniversary
```

Example 1.2   (Continued)

25	C:	Anniversary?
	A:	huh?
	N:	But maybe something something
	A:	huh?
	N:	Maybe just anniversary not wedding
30	A:	for him? or or=
	C:	=friend?
	Y:	if [he]
	N:	[no] because here, here (points to diary), he have golf
	A:	Yeah
35	C:	Yeah
	(laughter)	
	N:	No (.) Play golf
	Y:	So he married (.) Wedding anniversary
	N:	Maybe it's just, it just uh=
	A:	=write down
40	N:	Yeah
	Y:	Ohh
	N:	Yeah maybe ten years that he will be married (.) because he play golf not
	Y:	But daytime
	N:	Yes, but
45	Y:	Yeah his wife? I don't know
	(laughter)	
	C:	He married uh one year ago then he=
	N:	=Yeah maybe=
	A:	=Divorced
	C:	No don't divorce but he married uh maybe one month ago no one year ago and he still play with her
50	N:	Maybe
	A:	Or my, my opinion
	N:	Or may, oh sorry
	Y:	You see Paula is his wife
	C:	Yeah
55	N:	Yes, but why Paula send him this (showing document)
	Y:	He's busy (laughs)
	N:	(reading from document) Sorry I didn't meet you on Sunday
	C:	Yeah I think she is not wife
	N:	No (reading from document) because I was worried that somebody might see us together
60	C:	Huh?
	N:	(reading) Please forgive me
	A:	(reading) Call me [soon]
	N:	[call me] soon
	A:	No, not wife

65	C:	No, no
	A:	Huh? Wait (.) Somebody?
	N:	Yeah
	A:	Ahhh, he's married
	Y:	Yeah
	A:	He's married
70	C:	He's married
	A:	Ohh [wow]
	C:	[wow]
	A:	Sure?
	C:	Sure
	(laughter)	
75	Y:	Trust me
	(laughter)	

This extract illustrates one episode in a very early phase of the task-in-process, a phase in which the learners are exploring possible interpretations of part of the task materials. The instances of laughter, the number of overlapping turns and the sustained focus on one topic suggest a high level of engagement; much of the talk here is highly elliptical, possibly reflecting the shared frame of reference of the task materials, the social relationships among the participants, as well as the in-group flavour of this phase of the task, where ideas are being developed collaboratively in private, and not yet ready for public consumption. In terms of the workplan, we might expect that the demands of later phases of the task (presentation and justification of ideas to the rest of the class and the teacher; writing up final conclusions, for example) to give rise to other kinds of talk. But we cannot be sure of this from the workplan itself; nor can we be sure of this from this extract of this phase of one small episode of the task-in-process. The intricacy of the relationships between phases of the task-as-workplan and phases of the task-in-process and how those relationships relate to our understanding of the use of tasks in second language pedagogy and research is a recurring theme in this book, and we will be returning at various points to these examples later.

1.3   Features of tasks for second language learning

In this section we draw on the TIP task to illustrate a number of general features of second language tasks. First, as can be seen, the task is *holistic* in the sense that it requires learners to decide on potential relevant meanings, and use the phonology, grammar, vocabulary and discourse structures of the language to convey these in order to carry out the task.

A second feature of any task is the need to achieve *one or more meaning-ful outcomes*. This is essential for the dynamic of the task. In the TIP task, the learners were asked to come up with a description of the likely owner of the objects. Depending on the teacher's instructions this could take one of various forms: written, oral or possibly a non-verbal representation, such as a picture, set of notes or ID forms, selected from an array. What these have in common is a target outcome in the form of a verbal or non-verbal representation of information. That is, it is not sufficient for them to produce accurate language: they have to produce a pragmatically credible response.

Third, the task could not work without the *input material* – in this case, the objects and the instructions. Here, the input material is the springboard for all that follows. Changing the objects or the instructions could change the procedures the students follow or the target outcome, or both. Input material is therefore an essential element.

In following the instructions in order to work towards the task outcome, learners engage in a *process*. 'Task process' refers to any language process(es) used in working towards an outcome. This can include the language used to plan and organise the work, to distribute sub-tasks, to monitor progress, to identify and share information, to suggest or hypothesise missing information, interpretations or solutions; to evaluate, counter, agree/disagree; and to negotiate an outcome such as a conclusion, solution, report or graphic representation. Both the product and the process are by definition necessary: without a target product there is no call for the process. But equally, without a process learners cannot achieve a product. Sometimes particular task processes are targeted by the teacher, whether explicitly or implicitly. Sometimes they are shaped by the way the task has been designed. Sometimes task processes are left to the initiative of the learners.

The task also involves a number of different *phases*. This is one key dimension where tasks differ from analytical activities like drills or exercises, which once started involve the same operations from beginning to end. From a task-as-workplan perspective, the phasing of a task generally involves breaking down the overall task into a series of interlocking steps (see Example 1.1) with the aim of making the task more manageable. Here phases might be framed in terms of an initial search for information contained in or relating to the input material, an exchange and pooling of opinions and ideas relating to that information, leading to some form of synthesis based on the demands of the task. These phases reflect a route for moving through the task envisaged by a task designer or teacher. From a task-in-process perspective, however, the task is phased by the actual strategies that the learners use at different points in the activity. Possible examples here are an initial organisation and administration phase as learners orient themselves to the input material and to ways of engaging with it, followed by a phase of pooling, checking and exchanging preliminary ideas (as in Example 1.2), followed by a phase involving reorganisation and reworking of those ideas, a phase involving coordination and consolidation, a phase involving rehearsal and further reworking and checking, and finally a phase involving public presentation. These may or may not correspond with the phases set out in the workplan since the task-in-process is phased by the learners' need to make the content and the language manageable as the task unfolds. Phasing, then, is an element of the workplan and process and may be accomplished differently in each. An important point here is that the different phases of a task can serve different functions, and thus may give rise to different types of exchange and different types of talk. This means that generalisations about generic features of 'task interaction' or 'task talk' may be of limited value without reference to the phase of the task in which they occur.

Pedagogically, it is important for teachers to know what aspects of the language are being targeted, whether in terms of product or processes, since without this *knowledge/awareness* they cannot prepare and brief the students or provide relevant feedback. Likewise, in research terms, knowing the likely scope of a particular task with different kinds of students in different contexts is likely to be useful in developing the design and use of a repertoire of tasks. It may also shed light on second language learning. Language development is complex: it involves a number of distinct, though related processes such as social interaction, perception, ideational comprehension, motor control, contextual mapping and strategic control. Hence there are multiple ways in which a task can be exploited to contribute to development and a number of ways in which they can be researched. So although both the pedagogic use and the study of tasks start from the assumption that holistic activities in second language teaching are valuable, there are as many distinct ways of using and researching them as there are ways of conceptualising holistic language use and holistic language learning.

Another major factor that is important for pedagogical exploitation concerns *conditions,* which in any context influence the way people work. 'Conditions' can refer to the use and manipulation of external pressures, such as the imposition of time pressure, the use of competition or collaboration or both, and provision of pre-, while and post-task support. 'Conditions' can also include the atmosphere in and ethos of the class, the attitudes of the group members, their level of proficiency, how far teacher and students attend to the processes and outcomes of the task, and how far work on the task is perceived to contribute to learning.

Finally, the *different uses* of a task can be worth exploring. A task like TIP can fulfil a number of aims. For example, it can be used to raise awareness of a language area which learners need to get to grips with; it can be used to encourage them to use what they already know to communicate in an area they have difficulty with; it can be used to give them the opportunity to improve their handling of a particular area; or it can be used to give them a basis for reflection for a future task.

The features of a task such as TIP can be summarised as follows:

Concept 1.3   General features of a task

1. It involves holistic language use.
2. It requires a meaningful target outcome or outcomes.
3. It necessarily involves some individual and group processes.
4. It depends on there being some input material.
5. It is made up of different phases.
6. It is important for teachers – and at some point the learners – to know what is being targeted in the language learning purpose.
7. The conditions under which it is implemented impact on process and outcome and can be manipulated and variously exploited.
8. It can be used for different pedagogic purposes at different stages of learning.

1.4   The use of tasks for second language learning: some key questions

Apart from the first general defining characteristic, the remaining seven all make explicit a wide range of ways in which tasks can be exploited to contribute to language learning, and raise questions that we could usefully know more about.

For instance, in terms of process, we might find it useful to understand the ways in which students can work through a task, and how far any differences affect learning. It might help to know how far the task can be made to work at different levels of proficiency and what happens in each case. It could be enlightening to understand the different options that teachers have to introduce tasks, to monitor tasks and to provide post-task follow-up, and to see whether they work in different ways, and why. In the classroom from which Example 1.2 was taken, this task was used at the start of a cycle of work and was followed by teacher input. (A full description of a study of this task can be found Samuda, 2001: Part 2, 7.1). But the same task could be used in many other ways, so it would be valuable to see how it can be deployed at other points in a cycle of work, and how else it could be synchronised with the teacher's input. Also, we do not know how far a task of a particular format, such as this one, can be recycled to reuse language that is becoming familiar while introducing new language. And we do not know how this task differs from others.

So far we have characterised 'task' as a set of general elements, drawn from a single example; this has been done to sketch some of the broad questions that this book seeks to explore and to create a shared frame of reference for the background issues that we turn to next – influences from general education and human sciences research. However, later in Part 1 we return to the issue of what a task is and what it is not by exploring in more detail some of the ways that second language pedagogic tasks have been defined in the literature and some of the challenges that these definitions present.

1.5   Summary: the general elements of a task

We have noted that a task is a holistic activity, and that such activities are important to the extent that they target and enable the development of appropriate second language processes and appropriate language products. As we have seen, however, holistic activities of necessity involve the use of all aspects of language, and allow more choice than analytical exercises. This means that they can be harder for teachers and testers to use, since the language work will be relatively more complex and less predictable. For this reason it is worth attempting to understand how tasks work. A first step has been to identify some of the key elements involved. With these in mind, the aims of this book are to promote understanding of tasks for four main reasons:

1. To support development in the design of tasks.
2. To improve our understanding of how to select, adapt and use tasks in the classroom with different learners.
3. To increase our understanding of how to stimulate classroom language use.
4. To increase our understanding of the processes of language learning, and in particular the dynamic relationship between language knowledge and language use.

Our overall aim is to promote an empirical approach – to explore the use of tasks, their potential, ways of improving their design or use, and if necessary to seek out and develop alternative resources for achieving our aims.

2
Holistic Tasks in an Educational Context: Some Key Issues

Many of the principles underlying the design and use of what we now call 'tasks' in second language pedagogy owe their genealogy to developments in general education over the last century. In this chapter, we trace some of those developments. We start with the influence of Dewey and a number of issues that his work brings into focus. These are:

- experience as a catalyst for learning;
- the role of personal relevance and purposeful activity in mediating the world of the learner and classroom learning;
- the role of functional relevance in classroom learning;
- the roles of learners as active agents in their own learning.

Then through a series of brief illustrations we explore how these issues variously come into play in the work of educators centrally concerned with relationships between experience and learning, with examples from Freinet, Kilpatrick, Kolb and Freire.

From here we explore connections between these themes and aspects of the work of Bruner, focusing on:

- the organisation of knowledge and learning for use;
- the complementariness of the development of analytical and intuitive thought;
- the building of systematic relationships between concrete experiences and broader generalisation.

After this, we draw on the work of Barnes to explore aspects of these themes in relation to the role of classroom talk in the development of knowledge, focusing on:

- relationships between process and product in learning;
- the roles of exploratory and final draft talk in learning.

The themes brought into focus here, together with the pedagogic challenges that they pose, will recur in various forms throughout this book.

2.1   The influence of Dewey: experience and learning

Since the nineteenth century, educationists have been increasingly concerned to make school learning socially purposeful or functional. By 1913 Dewey was arguing that classroom learning needed to be focused and shaped so that it met the personally held interests that pupils brought with them, and the ends that they held in sight:

Quote 2.1   Dewey on means and end

The problem may be stated as one of the relations of means and end. Anything indifferent or repellent becomes of interest when seen as a means to an end already commanding attention. Or seen as an end that will allow means already under control to secure further movement and outlet. But, in normal growth the interest in means is not externally tied onto the interest in an end; it suffuses, saturates, and thus transforms it.
(Dewey, 1913/1975: 25–6)

In presenting material as a string of received facts unconnected to pupils' interests and personal goals, 'traditional' classroom learning was thus seen by Dewey as essentially 'abnormal'.

Quote 2.2   Dewey on traditional classroom learning

Learning here means acquisition of what already is incorporated in books and in the heads of the elders. Moreover, that which is taught is thought of as essentially static. It is taught as a finished product, with little regard either to the ways in which it was originally built up or to changes that will surely occur in the future.
(1938/1963: 19)

In this approach to education, a focus on 'finished product' treats learning as a simple accretion of items of knowledge, unconnected both from each other and from pupils' broader experiences of the world. It is based on a static body of knowledge which is backward-looking, at best reflecting the competencies of competent users, rather than those of learners. For Dewey, this leads to a fundamental misconception of the relationship between learning and the outside world:

Quote 2.3 Dewey on school learning

Almost everyone has had occasion to look back upon his school days and wonder what has become of the knowledge he was supposed to have amassed during his years of schooling, and why it is that the technical skills he acquitted have to be learned over again in changed form in order to stand him in good stead. Indeed, he is lucky who does not find that in order to make progress, in order to go ahead intellectually, he does not have to unlearn much of what he learned in school. These questions cannot be disposed of by saying that the subjects were not actually learned, for they were learned at least sufficiently to enable a pupil to pass examination in them. One trouble is that the subject-matter in question was learned in isolation; it was put, as it were, in a water-tight compartment. When the question is asked, then, what has become of it, where has it gone to, the right answer is that it is still there in the special compartment in which it was originally stowed away. But it was segregated when it was acquired and hence is so disconnected from the rest of experience that it is not available under actual conditions of life.
(Dewey, 1938/1963: 47–8)

Dewey argued for a congruent relationship between pupils' larger purposes and any narrowly focused learning activities. Here, personal relevance is the key. Thus in his view (1917/1963) a functional approach helped to make the subject as a whole relevant by connecting it to personal experience. The implication is that we need to seek out new ways of teaching so that the content is accessible, useful and relevant given the levels of experience and understanding of learners. Thus disciplinary content needs to be made available to learners in terms of their own experience, and how it relates to what they already know. To this end, we need to seek out ways that pupils may be brought into active mental engagement with new content and in ways that relate to what is already familiar. For Dewey, active mental engagement entailing the integration of what is known with what is new is necessarily effortful.

Quote 2.4 Dewey on good teaching

Good teaching, in other words, is teaching that appeals to established powers while it includes such *new* material as will demand their redirection for a new end, this redirection requiring thought – intelligent effort.
(Dewey, 1913/1975: 58)

Although experience provides the site for effective learning to take place, it also raises its own set of pedagogic challenges: how to uncover ways in which appropriate pedagogical experiences can be provided for learners in sequences that will make school subjects relevant. Some macro-element is necessary to provide a credible, motivating context for 'intelligent effort'. For Dewey, the macro-element for bringing together the learner's experience of the real world, the logic of the subject matter and the accumulated experience of educators was through the use of 'overt and executive activities', in which the learner learns through the interaction between thought and action.

Concept 2.1   Overt and executive activities

By 'overt and executive activities' Dewey was referring to activities in which the learner had to make some decisions or perform a skill, what others have referred to as the use of 'procedural knowledge'.
(Johnson, 1996)

The search for functional relevance grounded in experience and realised through holistic activity has underpinned the development of various pedagogic initiatives since Dewey's time; some of these have been directly influenced by Dewey's thinking and others have developed independently. To illustrate, we begin with two examples from the early part of the twentieth century: the work of Freinet, developed independently of Dewey's; and the work of Kilpatrick, developed with explicit reference to aspects of Dewey's thinking.

2.2   Experience and learning: some pedagogic examples

2.2.1   Freinet

Freinet, working in rural primary schools in France between the First and the Second World Wars, wrote:

Quote 2.5   Freinet on sense of purpose

L'enfant qui sent un but à son travail et qui peut se donner tout entier à une activité non plus scolaire mais simplement sociale et humaine, cet enfant sent que se libère en lui un besoin puissant d'agir, de chercher, de créer.

[The child who has a sense of purpose in their work and who can entirely give themselves over to an activity so that it is no longer schoolwork, but just social human activity – that child feels come to life a potent need to do, to search, to create.]
(Freinet, 1971: 88)

Freinet's pedagogic practices, which were embedded in the child's natural environment, amply illustrate this point. Here is an extract from a colleague's observation of his interaction with a group of children whom he had taken out of the classroom for a walk in the countryside they were familiar with. In this extract we see how Freinet exploited this familiarity to draw his pedagogic focus from the children's existing knowledge and experience, thereby making the task of producing descriptions of locations, or calculating measurements, functionally relevant:

Quote 2.6   Freinet drawing on his pupils' experience

- M'sieur, disait Lulu, là-bas, je vois ma mére dans mon champ!
- Où? Où?
- Explique bien, Lulu, disait le maître; explique, pour que nous la voyions aussi.
- Regarde, là-bas: tu vois la route? Tu vois le contour du pont? Eh bien, monte le petit chemin: tu vois le grand chêne? Eh ben! C'est un peu plus loin de ce côté. ...
- M'sieur, on est haut, ici!
- On est plus haut que le château?

Et des comparaisons s'ensuivaient des évaluations de distances, de mesures, des notions de longueurs, et voilà le point de départ d'une excellente leçon de calcul donnée à même la vie.'

- [Sir, Lulu says, over there, I can see my mother in my field!
- Where? Where?
- Explain it properly, Lulu, says the teacher; explain so that we can see her as well.
- Look, over there: see the road? See the edge of the bridge? Well, follow the little pathway: you see the big oak? Well! It's a bit further on along there.
- ...
- Sir, we are high up here!
- Are we higher than the château?

And comparisons followed on from the estimates of distances, measures, notions of length, and that was the starting point for an excellent lesson in arithmetic, based in life itself.]

(Freinet, 1971: 24–5)

In Freinet's work, then, learning arises from the learner's experience; it is given a purpose by that experience and is shaped by the teacher's mediating role in enabling connections between individual experiences and broader generalisations. Freinet's search for functional relevance is perhaps most famously exemplified in the printing press he set up in his primary school.

This, he believed, would help his pupils to see writing as socially functional and as a result enable them to become effective readers and writers – engaging children in the act of printing would bring them into contact with the act of writing, which itself could be grounded in the child's own priorities. By 1926, children in his primary school were producing printed bulletins to exchange with twinned schools, and some were starting to produce little illustrated books (Freinet, 1971: 55). Within a year or so of the first exchanges, newsletters were exploring questions which could still provide a focus for pedagogic task research today.

Quote 2.7   Freinet on the use of the printing press as a means of linking experience and learning: eliciting pupils' views

L'imprimerie dans ses rapports avec le travail scolaire:

a) Suivez-vous seulement l'intérêt dominant de la classe, selon le travail et les saisons, ou bien adoptez-vous des centres d'intérêt etablis d'avance? Comment procéder? Quels résultats semblent obtenus?
b) Comment lier l'enseignment à l'imprimerie? Notamment: quel parti tirer des imprimés journaliers ou bi-mensuels reçus par échange? Qu'en faire après la lecture? Quelle est l'utilisation possible? Peut-on supprimer des manuels? Lesquels? Comment?
c) Comment relier les imprimés? Quel est le format le plus pratique?
d) Quelle a été l'appréciation de votre I.P., de votre directeur, de la population?

[The printing press and its relationship to the work of the class:

a) Do you simply follow the main interest of the class, depending on the work schedule and the movement of the seasons, or do you instead adopt centres of interest drawn up in advance? How to proceed? What seem to be the outcomes?
b) How to link teaching to the printing press? In particular: how to exploit the daily or bi-monthly printings received in exchange? What to do with them after they have been read? How might they be used? Could we dispense with textbooks? Which ones? How?
c) How to bind the printed pages? What is the most practical format?
d) What was the evaluation of your school, your head teacher, the local population?]

(Circulaire de mai 1927, cited in Freinet, 1971: 61–2)

2.2.2   Kilpatrick and the 'Project Method'

Arguing in 1918 that 'the child needs the opportunity to purpose', Kilpatrick proposed that 'the purposeful act' should be made the unit of instruction. This would prepare the child for life as a democratic citizen while also constituting 'the present worthy life itself' (Kilpatrick, 1918, 1922).

The 'purposeful act' was realised pedagogically though four types of project work:

Quote 2.8   Kilpatrick on project types

Type 1: Purpose: to embody some idea or plan in external form (building a boat; writing a letter; presenting a play)

Type 2: Purpose: to enjoy some aesthetic experience (listen to a story; appreciate a picture; hear a symphony)

Type 3: Purpose: to straighten out some intellectual difficulty, or solve a problem (finding out how dew falls; how New York City outgrew Philadelphia)

Type 4: Purpose: to obtain some degree of skill or knowledge (learning the irregular verbs in French)

(Kilpatrick, 1918, 1922: 16)

At the broadest level, the focus on learner purpose suggests a resonance between this conceptualisation of 'project' and some of the current conceptualisations of pedagogic task mentioned above. For Kilpatrick the learner's purpose is made central through the nature of the pedagogic activities to be engaged with; and by schematising differences in the kinds of 'purposeful act' to be pursued, Kilpatrick is also schematising the potential for different relationships between project type and learner performance. Since he also argued that one project type could be used in relation to another as a means to an end, he also situates projects within a broader sequence of pedagogic activity. While admitting that there was perhaps an inevitable element of overlap in the project types, Kilpatrick nonetheless considered some form of overall classification valuable because of the light shed 'on the kinds of projects teachers may expect and on the procedure that normally prevails in the several types' (Kilpatrick, 1918: 16–17). Thus, projects were not to be seen as discrete activities, but in relationship with each other, and embodying patterns of typicality that could be recognised and anticipated by teachers.

As can be seen from these examples, Freinet and Kilpatrick were both concerned with issues of functional relevance and ways of making connections between school learning and the outside world. Both were also concerned with holistic learning through purposeful and relevant activity. However, there is some difference in their respective orientations to the pedagogic focus of such activity. For Freinet, pedagogic focus was what emerged naturally from interactions between learner, experience and activity, and thus we assume not necessarily predictable in advance. For Kilpatrick, the pedagogic focus was potentially embodied in the type of activity itself, thus enabling some element of predictability and planning both within that activity and across a sequence of activities. Interestingly, these differences in orientation prefigure differences in subsequent conceptualisations of task-based second language learning, and consequently, as we will see below and in Chapter 9, they are still reflected in current debates on the use of tasks in second language pedagogy.

Our next examples, drawn from approaches to experiential and participatory education, build on these themes by introducing elements of reflexivity and criticality as a means of bridging experience and learning.

2.2.3 Experiential education

A number of educational initiatives broadly rooted in Dewey's 'learning by doing' principle have come to be grouped under the umbrella term 'experiential education', as seen in Lewin 1(951) and Kolb (1984).

A number of different experiential education initiatives build on Dewey's view that certain elements need to be in place if learning is to proceed from experience.

Example 2.1   Elements of learning from experience

- Observation of surrounding elements.
- Knowledge obtained by recollection.
- Judgment which puts together what is observed and what is recalled to see what they signify.

(Dewey, 1938/1977)

One example of how these principles have been reflected across various approaches to experiential education is Kolb's four-phase model, which characterises learning in terms of an experiential cycle.

Example 2.2   Kolb's four-phase experiential cycle

1. Concrete experience.
2. Reflective observation.
3. Abstract conceptualisation.
4. Active experimentation (to test out newly developed principles).

(Kolb, 1984)

Although the number of phases in the experiential cycle may vary from model to model (Pfeiffer and Jones, 1975, propose five phases; Greenaway, 1995, three), experiential models all construe learning as leading from experience via a sequence of phases, crucially involving an element of concrete experience as starting and end points, and an element of reflection. Reflection on experience is thus seen as the key mediating factor between the experience itself and the types of learning it may motivate. It is through reflection on experience (usually guided and supported by the teacher) that learners develop meta-awareness of both the processes and the outcomes of learning, and through increased meta-awareness, gradually achieve greater autonomy and self-direction in their learning. Involvement in choosing, designing, evaluating and revising the activities they engage with is thus seen as a key element in experiential practice.

Kolb's model, and its various adaptations, have been applied across a diverse range of domains and disciplines, including (among many others) outdoor and environmental education (e.g. 'Outward Bound' programmes); cultural and community journalism (e.g. *Foxfire* magazine, grounded in local community and culture, written and published by secondary school pupils in southern Appalachia); pilot training (through the use of full flight simulators); sports training and music education (through the use of master classes). The work of Viljo Kohonen and colleagues in Finland is an example of how experiential principles have been applied in foreign language education.

Quote 2.9   Kohonen on experiential education

The learner is seen as a self-directed, intentional person who can be guided to develop his or her competencies in three interrelated areas of knowledge, skills and awareness:

(1) *Personal awareness*: self-concept and personal identity, realistic self-esteem, self-direction and responsible autonomy
(2) *Process and situational awareness*: management of the learning process towards increasingly self-organised, negotiated language learning and self-assessment, including the necessary strategic and metacognitive knowledge and the self-reflective interpersonal skills
(3) *Task awareness*: Knowledge of language and intercultural communication: the meta-knowledge of language at the various levels of linguistic description, providing an unfolding 'map' of the whole language learning enterprise.

(Kohonen, 2001: 36)

Kohonen's statement of experiential principles explicitly frames experiential learning as a developmental process involving guidance and support, which in turn suggests cyclical progressions of 'doing', followed by reflection on doing. It also implies a restructuring of conventional classroom role relationships and discursive practices. Practical examples of second language pedagogies that also embody these principles include Dam, 1995; Dam and Gabrielson, 1988; Legutke and Thomas, 1991; Finch et al., 2003.

2.2.4   Participatory education

Participatory education, rooted in an agenda for radical political and social change, offers a slightly different perspective on experience and learning. It grew out of mother tongue literacy programmes developed by Paulo Freire with non-literate fieldworkers and shantytown dwellers in Brazil during the 1950s. Here Freire sought to engage learners in dialogue about key words relating to problematic issues in their daily lives, and from this invited them to reflect on and critically analyse those issues, exploring the causes underlying the problems and possible ways of taking action to change them. The development of literacy was thus seen as a key for enabling marginalised members of society to become active participants in transforming social and political processes.

Quote 2.10   Freire on education

Education either functions as an instrument which is used to facilitate the integration in to the logic of the present system and bring about conformity to it, or becomes the practice of freedom, the means by which men and women deal critically and creatively with reality and discover how to participate in the transformation of their world.
(Freire, 1970: 15)

Central to this approach is a view of education as a 'participatory' and transformative process:

Quote 2.11   Auerbach on Freire's model of participatory education

Both the content and the processes of this model invite learners to become the subjects of their own education. Content centers on problematic issues from their lives so literacy is immediately relevant and engaging. Because this reality is problematized (presented in all its complexity without predetermined solutions), participants become the creators rather than the recipients of knowledge. They

---

Quote 2.11   (Continued)

engage in a process of reflection and dialogue, developing both an understanding of the root causes of the problem and generating their own alternatives for addressing it.
(Auerbach, 1992: 17)

In practice, this is enacted through a four-phase cycle of reflection and action.

Example 2.3   Freire's four phase process of participatory curriculum development

1. Initial identification/generation of a shared problem.
2. Dialogue about the problem, critical reflection on its root causes and generation of alternative ways of addressing it.
3. Decoding and recoding: focus on linguistic analysis in terms of relationships with learners' own lives and the problem identified in Phase 1.
4. Action: return to the problem identified in Phase 1, and work to change the conditions that give rise to it.

The starting point, then, is an aspect of the world as experienced by the learner. This leads to critical reflection on relevant underlying issues and possible ways of addressing them, which in turn leads to analysis of those aspects of language that may enable the learner to engage with and take action on the issues identified. Freire's phased cycle of experience, critical reflection, analysis and action not only situates the experiences that learners bring with them, but also provides a means for mediating and structuring those experiences for learning, for action and for political and/or social change. Freire's model has been adapted for use in very different contexts from those in which it originally evolved – for example, multicultural literacy in American primary schools (Ada, 2003), family literacy programmes (Ada and Campoy, 2003), second language instruction for adult immigrants and refugees (Wallerstein, 1983) and workplace learning programmes (Auerbach and Wallerstein, 1987) (Chapter 9).

As can be seen from these examples, the approaches to participatory and experiential education touched on here share a broad Deweyian concern with personal and social relevance as the touchstone for learning, and with education that is rooted in learners' actual and potential experiences of the world. Likewise, they illustrate some of the ways that the slipstream of experience may be distilled to serve as a springboard for learning through iterative phases of experience and reflection. However, a question worth exploring is the extent to which the phases highlighted in experientially-driven models such as those referred to here capture the full range of complex cognitive processes involved in learning from experience. In the next two sections, we consider issues relating to the kinds of support that may be necessary to enable learners make systematic connections between individual experience and broader generalisations, and some of the pedagogic challenges that this implies.

2.3   The influence of Bruner: learning for use

Some fifty years after Dewey, Bruner argued similarly that in any area of education learners need to have the target knowledge available. This knowledge needs organising mentally so that it is arranged in ways that dovetail with the ways in which the material will be needed in contexts of use. Or as Bruner put it, there is a distinction between learning general structures of patterns, and the ability to use them:

Quote 2.12   Bruner on learning for use

Whether the student knows the formal names of these operations is less important for transfer than whether he is able to use them.
(Bruner, 1960/1977: 8)

'Learning for use' leads us to situate the learner not simply in terms of the classroom, or of the target material, isolated from the social world. Bruner argued that pupils learning a subject in school (physics, for example) are hindered by having to master the 'middle language' of textbooks rather than being given the opportunity to engage with the discipline itself. In a famous formulation, he characterises learning not only as gaining control over information or skills, but also as joining a community of thought.

Quote 2.13   Bruner on learning

[I]ntellectual activity anywhere is the same, whether at the frontier of knowledge or in a third-grade classroom. What a scientist does at his desk or in his laboratory, what a literary critic does in reading a poem, are of the same order as what anybody else does when he is engaged in like activities – if he is to achieve

---

Quote 2.13   (Continued)

understanding. The difference is in degree, not in kind. The schoolboy learning physics *is* a physicist, and it is easier for him to learn physics behaving like a physicist than doing something else.
(Bruner, 1960/1977: 14)

Thus, the child should not be simply cast in the role of 'pupil', but encouraged to situate herself as a practitioner, albeit a novice practitioner, in a new domain: through cognitive involvement, educational engagement is seen as extending into participation within a community. Elements of what Bruner argues here are also found in the work of Wertsch (1985), Lave and Wenger (1991, and elsewhere) and reflected in applications of neo-Vygotskian thought to second language learning (e.g. Lantolf, 2000) as we see in Part 2.

In much of his early work, Bruner highlights the complementary nature of analytic and intuitive thinking in school learning, and emphasises the need to pay attention to the development of intuitive understanding, even in subject matter commonly associated with analytical thought:

Quote 2.14   Bruner on the complementarity of analytic and intuitive thinking

The development of effectiveness in intuitive thinking is an objective of many of the most highly regarded teachers in mathematics and science. The point has been repeatedly made that in the high school plane geometry is typically taught with excessive emphasis upon techniques, formal proofs, and the like, that much more attention needs to be given to the development of students who have a good intuitive feel for geometry, students who are skillful in discovering proofs, not just in checking the validity of or remembering proofs with which they have been presented. ... Similarly, in physics, Newtonian mechanics is typically taught deductively and analytically. In the judgment of many physicists, at least, there is too little attention to the development of intuitive understanding.
(Bruner, 1960/1977: 56)

The development of intuitive understanding may well depend on learners being given the space to confront problems, as well as their willingness to explore ways of engaging with those problems. This suggests a pedagogic climate which encourages effortful mental engagement with alternatives rather than the simple pursuit of a right answer.

Quote 2.15   Bruner on the development of intuitive thinking

It seems likely that effective intuitive thinking is fostered by the development of self-confidence and courage in the student ... Such thinking, therefore, requires a willingness to make honest mistakes in the effort to solve problems.
(Bruner, 1960/1977: 65)

However, Bruner argued that importantly linked to the kind of educational engagement envisaged here is the ability to seek out regularity or patterns of similarity across different experiences.

Quote 2.16   Bruner on regularity across experience

Children, as they grow, must acquire ways of representing the recurrent regularities in their environment, and they must transcend the momentary by developing ways of linking past to present to future – representation and integration.
(Bruner, 1973: 348)

What is highlighted here is the need for the child to be actively involved in making generalisations on the basis of different experiences, and for connections to be found across them. Bruner (1983) provides an illustration of how this might happen over time.

Concept 2.2   Formats and their role in learning

In studying the emergence of language in the young child, Bruner reports a number of studies from a longitudinal dataset which reveal a significant level of organisation in the discourse children experience, with a striking amount of repetition over time. Children repeatedly encounter a small number of structured discourses, which Bruner terms 'formats'.

By engaging with adults in these formats, children appear to go through a gradual process of acquisition. At first the focus is on the meaningful structure of the format, with the child grasping and responding to main meanings within the discourse. From an overall grasp of the sequence, the child then gradually comes to perceive and focus attention on particular sound sequences, words, phrases or utterances which occur at different points in the discourse. Since the formats recur, the sequences are also repeated, and the child is steadily able to recognise, recall and produce more and more of them. This suggests that multiple encounters with the kinds of activities we have been calling tasks can enable these connections to be made.

In common with aspects of Dewey's work, Bruner highlights not simply the importance of experience-based education, but also the need to create opportunities for the learner to build systematic connections between individual instantiations of concrete experience, and generalisation at a broader level of abstraction. The kinds of activities that learners engage with have an important role to play here. A full understanding of that role, however, implies an understanding of how those activities work, the kinds of talk they might generate and the learning they might give rise to. We consider some implications of these issues for second language task research and pedagogy in Chapters 7 and 9; we also return to other aspects of Bruner's work later in this chapter.

2.4   The influence of Barnes: classroom talk and learning

In a series of studies carried out in British secondary schools during the 1970s, Barnes explored relationships between two types of classroom talk and learning (Barnes, 1976; Barnes and Todd, 1977; 1995). Focusing on pupils' talk during group work in a number of curricular subjects, including English literature, history and science, Barnes distinguishes between talk that is 'exploratory' and talk that is 'final draft', and emphasises qualitative differences between the processes surrounding the two types of discourse and their roles in learning. Exploratory talk is characteristically (but not exclusively) associated with pupil–pupil talk in the absence of a teacher during collaborative group work; final draft talk is characteristically associated with 'well-shaped utterances' elicited by the teacher:

Quote 2.17   Barnes on exploratory and final draft talk

I call [pupils'] groping towards a meaning 'exploratory talk'. It is usually marked by frequent hesitations, rephrasings, false starts and changes of direction. I want to argue that it is very important whenever we want the learner to take an active part in learning, and to bring what he learns into interaction with that view of the world on which his actions are based. That is, such exploratory talk is one means by which the assimilation and accommodation of new knowledge to the old is carried out. [.....] The more a learner controls his own language strategies and the more he is enabled to think aloud, the more he can take responsibility for formulating explanatory hypotheses and evaluating them.
(Barnes, 1976: 28–9)

Final draft language is the contrary of exploratory: far from accompanying (and displaying) the detours and dead-ends of thinking, it seeks to exclude them and present a finished article, well-shaped and polished.
(Barnes, 1976: 108)

Whereas 'final draft' language is presented for evaluation, and seems to deny the possibility of revision and the learning processes that can go with it, 'exploratory' talk seems to allow, and indeed encourage, the active formulation and reformulation of hypotheses, engagement with under-standing of the material, and with the thought processes that enable that understanding. However, as Barnes points out, the normative order of a school does not easily give rise to contexts for the development of exploratory talk: 'When teachers entered the groups, asking questions intended to further their pupils' understanding, the style of speech shifted from the exploratory towards a style appropriate to showing the teacher that they had 'the right answer' (Barnes, 1976: 108). Peer collaboration on group tasks then is one context where exploratory talk may be fostered.

Quote 2.18   Barnes and Todd on types of exploratory talk most likely to contribute to learning

[The types of group talk most likely to contribute to learning was when pupils engaged in]:

a) solving a problem
b) interpreting texts
c) making choices on the basis of evidence
d) applying a principle to new cases
e) planning and carrying out a productive activity to fulfil criteria which may either have been given or defined by the students themselves
f) exploring an issue for which there is no single right answer

(Barnes and Todd, 1995: 88)

Barnes argues that different tasks seem to give rise to different strategies on the part of individuals and their groups, and the studies show how group tasks can be designed and used to generate exploratory talk which participants use to seek out responses to problems. Barnes is therefore charting a significant distinction between process and product, one to which we return at the end of this chapter. At the same time, he traces connections between the surface discourse produced by the groups and the underlying thinking which drives it. The tasks that pupils undertake can thus be seen as creating space within the classroom for the develop-ment processes needed to engender understanding and conceptual mas-tery: this means that final draft language is not abandoned, but rather that significantly more space is created for learners to work their ways towards a satisfactory final draft. In other words, tasks are used here to open up the dynamics of learning to the attention of learners and to teachers, not merely to structure 'final draft' performance. Importantly though this is not to deny a role for final draft talk, and Barnes outlines a pedagogic model that places the two types of talk in relation to each other in a sequenced progression of stages.

Example 2.4   Barnes' model for sequencing exploratory and final draft talk

1. *Focusing Stage*: Topic presented in full class, and pupils encouraged to verbalise necessary preliminary knowledge as a basis for group work.
2. *Exploratory Stage*: Pupils in groups carry out any necessary manipulation of materials and talk about issues that their attention has been directed towards on the basis of current knowledge and understandings.
3. *Reorganising Stage*: Teacher refocuses attention, tells groups how they will be reporting back and how long to prepare for it.
4. *Public Stage*: Groups present their findings to one another and this leads to further discussion.

(Based on Barnes, 1976: 197)

Discussing relationships between aspects of the tasks that pupils engage with and the nature of the talk that may be produced, Barnes distinguishes between tasks based on 'well-formed problems' (open to single solutions, the validity of which can be demonstrated) and tasks based on problems where many different 'answers' are possible. Barnes argues that in tasks of the latter type, pupils need to decide for themselves on what principles the data will be selected and ordered, while in 'well-formed tasks' this is largely decided for them. Thus, speech is likely to have a more complex part to play in learning in problems that are not well formed, and indeed, as Barnes points out, most of the choices that we make in everyday life are based on problems that are far from well formed. This raises an important pedagogic challenge regarding the amount of structure inherent in the tasks pupils engage with: too little structure and pupils don't know what to do; too much and 'we interpose ourselves between the children and the experience we want our pupils to recode' (Barnes, 1976: 194). Paradoxically, in their different ways, both extremes can have a restricting effect on the ways pupils carry out the task.

Quote 2.19   Barnes on the teacher's dilemma

This is every teacher's dilemma: how can one support pupils with a framework which does not at the same time constrict their participation? How can one enable the learner to order his own learning without abandoning him in a trackless wilderness? (Barnes, 1976: 88)

This dilemma, rooted as it is in a tension between freedom and control, brings us back to many of the issues raised earlier by Dewey. As Dewey himself recognised, reconceptualising traditional practices does not in itself offer solutions, but in fact brings into focus a different set of problems that need to be understood in their own terms. For example, Dewey famously argued that both the advocates and the opponents of progressive education appear to share the same mistaken assumption (albeit for different reasons) that the use of holistic activity implies that learning is left unguided; this assumption, Dewey argued, leads to two extreme, but equally erroneous, positions about the nature of holistic learning activities.

Quote 2.20   Dewey on chaos and magic

One extreme is to neglect [holistic learning activities] almost entirely, on the grounds that they are *chaotic* and *fluctuating* ... The other extreme is an enthusiastic belief in the almost *magical* educative efficacy of *any* kind of activity..
   When we vibrate from one of these extremes to the other, the most serious of all problems is ignored: the problem, namely, of discovering and arranging the forms of activity ... which are most congenial, best adapted [to the learners].
(Dewey, 1910: 44)

The two opposing perspectives on holistic activity highlighted here are also relevant to understandings of second language pedagogic tasks. As we shall see, on the one hand, there appears to be a belief that second language pedagogic tasks engage learning processes as if by magic simply through interaction, and any attempt to shape the way learners carry out a task, whether through design or implementation, is to intervene in the those processes. On the other hand, there is a belief that task engagement is too chaotic, fluctuating and inconsistent to provide a basis for a systematic pedagogy. Dewey, however, was arguing for a more constructive though more difficult way forward through a *systematic* approach to the use of holistic activities:

Quote 2.21   Dewey on 'organising' experience

The problem for progressive education is: What is the place and meaning of subject-matter and of organization within experience? How does subject matter function? Is there anything inherent in experience which tends towards progressive organization of its contents?
(Dewy, 1917/1963: 20)

That is, while traditionalists are mistaken to insist exclusively on teacher-led learning, and progressivists are right to wish to bring learner-driven activities into the classroom, progressivists are wrong to advocate total learner control, and traditionalists are right to argue for the teacher's role in developing coherence through the curriculum. The flaw is to believe that learner-driven activities are not amenable to systematic use by the teacher: we need to explore how the logic of our disciplines can be brought into contact with our learners' experiences of the world. Planning, then, 'must be flexible enough to permit free play for individuality of experience and yet firm enough to give direction toward continuous development of power' (Dewey, 1938/1963: 58). What we are calling 'tasks' can thus be seen as a means of creating experience-based opportunities for language learning; the management of those opportunities however remains an enduring pedagogic challenge.

2.5   Summary: holistic, experience-based tasks in an educational context: the case for a systematic pedagogy

Thus far we have highlighted some key recurring themes from general education. In particular, we have noted that for there to be a connection between learning activity and the learner, there needs to be a connection between learning activity and learning, and more specifically between learning activity and behaviour. This implies seeking congruence between the whole learner, particular learning activities and particular learning behaviours. That is, there needs to be a relationship between activity and learning. In second language education, this entails the creation of opportunities for learners to associate the target language with action and the need to achieve some goal, and through this, thought about how to accomplish it and reflection on the outcomes. Activities like Dewey's 'overt and executive activities' have a significant role to play in enabling such connections to be made. But in second language education, as in general education, the design and implementation of those activities is dependent on an understanding of how they work.

3
Holistic Tasks in a Research Context: Some Key Issues

The use of holistic activities fits not only with educational thinking. Since at least the middle of the twentieth century, holistic tasks have been used in human sciences research (including applied language study) as a means of eliciting and sampling behaviour. In what follows we distinguish between the study of tasks in what might be considered relatively stable, 'bounded' contexts, and the study of tasks in the broad social context in which they occur. From examples of research carried out on holistic tasks in both contexts, we explore a set of issues relating to the use of holistic tasks for research purposes:

- consistency of research focus;
- impact of task type on task performance;
- participant vs. researcher interpretation of the task as given.

These issues bring into focus a number of implications for ways of researching second language tasks and for understanding learners' performance on those tasks.

3.1   The study of tasks as 'bounded' contexts

For many researchers in the human sciences, holistic tasks are of interest because they provide a bounded context with a goal (asking people to recount their 'near-death' experiences, as in Labov, 1972; Labov and Waletzky, 1967; or asking chess grandmasters to build on opening moves in a chess game, as in de Groot, 1978). Within these boundaries, researchers can focus on aspects of task performance and use them, if desired, as a basis for comparison (e.g. how different people carry out the same or different tasks). Performance on tasks can thus create a window on observable facets of performance itself (discourse patterns in near-death experience stories) or on underlying cognitive processes (charting the eye movements of a chess grandmaster scanning the next move to tap into mental representations of expert knowledge). Performance can be on novel tasks (as in the near-death stories) or on typically occurring tasks in a familiar domain (as in the chess example), or on combinations of both (a novel task in a familiar domain, for example).

Importantly, however, although the context of the task may be bounded, instructions given to participants may be open and non-directive. An example of this is a well-known applied language study.

Example 3.1 Similarities in organisational structure in task performance

Linde and Labov simply asked participants to describe their apartments, and investigated the strategies that speakers used. They found that well over 90 per cent of all interviewees structured their descriptions as though they were giving a guided tour, walking with the interviewer through the apartment from one room to another.
(Linde and Labov, 1975)

Interestingly, then, although the interviewer's question was extremely simple and very open, nearly all the speakers spontaneously chose to follow the same organisational structure. Also using a holistic task in a bounded context, Levelt (1989) reports a study focusing on a central problem in speech and writing, that of 'linearising' information. All speech and writing is inevitably linear. This creates a potential problem because semantic content can be sequenced in numerous different ways, and in fact is not sequenced until it is transformed into language (something which anyone who has ruined a good joke by giving away the punch line too early will be painfully aware of).

Example 3.2 Similarities in processing in task performance

To study the ordering of words in speech, Levelt asked participants to describe an underground route on a map, and found that it was possible to identify the points at which speakers were making decisions of sequencing, and the kinds of information which were problematic (such as the placement of prepositional phrases indicating direction and destination).
(Levelt, 1989)

Example 3.3   Similarities in processing in task performance

Kellerman and van Hoof asked speakers of different language backgrounds to recount part of a film, and carried out a micro-analysis of the speech and gestures they used in describing a series of movements. The study shows interesting patterns of synchronisation of speakers' gestures of movement with the words denoting direction. Speakers whose languages expressed the direction of movement in the verb (such as French, Spanish, Italian – e.g. 'Marie a traversé la rue en courant') timed their gestures to coincide with the verb; speakers whose languages expressed the direction of movement in the preposition ('Mary ran across the road') gestured at the point of uttering the preposition.
(Kellerman and van Hoof, 2003)

Studies such as these highlight how holistic language production on tasks can reflect similarities in processing, whether at the schematic level (the way people described their apartments in Linde and Labov's study) or at the lexical and syntactic levels (in Levelt's and Kellerman and van Hoof's studies). We return to the implications of findings such as these for second language task research in Part 2.

3.2   The study of tasks in their social context

In contrast to studying performance on bounded tasks such as those cited above, other researchers focus on tasks in terms of the broader, constantly evolving social contexts in which they are situated. For example, in studying expertise in the context of the workplace, Engestrom and Middleton characterise expertise as the 'ongoing collaborative and discursive construction of tasks, solutions, visions, breakdowns, and innovations' (Engestrom and Middleton, 1998b: 4) rather than as individual performance on stable, well-defined tasks, as in the chess grandmaster studies mentioned above. Laufer and Glick (1998) make this point explicitly.

Quote 3.1   Laufer and Glick on researching problem-solving in real-world activities

The focus of [expertise] research has generally been on problem solving in 'well structured' problem domains that lend themselves readily to problem descriptions and identification of linkages between problem representations and linear solution strategies. But does this logical/rationalist model of thinking apply to the more mundane tasks that people face in their everyday life and work? What constitutes problem solving in real-world activities?
(Laufer and Glick, 1998: 177)

Goodwin and Goodwin (1998), researching social cognition in workers in an airport characterise the issue thus:

Quote 3.2   Goodwin and Goodwin on researching cognition in the workplace

In order to focus as clearly as possible on some of the issues involved in the analysis of cognition in the workplace, this chapter will investigate a single, very simple, but very pervasive, activity performed by different kinds of workers in a medium-sized airport: looking at airplanes. Despite the brevity of individual glances, they are in no way haphazard. Workers look at planes in order to see something that will help them accomplish the work they are engaged in. Understanding that looking, therefore, requires analysis of the work activities within which it is embedded. (Goodwin and Goodwin, 1998: 61)

Different people may 'look' in different ways, and this involves understanding their seeing 'in an appropriate task-relevant way' (1998: 61). But this can only be understood in the global context of people's work.

Quote 3.3   Goodwin and Goodwin on 'seeing'

By looking at how participants actually accomplish relevant seeing within specific tasks in local environments we will provide detailed analysis of ... performances.
...
   Consider the tasks faced by someone responsible for loading baggage on an Atlantic Hawk flight to a specific destination, say Oakland. On the field in front of her are ten identical Atlantic Hawk planes ... . How is she to determine which plane to load, i.e., how can she see which of the ten planes is going to Oakland? Seeing the plane itself is not enough, since the plane she is looking for looks just like all of the other planes in her field of view.
   For airport personnel, planes do not stand alone as isolated objects. Instead, they are defined by their positions in larger webs of activity.
(Goodwin and Goodwin, 1998: 62)

One of the challenges for the study of tasks in a broad context like the workplace is that work activities 'are rarely straightforward individual actions', but often require continuous switching among activities embedded within each other during a limited time period, and are commonly interwoven with (and thus dependent on) the contributions of co-workers (Rogers and Ellis, 1994). One way of addressing this challenge has been to study workplace activity in terms of the 'distributed cognition' of groups of workers involved in collective routines rather than in terms of individual performance on isolated, serial tasks. An interesting example is Hutchins' 1995 study of the navigation of a ship:

Example 3.4   Distributed cognition and task performance

Hutchins shows how the accomplishment of many routine navigation tasks (for example, taking a bearing when moving near land) involves the coordination of a number of discrete activities carried out by different members of the ship navigation team (for example, searching for landmarks on the shore; measuring the bearings of the landmarks; reporting the readings to the bearing time-recorder; logging the bearings; transmitting the bearings to the ship's pilot; plotting the bearings on a chart through the use of various instruments). By themselves these various activities may not amount to much, but when carried out in conjunction with each other and in the correct order they constitute 'the computation of the ship's position'. (Hutchins, 1995)

Interestingly then, even within broad webs of collective activity, we can see that the construct of 'task' provides an important mediating context. In the case of the Engestrom and Middleton study, the task is a reference point for understanding what constitutes a solution, a breakdown or an innovation; in the case of the Hutchins study, it is also a reference point for highlighting interdependence among sub-tasks.

3.3   Some issues arising from the use of holistic tasks for research purposes

Whether the research task is construed as a bounded context or is studied in its social context is an issue of relevance to the study of second language pedagogic tasks. In Chapter 7 we make the point that the context in which a task is studied – whether bounded, in controlled conditions and conducted outside the classroom, or in the situated context of naturally occurring activities within an intact classroom – does not *in itself* entail the use of any one theoretical framework or paradigm, and explore in some detail a number of assumptions about relationships between research context and research paradigm. In this section, we briefly focus on some issues arising from the use of holistic tasks in both bounded and situated contexts of research, and also relevant to the study of second language pedagogic tasks. These are:

1. the extent to which the use of a holistic task provides a sufficiently stable basis for research purposes;
2. the impact of the type of task used on the way it is carried out;

3. the extent to which participants in research studies re-interpret the task in ways that may be at odds with the researcher's intentions.

3.3.1   Holistic tasks and consistency of research focus

A recurrent concern with the use of holistic tasks in human sciences research relates to the consistency of behaviour elicited. For example, to what extent can unscripted, holistic tasks, like those used in the studies exemplified above, provide a stable enough basis for generalisation or comparison? In what ways might we expect the holistic nature of such tasks to undermine of the consistency of the research focus?

Interestingly, a number of studies have shown that even when engaging in an open, spontaneous task, participants respond with a degree of consistency. In some cases, this is a reflection of cultural patterning. For example, in a much cited study, Bartlett (1932, in Baddeley, 1991: 335) showed that people unfamiliar with Native American culture would very consistently have the same difficulties recalling the same details of Native American stories they were asked to recall. Cultural influences can also affect consistency in the ways that children respond to tasks. Bruner cites the following case.

Quote 3.4   Bruner on the influence of cultural background

Indeed, each culture has certain unique ways of dealing with the relation of the three systems [i.e. iconic, enactive, symbolic]. In [Greenfield's] field studies in Senegal, she found that Frank's screening procedure, so successful in a Western setting, had little effect with Senegalese children. What could produce change was giving the children conservation tasks in which they themselves rather than adults manipulated the materials, largely because the children expected magic powers of adults, but not of themselves.
(Bruner, 1973: 323)

A different kind of example can be found in Tannen (1980).

Example 3.5   The influence of cultural background

Tannen studied how Greek and American-English speakers reported a silent film which they had watched individually. She found a very strong tendency for the American speakers to treat the task as a memory test, while the Greek speakers were very much more likely to handle the task as requiring them to provide a dramatic oral account of what they had seen. Although this study showed that the two cultural groups responded very differently, it also demonstrated there was a high degree of predictability regarding the kind of discourse that they would produce, given their distinctive orientations.
(Tannen, 1980)

In other words, general knowledge affects comprehension processes. Since much of our general knowledge is culturally shaped, it differs across different cultural backgrounds. For example, given that background knowledge is one important element, and that background knowledge is partly culturally shaped, it is perhaps not surprising to find that studies have shown that people can respond differently, but consistently, to tasks according to their cultural background.

Our more general point is that when given holistic comprehension tasks, people spontaneously encounter very similar comprehension problems. From such studies, it is possible to infer the kinds of processes that occur and major ways of resolving comprehension problems. Furthermore, spontaneous attempts to resolve problems can be consistently interpreted in terms of over-assimilation as in Bartlett's study, or over-accommodation, as in foreign language studies where rather than over-assimilating, readers are often found to ignore their personal stores of general knowledge, and attempt to work out the meanings of texts purely on the basis of the literal meanings on the page – a form of over-accommodation. What is relevant for our purposes is that tasks can be devised to engage text comprehension processes which enable researchers to infer the kinds of sub-processes that are involved, to identify different types of processing problem and to interpret the different kinds of strategies that people use. That is, the tasks are deliberately holistic to ensure that normal processes are engaged; yet, they are also focused to target particular parts of the process. Holistic tasks then can be used to show that we all use similar processes in producing or comprehending language.

However, holistic tasks have also been used to study individual differences, and as such can be seen as an anchor for focusing on differences in the ways that people carry out the same task, as Bruner et al. show.

Example 3.6   Individual differences in approaches to problem-solving

Bruner et al. set children a questioning task involving cards each with a drawing made up of a different combination of elements (for instance, a man, with or without a hat, with or without a stick, with or without very big shoes). He found that children differed in the extent to which they gambled on rapid success, or slowly worked out the solutions by a process of logical elimination. He concluded that there were distinct approaches to this kind of problem-solving, some highly conservative, attempting to avoid any incorrect guesses at the cost of considerable work, some highly risky, going for the solution by one-off guesses, willing to carry the cost of many errors.
(Bruner, Goodnow and Austin, 1956)

Tasks of the sort described here are holistic in the sense that participants have to sort out what to say, how to say it and in what order, bringing together the formulation of particular utterances into a whole discourse strategy. Learner differences occur, but there is no reason to think that these are infinite in number. For instance, elsewhere Bruner comments on reading strategies, as revealed through story retelling tasks:

Quote 3.5   Bruner on story telling tasks

One gets a sense of the psychology of genre by listening to readers 'tell back' a story they have just read or spontaneously 'tell' a story about a 'happening' in their own lives. 'Telling back' a Conrad story, one reader will turn it into a yarn of adventure, another into a moral tale about duplicity, and a third into a case study of a *Doppelganger*. The text from which they started was the same. Genre seems to be a way of both organizing the structure of events and organizing the telling of them . . .
(Bruner, 1986: 6)

The examples from human sciences research noted here suggest then that it is possible to capture elements of difference in the ways that holistic tasks are carried out by individuals, but that it is also possible to capture patterns of consistency.

3.3.2   Impact of task type on task performance

Another recurring question about the use of tasks for eliciting performance is the extent to which the type of task selected artificially pushes the type of behaviour it elicits: to what extent can task performance be taken as a reflection of performance in other contexts, and to what extent an artefact of that particular task? In communication strategies research (Bialystok, 1990; Kasper and Kellerman, 1997), where the focus is on the ways that individuals deal with communication problems – misunderstandings, breakdowns in communication, seek clarification, and so on – the issue is brought into focus in different ways.

Quote 3.6   Bialystok on tasks in communication strategies research

There are few studies that compare performance of a single subject across methods, since each researcher tends to use only one procedure. Comparisons across tasks, then, tend to be highly inferential.
(Bialystok, 1990: 50)

In a study of her own, Bialystok found that while task type affected the quantity of language produced, it had no significant effect on the frequency or type of communication strategies elicited. In spite of this, she argues that elicitation type almost certainly has some impact on results, and, by implication, we can assume that in the classroom it is likely to influence learning.

Williams, Inscoe and Tasker (1997) argue that weaknesses in earlier communication strategies research were essentially due to the type of task selected: 'the selection of CSs [communication strategies] is determined by the nature of the situation – the interactive goal – as well as the role of the participants – 'expert' versus needing information' (1997: 306). For this reason they adopted a different type of task for their study, one typical of non-language learning contexts (tutoring interactions in the organic chemistry laboratory) and in which the NNS is the expert and the NS the non-expert:

Quote 3.7   Williams et al. on impact of task type in communication strategies research

[This approach] extends the notion of CS to situations involving other kinds of gap in knowledge, for example, gaps which are primarily *information*-based, rather than *code*-based. Specifically, we look at episodes in which either the NS or the NNS fails to comprehend some aspect of the task or another participant's actions and must seek some way of resolving the problem. . . . Secondly, such gaps in knowledge tend to show up in *comprehension* problems rather than in production. ... We will examine the CSs of *both the NNSs and NSs* because we believe that the achievement of comprehension is a joint process. While the NNSs and NSs do appear to have different strategies, they must be viewed together, rather than separately.
(Williams, Inscoe and Tasker, 1997: 306–7)

The key point here is that the design of the task has a central role since it is informed by the researchers' conceptualisation of communication strategies. The same would be true if we were to substitute the word 'teacher' for 'researcher'. The issue of the impact of task type can be further illustrated with reference to elicitation material originally designed by Krauss and Weinheimer (1964) and subsequently used in the study of adult first language communication (Clarke and Wilkes-Gibbs, 1986; Bongaerts and Poulisse 1989).

Example 3.7   Impact of task type on strategy use

In this study, the material consisted of twelve unconventional shapes, which participants were required to refer to in order to complete a task. The fact that they were unconventional meant there was no pre-existing word or phrase available to refer to them, hence requiring the speakers to find some verbal strategy to manage the task. One speaker was asked to instruct the other to lay the twelve figures out in an array of their choice. Two types of strategy were used – an analogical strategy, likening the shapes to something familiar of a roughly similar shape; and a literal (or analytical) strategy, describing the parts of the figures. Bongaerts and Poulisse found that Dutch speakers used similar strategies in both their L1 and their L2. (Bongaerts and Poulisse, 1989)

Although the results of this study are not in question, it is worth pointing out that the nature of the strategies elicited could be strongly influenced by the kind of task employed. If both speakers are able to see the figures on the table, the chances are this will severely reduce the use of inventive strategies. If, on the other hand, one speaker is asked to describe a figure so that the other can draw it, this is very likely to bias the speakers towards the use of analytical strategies, since an analogical strategy is bound to neglect some important elements of the figures. Hence in language elicitation, task design is crucial in targeting the kinds of behaviour that are of interest.

Studies of child language development have also demonstrated some effect of task on performance which could explain some of the historic results reported by Piaget (e.g. Piaget and Inhelder, 1956). Research by Kahan and Richards (1986) into the referential communication of children and college students demonstrated that the context within which language was presented significantly affected the way both the children and the adults handled the task. In other words task type affected performance. Other research has shown more direct educational relevance:

Example 3.8   Impact of task type

Snow et al. studied the ability of multilingual primary school children to produce formal (i.e. decontextualised) and informal definitions of words. They found evidence to suggest that the quality of children's decontextualised definitions related closely to both their overall proficiency (written as well as oral) and to academic ability. In other words, the ability to manage decontextualised definitions could be seen as related to the extent to which they were specifically socialised into that activity. That is, familiarity with the specific type of task seemed more important than oral proficiency in the language. (Snow et al., 1989)

As we shall see in Chapters 7, 8 and 9, the impact of task type on task performance is a topic of considerable interest to second language task researchers. This should not be surprising: if tasks are a pedagogical tool for generating language work, then the kind of language that arises as a result of their use is bound to be of central interest to teachers, learners, designers and others who consider their use to promote language development.

3.3.3 Participants' re-definition of tasks

Many studies of task performance appear to assume convergence between the aims of the researcher setting the task and the aims of the participants carrying it out. However, referring to the issue as 'one of the skeletons in the psychologist's closet', Bruner et al. (1956) make the point that participants in research studies cannot be expected to share the same agenda as the researchers setting the task. It is possible, indeed likely, that they will have different interpretations of the objective of the task, and different understandings of what is required to accomplish it. This opens up the possibility that the task may be 'redefined' in ways that make sense to the individual carrying it out, but that may be at variance with the researcher's original intentions. This in turn implies that any task can be transformed into something individual and unique each time it is carried out, and thus calls into question many of the assumptions about tasks as stable contexts for studying behaviour discussed above.

Interestingly, as Bruner et al. suggest, although the extent to which a research task can be viewed as external to the person carrying it out and imposed, and the extent to which it can be viewed as internal to, and defined by the performer, is recognised as an issue that needs to be confronted in human sciences research, it is not widely discussed or accounted for in research reports. The quotes and examples that follow, however, illustrate some of the ways that human sciences researchers have acknowledged and confronted those issues.

Quote 3.8   Pepinsky and Pepinsky on the 'official' and the 'private' task

We can anticipate the necessity of distinguishing between the task as defined by (a) the actor to whom it is assigned and (b) the setter who assigns it.
(Pepinsky and Pepinsky, 1961: 219–20; cited in Hackman, 1969)

Example 3.9   Understanding the 'objective' and the 'redefined' task

Hackman argues that since a research task is inevitably transformed when carried out, task redefinition should be viewed as a normal part of the performance process, with 'objective' and 'redefined' tasks occupying different temporal positions in the performance sequence.

For Hackman, both objective and redefined tasks are nonetheless still 'tasks', and can be differentiated on the same dimensions. This implies the 'objective' task, as assigned by the researcher, can function as an anchor for exploring ways in which the task is actually reinterpreted and redefined by task participants. To this end, Hackman proposes a framework broadly corresponding to the different aspects of the objective task, and which he argues can be used as reference points for tracing both what was intended by the researcher, and what actually happened.

(Hackman, 1969)

Working from a different theoretical perspective, Griffin et al. (1982) discuss problems of 'locating' tasks within the larger social networks within which they are carried out. With reference to their study of children's problem-solving in a range of contexts, they comment that recognising where a task began and ended was clear-cut in test conditions, relatively clear in classroom conditions, but impossible in 'club' contexts (i.e. in school but out of the classroom), where things got done (cakes baked, plants grown, etc.), 'without anyone doing anything that a cognitive psychologist could recognize as thinking' (1982: 4). They argue that the source of this difficulty lies in the social constraints operating on people when carrying out a task/solving a problem:

> The larger social context within which the 'same task' was embedded placed very different constraints on the individuals participating in the scene. As a consequence, the individuals were more or less free to change the conditions of the task, even to the point of making it go away, depending upon what social context it appeared in. (Griffin et al., 1982: 5)

To address the problem, Griffin et al. propose the introduction of 'tracer elements', which can be subsequently used as a basis for constructing a model system of what the task is. A tracer element might take the form of a topic or problem that children encounter in lessons, peer work, tutorials or in club settings, and thus the topic or problem can serve as a trace of the task being searched for. In this way, Griffin et al.

argue, it is possible to locate recurring situations where a goal can be isolated; that is, we can identify it via its relation to the tracer.

Quote 3.9   Griffin et al. on the use of tracer elements in research tasks

By having a tracer element, we have a clearer chance to see what is varying: we can see how the researcher/teacher/club leader's plans concerning the task are transformed to create the task that the participants perform.
(Griffin et al., 1982: 10)

Thus by providing a window on the task as planned and on ways that it is variously interpreted, tracer elements offer a means to capture the slipstream of individual task enactment. From Griffin et al.'s perspective, this would enable a theory that is 'simultaneously a theory of what the task is, what the relevant behaviors are, and the relationships between elements of the tasks and elements of behavior' (1982: 8).

We might have easily substituted 'second language learner' for 'participant' and 'actor' throughout this discussion, since the issue of how learners reinterpret and redefine tasks is highly relevant for task pedagogy and research, and has been widely recognised in recent years. As we saw above, it is brought into focus through Breen's (1987) distinction between task-as-workplan and task-in-process; it subsequently emerged in relation to neo-Vygotskyian perspectives on language learning, where the distinction has been framed in terms of 'task' (the task as planned) and 'activity' (the task as enacted by individual learners) to highlight how the 'official' task may be uniquely transformed by the learners carrying it out (Coughlan and Duff, 1994; see also Lantolf, 2000; Donato, 2000). As we shall see in Chapter 7, for some neo-Vygotskyians the issue represents a major stumbling block for both task research and the development of a systematic task pedagogy. However, if we accept task reinterpretation and redefinition as inevitable elements in the enactment of tasks of any kind, as suggested in the examples from human sciences research cited above, then it is possible to envisage ways around the problem – for example, exploring the extent to which the notion of a 'trace' might apply to features of pedagogic tasks, and ways in which it could be used to provide stable points of reference for exploring potential divergences between the workplan and the task in action.

Nevertheless, the pedagogic and theoretical implications of how tasks are redefined and reinterpreted in action cannot be understood fully without also taking the perspectives of task users into account. Unfortunately, to date most of the empirical work relating to task reinterpretation has been based on researchers' interpretations of learners' reinterpretations of tasks (Coughlan and Duff, 1994), and very little has focused on the issue of reinterpretation from the learner's own perspective. Likewise, there has been very little work carried out on teachers' interpretations of tasks from their own perspectives, or of task designers' intentions from theirs. Taken together, we might expect the various perspectives of learners, teachers, designers and researchers to permit richer accounts of the capacity of the workplan, and richer conceptualisations of the boundaries between workplan and enactment. This remains an under-explored aspect of task research, and a topic to which we shall return in later chapters.

4
Tasks in Second Language Pedagogy

Having traced some of the educational antecedents for the kinds of activities we are calling second language pedagogic tasks, and having considered some of the ways in which those activities have been used in human sciences research, we narrow the focus to concentrate more closely on the development of tasks as a significant force in language teaching. First, we consider the impetus communicative language teaching gave to the development of task-type activities, looking more closely at their roles within different types of communicative language teaching programme. We then turn to closer consideration of the emergence of tasks as a key element of interest.

4.1 The development of Communicative Language Teaching (CLT)

For many second and foreign language teachers, the broad principles underpinning the use of holistic activity in classroom activity were brought into concrete focus by Communicative Language Teaching (CLT) during the mid-1970s in the UK and Europe and somewhat later in North America. Earlier approaches to language teaching had been developed mainly in order to teach different types of language feature, such as pronunciation, grammar, vocabulary, conversational structures, functional elements. To do this they drew largely on a behavioural model of learning, based on the fundamental processes of presentation of input (involving learners' perception and comprehension), practice (involving the learners' reproduction and manipulation of the input) and production (involving learners' free strategic and exploratory use of the input material), a pedagogic procedure widely referred to as P, P and P. CLT aimed to break from this paradigm, on the grounds that there was a fundamental qualitative difference between the kinds of learning that had been promoted so far within classrooms on the one hand, and the kinds of second language learning that can occur in the target language community on the other.

Communication needed to become a touchstone for language teaching and learning in two main ways. First, it emphasised the central role of communication activities in all the main learning processes. Even if comprehension and production have distinct roles in language learning, communication should be central to both. Second, it questioned the viability of a pre-constructed syllabus, since learners have different levels of readiness and learn at different rates. That is, proponents of CLT argued that communication should determine both the content and the mode of learning. For many advocates of CLT theory, this implied a radical reconstrual of traditional classroom role relationships, with teachers and learners increasingly seen as co-participants (Candlin, 1987) and the role of the learner as an active agent in her own learning strongly emphasised (Breen, 1987). It was argued by some CLT proponents (notably Breen and Candlin, 1980) that issues normally considered the purview of the teacher/syllabus/institution (e.g. content, topic, classroom configuration, modes of evaluation, etc.) could now be seen as open to negotiation among learners and teachers, and importantly, space for learners to reflect on the route and processes of their own learning could be opened up.

4.2   Communicative activities and tasks

This theoretical approach gave rise to various principles intended to guide the structuring and management of second language programmes. It was also fuelled by, and in turn inspired, the development of a number of novel techniques for designing second language classroom activities which would engage learners in communication, widely referred to as 'communicative activities'.

Widdowson (1978) and Brumfit (1984a), both closely associated with the development of CLT, outlined principles, activities and practices for an emerging communicative approach. However, at that time, they rarely if ever used the term 'task'. Allwright (1984), another important influence on the development of CLT, was concerned to elaborate an account of the language classroom in which communication entered into the teaching and learning processes at a whole series of levels. 'Task' is one such level, but for him 'task' referred to any activity which a teacher might require of a student, down to answering a question. However it is possibly

Johnson (1979) who was the first explicitly to articulate the need for a concept of 'task' to incorporate the dimension of language processing into materials and as the orientation for teaching.

Quote 4.1   Johnson on task-oriented teaching

[M]ethodologies should be based not only on *linguistic* insights as to the nature of 'knowledge of a language', but also on *psycholinguistic* insights as to the processes involved in its use ... It is for reasons such as this that fluency in communicative process can only be developed within 'task-oriented teaching' – one which provides 'actual meaning' by focusing on tasks to be mediated through language, and where success or failure is seen to be judged in terms of whether or not these tasks are performed.
(Johnson, 1979: 198, 200)

There is room for discussion as to whether success or failure can be judged only in terms of task completion: as in all learning, completion is not the only concern in performing a language task. Swales, for instance, while endorsing the use of tasks as a central element in language teaching, is comfortable to admit 'the analysis and discussion of texts and situation, and the teaching and practice of form' (1990: 72). However, Johnson makes a crucial step in highlighting the need for materials not only to focus on relevant language, but also to engage the learners in developing the skills of using it in relevant ways.

4.2.1   Tasks in the teaching of language for specific or academic purposes

Johnson's view of 'task' was especially explored by educationists working in the teaching of language for specific or academic purposes (LS/AP). The purpose of LS/AP programmes is to provide language training for non-language specialists who need it for academic or professional purposes, but have limited time. Central to LS/AP work is the concept of needs analysis (Munby, 1978) as the basis for the specification of the type of content and the type of task relevant to learner needs and purposes. Thus, in LS/AP the notion of genre skills and situational demands goes somewhat further than Johnson's position, sharpening the criteria for task development.

A central concern then is relevance of language *and* relevance of activity. However, as Swales (1990) points out, it is possible to teach relevant language but in ways that are quite unsuitable.

> ## Quote 4.2   Swales on task appropriacy
>
> I used to teach an EAP course for students entering the largely English-medium Faculty of Law at the University of Khartoum in Sudan. One of the main genres that I used were Sudanese case reports, and for this choice I could put forward an elaborate justification. ... However, the comprehension tasks I invited the students to undertake were misconceived because they were designed to help the students to understand the *stories*. It was only when I attended classes given by a Criminal Law professor that I belatedly came to realize that the reading strategy required in legal education was not to understand – and retain the gist of – a narrative, but to spot the crucial fact on which the decision (rightly or wrongly) rested. The problem-solving law professor's questions were quite different to my own. Because I had failed to appreciate the role of the genre in its environment, the reading strategies I was teaching, however well-founded in terms of ESL methodology, were probably doing the students more harm than good.
> (Swales, 1990: 72–3)

The language being taught was appropriate, but the task type was not. With this in mind, authors increasingly became concerned to develop materials which not only provided exposure to appropriate types of language (e.g. McEldowney, 1982; White, 1978, 1979; Moore, 1979, 1980), but also to engage appropriate types of *processing* (e.g. Hall and Kenny, 1988; Morrow, 1980; Scott, 1981).

4.2.2   Tasks in content-based instruction

'Task' has also been an influential organising factor in the design and provision of content-based instruction (CBI). There are many approaches to CBI, but what unites them is a focus on content, with language teaching subsumed to the learning of content and arising out of engagement with that content. Tasks have been widely used in CBI in second and foreign language teaching (as seen in the project work described in Legutke and Thomas, 1991, and illustrated later in this book), and also play an important part in programmes providing language minority students with access to academic curriculum content in primary and secondary schools (e.g. Mohan, 1986; Leung, 2001; Dufficy, 2004; Van Avermaet, 2006), as well as in post-secondary education (Mohan and Marshall Smith, 1992; Snow and Brinton, 1997). Tasks are also an important organising principle in many approaches to adult basic education, particularly in immigrant and refugee programmes (e.g. the Australian Adult Migrant Education Program (AMEP), and the Flanders Centre for Migration and Learning). We describe some of the work developed in these contexts in Chapter 9.

In content-based instruction, then, content is organised around real-world themes or topics that learners encounter outside the language classroom and the kinds of tasks that they will need to engage with; thus it is possible to see the curriculum as part-content, part-process. This enables a distinction to be made between materials which introduce learners to the conceptual and thematic content of a scheme of work and materials which engage the learners in learning and communication processes. This has the merit of creating a dual teaching and learning perspective for any aspect of the curriculum: the dual focus enriches the coherence and hence the motivational appeal of the curriculum.

Quote 4.3   Van Lier on the relationship between task-based and content-based education

Task-based and content-based language teaching really go hand in hand, since a progression of tasks without some continuity or systematicity in terms of content progression (or coherence) would lead to a very disjointed, 'scattergun' syllabus. Conversely, content-based teaching in which little or no thought has been given to the design and sequencing of tasks will be a transmission, most likely in lecture or IRF form, of lesson material ... Therefore, task and content should be seen as a unity. (Van Lier, 1996: 205–6)

In a number of educational contexts, however, responsibilities for the teaching of content and language are divided: the 'content' teacher (e.g. of geography or physics) is responsible for the learning of the curriculum in his or her specialist area, and the language teacher is responsible for pupils' language development across those areas. This has been common practice, for example, in the provisions made for English as an Additional Language (EAL) in a number of British schools (Mohan, Leung and Davison, 2000), as well as in adjunct models of post-secondary CBI in North America (Brinton, Snow and Wesche, 1989). In contexts such as these, the adoption of a task-oriented approach can be a means of easing potentially awkward relationships between the specialist knowledge and expertise of the content teacher on the one hand, and the specialist knowledge and expertise of the second language teacher on the other.

Quote 4.4   Leung on the potential for tasks to clarify the roles of content teachers and language teachers

The task-based approach creates a common platform for the two teachers to share their expertise: from the content teacher his or her knowledge and skill of the subject matter (which inevitably involves language expressions) and from the ESL

Quote 4.4   (Continued)

teacher his or her knowledge and skill in developing pupils' target language appropriately within the task context. The content teacher can inform the ESL teacher what a task entails in terms of thinking processes, practical activities and specialist language use; the ESL teacher can use the task to promote understanding of the content knowledge and content-related language, and to generate language development opportunities.
(Leung, 2001: 187)

By the same token, tasks can provide an effective reference point for teacher development projects, as Cameron, Moon and Bygate (1996) have noted.

A further virtue of this approach is that it highlights the desirability of developing a systematic approach to the design, use and research of task types in their own right, and to the exploration of the extent to which they have consistent effects on language use and language learning irrespective of topic.

4.3   The emergence of 'task' in general language purpose language teaching

As we have seen, the use of holistic tasks has been a key element in CLT, LS/AP and content-based instruction for some time. Over the years, however, the term 'task' began to emerge in its own right as the centrepiece for specialised pedagogic initiatives, as in the various approaches to task-based learning and teaching (TBLT) described below.

The concept of task came to be of interest to second language researchers, teachers and methodologists for a number of reasons. For many, an interest in 'task' as a central guiding pedagogical principle grew out of a dissatisfaction with the ways in which mainstream CLT appeared to be developing, and in particular with CLT's apparent inability to harness issues relating to the content of learning with issues relating to modes of learning, as reflected in many (but not all) commercially produced CLT materials and in much (but not all) pedagogic practice. For example, although many CLT materials framed syllabus content in terms of communicative function (apologies, requests, and so on) rather than linguistic form, the procedures for bringing learners into engagement with that content continued to reflect a view of learning as a gradual accretion of individual, pre-selected items, mediated through orchestrated pedagogic sequences, proceeding from teacher presentation to controlled and less controlled practice and finally to free production. Thus for many researchers, teachers and methodologists the possibility of a pedagogic initiative driven by engagement with meaningful and relevant *tasks* offered a promising way through the communicative content/communicative procedure impasse that CLT seemed to have arrived at, and thus seen by many as an opportunity to return to the conceptual foundations of CLT (as outlined in Breen and Candlin, 1980), rather than a radical departure or innovation. From the mid- to late 1980s, the term 'task-based' was increasingly adopted to describe this alternative. The potential 'rewards' that task-based learning was seen to offer are summarised by Candlin.

Quote 4.5   Candlin on the rewards of task-based learning

- A *restructuring* of the relationship between curriculum and syllabuses
- A *re-evaluation* of the relationship between data, resources and processes in task content and task action
- A *re-estimation* of the relationship between goal-based and norm-referenced evaluation
- A *review* of the role relationship of 'teacher' and 'learner' in task co-participation
- A *re-emphasis* of the potential of the classroom as a place for experimentation into language and language learning
- A *renewing* of a critical perspective on the understanding of the second language acquisition and the place of language learning in the social identity of the learner

(Candlin, 1987: 22)

More recently 'task-based' has come to be rather loosely applied as an umbrella term to refer to any context in which tasks are used, whether as an occasional activity to fill a gap in a lesson plan, or as the central mode of instruction. 'Task-based' has also been widely used in the marketing of English language teaching materials, and as a broad descriptor for curriculum proposals (e.g. the Hong Kong SAR Target Oriented Curriculum, Curriculum Development Council, Hong Kong, 1999). As a result, it is not uncommon to find 'task-based' materials that would not meet the task criteria set out at the beginning of this chapter, or 'task-based' curricula that are broadly communicative in content, but not in mode of learning. This catch-all approach is unfortunate, partly because of the confusion and scepticism it has created in the teaching profession, and partly because it devalues 'task' as a distinct pedagogic construct. Thus, in our view, it is more useful to focus on the different ways that tasks can be used in a syllabus, whether centrally or peripherally. To this end, we can think of approaches to the use of tasks as *task-based*, *task-referenced* and *task-supported*.

4.3.1   Task-based learning and teaching (TBLT)

We use the term 'task-based' teaching and learning (TBLT) to refer to contexts where tasks are the central unit of instruction: they 'drive' classroom activity, they define curriculum and syllabuses and they determine modes of assessment:

Concept 4.1   Task-based learning and teaching

- Tasks define the language syllabus, with language being taught in response to the operational needs of specific learners.
- Tasks are seen as essential in engaging key processes of language acquisition.
- Tasks are selected on the basis that they replicate or simulate relevant real-world activities.
- Assessment is in terms of task performance.

Well-known examples of somewhat different approaches to this view of TBLT are Long and Crookes (1992), Skehan (1998) and Willis (1996), and are discussed in Part 2. TBLT has also come to be strongly associated with the strand of second language acquisition research that has focused on ways that task interaction can give rise to opportunities for the negotiation of meaning, the provision of feedback on output and focusing on form (Gass and Varonis, 1985; Long, 1985; Pica and Doughty, 1985).

Even after two decades, TBLT as outlined above continues to be extremely controversial and has attracted a number of highly vocal critics and detractors, notably Sheen (1994); Bruton (2002a, 2000b) and Swan (2005), who argue that TBLT has been imposed on teachers on the basis of limited research findings, generalised from laboratory-based studies in conditions that do not reflect the realities of the average teaching situation worldwide. Other critiques of TBLT from various perspectives include Aston (1986), Seedhouse (1999, 2005), Cook (2000), Mori (2002), Hampshire and Aguareles Anoro (2004) and Slimani-Rolls (2005). We return to the issues these raise in later chapters.

4.3.2   Task-referenced learning and teaching

We use the term 'task-referenced' (Bygate, 2000) to refer to contexts where progress through the syllabus is measured by performance on target achievement tasks. This is widely associated with various forms of 'outcomes-based' approaches, as adopted for example in adult migrant education in Australia and in parts of North America. Learners are assessed on 'competencies' or 'attainment targets', which they must meet in order to progress through the programme. In the Australian Adult Migrant Education Program (AMEP), for example, typical targets include 'can participate in a casual conversation; can respond to spoken instructions' (Brindley and Slatyer, 2002), and are broken down into subcomponents. Our use of the term 'task-referenced' thus highlights the use of tasks for assessment and for setting achievement targets, but makes no assumptions about the extent to which tasks may be used in teaching.

Concept 4.2   Task-referenced learning and teaching

- The curriculum and learner achievement are defined in terms of a series of selected target tasks.
- Teachers use whatever means are most suitable for preparing students for target assessment.

In other words, a task-referenced approach is one that uses tasks to set achievement targets and to evaluate learning, but may draw on a range of teaching procedures to attain those targets, and is not *necessarily* restricted to the types of activity that would conform to our definition of task at the beginning of the chapter.

4.3.3   Task-supported learning and teaching

In a task-supported (Ellis, 2003; Bygate, 2000) approach to the use of tasks in the syllabus, tasks are used as a key element in the learning cycle; they are used to actualise part of the curriculum, to enrich the syllabus or to provide additional learning opportunities (Ur, 1982; Brumfit, 1984; Nunan, 1995, 2001). However, tasks are not necessarily used for assessment purposes and the syllabus itself may be defined by categories other than tasks (Nunan, 1995, 2001; Richards et al., 1997). In task-supported teaching, then, tasks are seen as tools to be exploited by teacher and learners in the service of particular language aims and objectives, with the teacher providing support through briefing, on-line support and selective feedback.

Concept 4.3   Task-supported learning and teaching

- Tasks are an important, but not the sole. element in a pedagogic cycle.
- Tasks are used in conjunction with different types of activity.
- Tasks are one element in the syllabus, but not necessarily the defining element.
- Tasks may be used as an element of assessment, but not necessarily as the defining element.

The overall point we wish to emphasise here is that tasks themselves can be seen as neutral with respect to overall syllabus type or teaching approach. This reflects some of the ways that language teaching has evolved away from a technicist concern with 'method'. In a timely paper, Kumaravadivelu (1994) argued that the communicative movement had effectively given rise to a 'post-method' phase in language teaching. Rather than work with entirely pre-packaged methods, teachers could now negotiate content, sequence and activity type with learners from a range of resources. This account can be seen as being largely underpinned by the twin emphases of CLT proponents on principle rather than method, and on learner rather than teacher. In this context, the task becomes a resource, and a range of tasks a repertoire, which teachers can draw on in the light of experience and learners' preferences and needs. From this perspective, the study and use of tasks does not of itself entail the adoption of one particular type of approach to language teaching and learning. Rather, tasks can be seen as a pedagogic tool that can be used flexibly in different ways depending on purpose, setting and context, rather than as part of a pre-packaged set of a priori procedures and assumptions. In our view, the distinctions between task-based, task-referenced and task-supported are useful because they highlight both the flexibility of task as a pedagogic tool and the range of roles that tasks *can* fulfil, rather than narrowly focusing on one specialised use, as for example associ-ated with Long and Crookes' (1992) conceptualisation of task-based syllabuses.

A key consideration for teachers, however, remains the issue of the pedagogic focus of tasks. We use the term 'pedagogic focus' here as a means of highlighting four key domains where tasks can help focus learners' attention. These are:

1. aspects of the target language (Newton and Kennedy, 1996);
2. aspects of language processing (Anderson and Lynch, 1988);

3. aspects of the learning process (Bygate, 1996, 2001; and in relation to the development of learner autonomy, Kohonen et al., 2001; Breen, 2001);
4. socio-affective dimensions (Legutke and Thomas, 1991).

In a task-*based* approach, the pedagogic focus of the task is seen as that which arises naturally out of task performance in response to learners' evolving needs, very much in line with aspects of Freinet's approach described earlier. Any attempt to target specific language features pre-emptively (dubbed 'structure-trapping' in Skehan, 1998) is seen as an artificial intervention into the naturalistic learning processes that task interaction seeks to engage. On the other hand, the use of tasks in task-*supported* and task-*referenced* contexts could be seen as offering greater potential for flexibility in ways of introducing and exploiting the pedagogic focus of a task (including, but not necessarily restricted to, a pedagogic focus emerging naturally out of task enactment). However, as we saw earlier in relation to our discussion of Dewey, balancing the timing, role and nature of the pedagogic focus with task-oriented activity is complex, and we return to the topic in more detail in later chapters.

5
Defining Pedagogic Tasks: Issues and Challenges

At the beginning of this book, we proposed a set of general elements to describe what we broadly mean by 'task'. We did so to provide an initial point of reference for talking about issues relating to the use of tasks in general education and human sciences research. As we further narrow the focus in our consideration of tasks as a pedagogic tool for second language learning, we revisit the construct of 'task' and attempt a more precise definition than the general elements we offered in Chapter 1. To this end, we:

- Invite consideration of why a more precise definition might be desirable.
- Explore some of the ways that task have been defined in the literature.
- Highlight issues and challenges involved in arriving at an adequate task definition.
- Offer a working definition of our own.

5.1   Approaches to task definition

In order to distinguish between activities that are tasks and those that are not, and to focus our attention on using and studying them, a widely agreed definition of the term is both desirable and necessary. But arriving at such a definition is not straightforward – a considerable part of the second language task literature has long been concerned with the search for a precise, yet comprehensive definition of 'task', and the sheer volume of resulting definitions, redefinitions and counter-definitions that have proliferated must come as something of a surprise to colleagues working in other areas. The sources quoted in Kumaravadivelu (1993), Skehan (1998), Bygate, Skehan and Swain (2001), Johnson (2003) and Ellis (2003) all give a sense of the range covered by these definitions, as well as various points of convergence and divergence. Some of the most widely cited include the following:

Quote 5.1 Candlin defining 'task'

One of a set of differentiated, sequencable, problem-posing activities involving learners and teachers in some joint selection from a range of varied cognitive and communicative procedures applied to existing and new knowledge in the collective exploration and pursuance of foreseen or emergent goals within a social milieu.
(Candlin, 1987: 10)

Quote 5.2 Long defining 'task'

A piece of work undertaken for oneself or for others, freely or for some reward. Thus examples of tasks are painting a fence, dressing a child. 'Tasks' are the things people will tell you they do if you ask them and they are not applied linguists.
(Long, 1985: 89)

Quote 5.3 Prabhu defining 'task'

An activity which required learners to arrive at an outcome from given information through some process of thought and which allowed teachers to control and regulate that process.
(Prabhu, 1987: 24)

Quote 5.4 Skehan defining 'task'

An activity in which: meaning is primary; there is some communication problem to solve; there is some sort of relationship to comparable real-world activities; task completion has some priority; the assessment of the task is in terms of outcome.
(Skehan, 1998: 95)

We have chosen these examples because they illustrate ways in which definitions can vary in terms of the different dimensions of 'task' that are brought into focus. Candlin, for example, highlights the contextualisation of tasks as a jointly constructed activity in the social setting of the class-room, and reflects the critical, problem-posing stance of participatory educators like Freire, while Long highlights connectedness with 'real-world' activity; Prabhu's definition emphasises the cognitive demands placed on learners and the regulating role of the teacher, while Skehan's is applicable to tasks for use in research and assessment, as well as in the classroom. The focus of a definition may be deliberately selective (as in Long's alignment with the world outside the classroom) or deliberately inclusive (as in Candlin's enumeration of all the things that a task *could* be).

The way a task is defined, then, may depend on the perspective of the person making the definition and the purposes for which the definition is being made, a point raised in Bygate et al. (2001). For our purpose, however – a generic definition of second language pedagogic 'task' – we are faced with a choice: either to seek a definition that highlights those features that a task *could* have, or to work more parsimoniously with a definition that highlights only those features that a task *must* have. The advantage of the former is that it lays out the full set of options potentially available – a complete conceptual toolbox for task design and selection; the advantage of the latter is that it defines a task in terms of its bare essentials – the minimum requirements that must be present. There are obvious pluses and minuses to each approach, and although the minimalist option may be seen as considerably less ambitious, it is this approach that we follow here. We do this on the grounds that paring down a task to its essentials provides a more realistic, less idealised, more manageable and hence potentially more constructive basis for the exploration of tasks; for distinguishing among tasks and other types of pedagogic activity; and for exploring with teachers ways of working with tasks.

5.2   Criterial properties of a task: Ellis

Ellis (2003) is an example of a bare essentials approach to task definition. Based on a detailed study of a number of previous definitions (including among others those cited in Quotes 5.1–5.4), Ellis's definition is framed in terms of a set of essential, criterial properties:

Quote 5.5   Ellis's definition of 'task'

1. A task is a workplan.
2. A task involves a primary focus on meaning.
3. A task involves real-world processes of language use.
4. A task can involve any of the four language skills.
5. A task engages cognitive processes.
6. A task has a clearly defined communicative outcome.

(Ellis, 2003: 9–10)

Since the properties highlighted here are based on points of convergence across the definitions Ellis surveyed, this definition could be taken as representative of areas of general agreement, although inevitably this also means that some aspects of existing definitions (e.g. 'task' as a jointly constructed social milieu) are not overtly represented here. Nevertheless, to explore the scope of Ellis's approach to definition as it stands, we'll take a look now at each of his criterial properties, point by point.

5.2.1   Task as workplan

Like most definitions, Ellis's begins with a generic term, 'workplan', here echoing Breen's distinction between task-as-workplan and task-in-process distinction. However, by framing his definition in terms of 'workplan', Ellis uses the definition to refer explicitly only to the *intentions* of the teacher (and possibly the materials writer), and thus excludes the activities the students actually engage in. That is, the definition enables 'task' to be defined in terms of pedagogical intention, but not in terms of what happens in practice. However, other elements of the definition are not consistent with this position. Points 3 and 5, for example, are not helpful as criteria unless we can show what kinds of *processes* occur. At the very least, we have to be able to show that the task as designed does give rise to real-world processes of language use and that it engages cognitive processes. As noted earlier, this means that it is not enough to look at the activity on paper; we need to observe what happens when learners engage with it.

In fact, the definition of the term 'task' needs to accommodate the different ways in which it is used. For example, teachers and teacher educators will commonly ask questions of the kind: What did you ask the class to do? This is frequently directed at trainee teachers, for instance. Where a task is concerned, it refers to the task-as-workplan. The reason why it is relevant for trainee teachers is that they can often benefit from being encouraged to reflect about the choice and/or exact formulation of task instructions, and their relationship to the activities that learners actually engage in. In other words, teachers are encouraged to reflect on what they ask students to do, since it affects what they end up doing. Thus we need also to reflect on task as action and process.

A second type of question frequently asked by teachers of each other is: How did the task work? Or: How did your group get on with the task? Here the central concern is with what learners actually did. This refers rather to the task as 'task-in-process', but it is worth noting that the question is asked in the light of what they were asked to do.

From these two examples, we can argue that in educational contexts we are never simply interested in the task as workplan or the task in process: we are only interested in each in so far as it relates to the other. In other words, we need the term 'task' to refer to both dimensions of the activity, just as the word 'activity' itself, like words such as 'game, set and match', can refer both to the plan prior to the event, and to the events of the plan-in-action. All the more so in the case of language learning tasks, since without attention to both the plan and the process, the pedagogic principle is lost. Thus to understand tasks, far from ignoring what learners actually do with them, it is essential that we study how learners respond to and engage with tasks, and how they modify and reinterpret the workplan themselves.

Hence, rather than defining tasks as 'workplans', we propose that they can be more usefully defined as *a holistic type of pedagogical activity,* a term which can encompass both the plan itself (the task on paper) and how that plan is subsequently interpreted and enacted by learners and teachers.

5.2.2   Language use

Items 2, 3 and 4 in the definition are all concerned with language use. However, we could argue that items 2 and 3 are implied by item 4. That is, the phrase 'language use' implies both 'real world' and 'a primary focus on meaning'. While it might be useful to specify that tasks can involve the use of all four language skills, this is not strictly necessary, and is in any case implied in 'holistic' pedagogic activity. Given this, the phrase 'language use' can also be taken to imply that language is socially and interpersonally mediated. Hence we argue that *language use* is the key element of the definition.

5.2.3   Cognitive processes

Item 5 introduces the notion of cognitive process. As Ellis points out, this term has two meanings. On the one hand, any use of language involves some kind of cognitive activity; on the other, the term is often associated with problem-solving. Interestingly, many tasks used in second language pedagogy have a problem-oriented dimension, although it is worth noting that this dimension can be either problem-*solving* or problem-*posing* in its orientation. For example, in the former, a problem is typically set externally by the task designer with a solution to be found by the learners, as reflected in examples of problem-solving tasks in Prabhu (1987); in the latter, a problem may be jointly created by the learners themselves on the basis of personal experience, and used as a springboard for collaborative exploration of underlying issues rather than direct solution *per se*, as reflected in problem-posing tasks based on Freirean principles (see section 2.2.3 above) in Wallerstein (1983). In both cases, despite obvious differences in orientation towards problem resolution, it is nonetheless engagement with some kind of 'problem' that functions as a catalyst for learning. With this in mind, let us consider what this could entail in terms of task processes.

Quote 5.6   Bereiter and Scardamalia on problem-solving

... goal-directed activity in which a path to the goal is not known in advance and has to be discovered.
(Bereiter and Scardamalia, 1993: 129–30)

Here we have a more precise characterisation of some of the cognitive processes subsumed in Ellis's definition. But does this imply that for a problem-oriented task to be pedagogically effective, participants must know at least some of the relevant paths to the goal? Certainly knowing *none* of the relevant paths would create too heavy a learning load, and so we might expect that only a proportion of the paths should be unknown in advance. This much is common sense, perhaps. But are Bereiter and Scardamalia also implying that a problem-solving activity must involve the creation of a *new* path? If so, does this mean we risk ruling out the use of problem-oriented activities that focus on fluency development? Perhaps one way of avoiding risks such as these would be to expand this definition of 'problem-solving' to encompass improvement in the use of familiar paths, as well as the use of existing resources to complete the activity. An example from second language pedagogy is Samuda's (2001) distinction between 'knowledge-constructing' and 'fluency-stretching' tasks, discussed in Chapter 8.

A further puzzle for second language pedagogy is Bereiter and Scardamalia's statement that paths have to be 'discovered'. How does this relate to a teacher's decision to use a task to raise learners' awareness of the problem and to create a mental space for new relevant material to be introduced, rather than expecting them to discover the path for themselves? Questions such as these suggest that a problem-oriented dimension is not intrinsic to any particular task, but is a function of the relationship between the task and the knowledge state of the learners.

To return to Ellis's task definition, we propose that the following adaptation of Bereiter and Scardamalia's characterisation of problem-solving provides a richer conceptualisation of the cognitive processes that may be engaged through working with tasks: *a task is used to create some challenge aimed at promoting language development.*

We propose that this reworking of the original definition allows for the following possibilities: raising participants' awareness of the need for a new path; enabling them to understand and appropriate new resources which will enable them to follow a new path; or enabling them to reorganise familiar resources to track a new path, or to improve their use of familiar resources for a familiar path. (We note, though, that each of these possibilities may not always engage conscious cognitive processes.)

5.2.4   Outcome

By highlighting the need for 'a clearly defined communicative outcome', Ellis focuses attention on the importance of a meaningful outcome. As we saw in the case of the TIP task, this is an essential element of a task. The outcome of a task can be described as meaningful in the sense that it can be interpreted and evaluated in a number of pragmatic ways – for instance as true or false, as more or less informative, as more or less persuasive, or as more or less amusing, interesting or sad.

However, Ellis's notion of 'a clearly defined communicative outcome' is problematic. For example, how clear is 'clear' and who decides? (One might reply 'the students, of course', but students do not necessarily agree.) In addition, what counts as a 'communicative outcome'? Is a number, a communicative outcome? Or a diagram? Or a performance? Or a report? Or cake? A piece of music? A poster? In order to navigate these problems, we propose some alternative phrasing here: an *explicit non-linguistic outcome, that is a language (and/or semiotically) mediated outcome that is not in itself a language focus.*

By 'explicit' we mean an outcome that is somehow signalled or stated. By 'non-linguistic' outcome we mean a *pragmatic* conclusion to the task. This can take many forms, for example, laughter, the communication of information, the production of a persuasive stretch of talk or writing, a poem, a list, a brochure, a meal, a T-shirt design, a mural, a song, a diagram, a map, a chart, and so on. We use 'outcome' in a generic sense, denoting it as one of the essential requirements of a task, although we recognise that it is in many cases possible and desirable for a task to have more than one outcome signalled in more than one way.

There is, however, another problem. A challenge for designing educational activity in any discipline is that pedagogic activity simultaneously seeks to engage two types of learning: outcome (content) learning and process (procedural) learning. In many educational activities the emphasis is on outcome learning, although this is always accompanied by some process (or procedural) learning. In language education, however, activities are often deliberately designed, selected and used with the purpose of engaging learners in the *use* of language in order to achieve an outcome. Unlike other disciplines, then, language is both means and end. Language learning tasks are concerned with two types of pedagogical significance: first, that associated with the immediate outcome; second, that of language development. Opportunities for language development may be targeted through the 'product' of the task via the outcome (e.g. feedback on the poster summarising conclusions at the end of the TIP task) or through the process of arriving at that outcome (e.g. feedback on the language used in small group discussion speculating on the objects in the TIP task), or through both. Hence we propose that tasks need to have a non-linguistic outcome and that they are used to promote language development through process or product or both.

5.3   A working definition of 'task'

Our exploration of the implications underlying the six aspects of Ellis's task definition has highlighted some of the challenges and issues involved in defining what a pedagogic task is in terms of its bare essentials. In attempting to speak to these issues and challenges in light of the general elements of a task we established earlier in the chapter, we offer some modifications to Ellis's original:

- A task is a holistic pedagogical activity.
- A task involves language use.
- A task has a pragmatic, non-linguistic outcome.
- A task is used in such a way as to create some challenge aimed at language development.
- A task is aimed at promoting language learning through process or product or both.

These can be expressed in a single sentence:

Concept 5.1   A working definition of a second language pedagogic task

A task is a holistic activity which engages language use in order to achieve some non-linguistic outcome while meeting a linguistic challenge, with the overall aim of promoting language learning, through process or product or both.

Although the aim of a generic minimalist approach to definition is to distinguish broadly a task from other types of pedagogic work, a study of tasks necessarily must extend well beyond these minimum features to include relationships between task characteristics and language; task implementation and language; students, tasks and language; task characteristics, task implementation, students, and learning; task and social context.

With our working definition of 'task', we have begun to narrow our focus from the use of holistic tasks in general education and in human sciences research to the use of tasks in second language pedagogy and research. We now narrow the focus again to explore the pedagogic context in which tasks came into prominence in second and foreign language teaching.

6
Engaging Learning Processes: Implications for the Use of Second Language Tasks

To round out our discussion of the role of tasks in second language learning, we re-situate issues raised in this section in relation to broader conceptualisations of learning in two ways. In this, we:

- revisit aspects of learning and problem-solving;
- revisit issues of general learning processes.

In both cases, we then narrow the focus again to:

- highlight key factors in understanding ways that tasks can relate to second language learning,

first, by revisiting aspects of learning and problem-solving; and second, by revisiting the issue of general learning processes. In both cases, we narrow the focus again to highlight key factors in understanding ways in which tasks can relate to second language learning.

6.1   Real-world activities, holistic tasks and learning: some issues

As we have seen, one issue raised repeatedly since Dewey is how pedagogy can be related to real-world activity. In what ways can the slipstream of real-world experience be appropriately harnessed as a tool for learning? One dimension worth exploring is the element of structure already inherent in some types of real-world activity, and the elements of structure inherent in the sequences in which those activities may be typically encountered. Lave (1990), in a study of tailors' apprentices learning in the context of the workplace, describes how the apprentices worked through a progression of workplace experiences starting with activities that provided access to *overall* goals for performance. For example, by starting with tasks like finishing and ironing completed garments the apprentices were able to develop an understanding of the expected requirements and standards for the whole task, including level of finish and the shape of components. From this they typically moved on to activities providing access to requirements for *particular* performances, for example, specific procedures for constructing garments. The apprentices' workplace learning thus appeared to progress from engagement with low accountability tasks (some tolerance of error) to engagement with high accountability tasks (no tolerance of errors because of significant consequences). In citing Lave's study, it is not our intention to imply that there is a necessary connection between apprenticeship models of learning and the use of tasks in second language pedagogy. Rather, what is of interest is that inherent in the progression described by Lave is a movement that starts with a focus on 'the big picture' – the demands of the whole task – and continues towards a focus on the details of its parts. The 'whole to parts' progression illustrated here is an option that might be usefully exploited in the use of tasks for classroom learning (see Chapters 7 and 9).

However, as Ericsson and Hastie (1994) point out, we also need to take into account that, beyond a certain point, learning in real-world situations may be less efficient and less effective than in deliberately structured learning situations. Ericsson and Hastie identify two reasons for this. First, in everyday activities – whether in work or play – learning opportunities may occur randomly and many of them only occasionally. Second, whether in work or play, the purposes and rewards of the activity are generally not conducive to learning. In work, the main demand is for efficiency, while in play the search for the pleasures of 'flow' leads the participant away from practice at eliminating errors. Both factors work against learning. A pedagogy that uses holistic or real-world activities in the classroom thus needs to take this in account.

A number of findings from the study of problem-solving highlight more precisely what it is that needs to be taken into account and how. In a survey of studies of children's cognitive development, Ellis and Siegler (1994) highlight factors that seem significant in children's development in problem-solving in their mother tongue. Interestingly, a number of the issues that Ellis and Siegler bring together could be related to a number of the themes we have been highlighting. With this mind, we briefly summarise some of the issues they raise and explore their potential relevance for the use of tasks in second language learning.

Ellis and Siegler focus on three aspects of the development of problem-solving:

1. formation of strategies;
2. representation;
3. self-regulation.

In this they highlight three main kinds of 'representation':

1. memory for past occurrences;
2. language;
3. external representations.

'Self-regulation' is seen in terms of:

- planning;
- private speech;
- dialogue.

While these processes are all important, Ellis and Siegler's survey offers evidence to suggest that learning does not occur without an appropriate task structure or facilitative learning conditions (see Example 6.1).

Example 6.1   Issues arising from research into the development of problem-solving abilities

1. *Planning needs support*: Planning involves preparatory reflection, which can be broken down into a number of sub-features, influencing behaviour in a series of ways. Children are unwilling to plan, but planning seems to increase as a function of their sensitivity to the nature of task demands. Nonetheless, planning needs encouragement.
2. *The role of feedback and collaboration*: 'Good ideas do not automatically win out over bad' (Ellis and Siegler, 1994): Working with a partner, receiving feedback and working with a partner who used the target rule across a series of practice problems, was far more likely to lead to correct rule formulation, and to adoption of the rule. This is one reason why it may be important for learners to know the language learning purpose as well as the intended task outcome.
3. *Problem/task structure*: Understanding the goals that strategies must meet is critical to avoiding random trial-and-error behaviour. This implies that both problems and learning purpose need to be clearly defined for learning to take place.

Example 6.1   (Continued)

4. *Problems and strategy development*: Experience of solving particular problems leads to the development of multiple strategies for solving that class of problem. This suggests that a systematic pedagogy would need to group task types.
5. *Interaction type*: Beneficial effects do not follow automatically from working with others, but rather depend on the nature of the interaction. Studies of the way in which collaborative interactions actually occur suggest that the desired types of collaborative interaction are exceptional. If partners work in parallel, or one partner dominates the interaction, collaborations are no more productive than one individual working alone. Further the reluctance of the older, more expert children to relinquish control of the task to the younger, less expert one is a block to the less expert participant's learning. In contrast designed activities which structure and support particular types of interactive questioning are effective.
6. *The positive role of activity as context*: Decontextualised briefing for problem-solving is ineffective because hard to transfer. In contrast, contextualising support within tasks is effective because they are applied to specific tasks, are open to joint contributions, and as a result are more motivating, allow active participation, deep processing and enable application of skills to a variety of sample tasks, encouraging generalisation.

As we can see, the research reviewed by Ellis and Siegler suggests that tasks are valuable because, in line with Dewey and Bruner, they contextualise learning. However, design, language learning focus, planning, feedback, interaction types and guidance are all essential. In other words, as Ericsson and Hastie point out, naturally occurring activities, however meaningful, are not of themselves necessarily good learning environments.

Further, the research reviewed by Ellis and Siegler suggests that tasks do not necessarily lead to learning if students are not provided with feedback through practice tasks (if students are working alone or with another novice), or if one of the students does not already use the pattern. It is common for the 'expert' child not to enable other participants to become actively involved in the task. This research also shows that productive interactions do not occur spontaneously, but need modelling, structuring or prompting. It also appears that children have difficulty finding strategies to solve problems if the goals are not clear. Children, Ellis and Siegler argue, may be naturally unwilling to plan.

All this suggests that a second language pedagogy of tasks will be viable only if it seeks out systematic relations between tasks and language learning (issues of design, learning focus and interaction types), and the ways in which tasks are implemented in the classroom to promote learning (notably the use of planning, feedback and teacher guidance and support).

It is tempting to think of tasks as engaging language learning processes as if by magic (cf. Dewey 1910). However, Ellis & Siegler suggest that there are reasons for us to develop a critical stance regarding how tasks work to promote learning.

This raises some searching questions regarding the design and use of tasks for language learning:

1. Is the goal of the task clear and do the students know what kind of learning they are supposed to be aiming for? In particular, if the goal is linguistic, do they know what language they are trying to work on? If it is not linguistic, what is the role of any eventual goal achievement?
2. Is planning presented as strategically valuable, and if so what is it focused on?
3. Is formative feedback provided?
4. If feedback is not provided, are dyads formed so that one of the pair is already an expert in the target domain, and if so, is the expert briefed to allow the novice to participate actively?
5. Is the desired type of group- or pair-interaction supported or prompted; and are the guidelines contextualised within particular tasks?

In other words, research in both education and social psychology provides grounds for thinking that it is inadequate to simply provide tasks for learners to do and hope that valuable interaction or learning will take place. This would be task-as-magic, and it would be understandable if such an approach were seen as 'task-as-chaos'. Instead, questions such as 5 above might point in a direction which could help us to answer Dewey's question: how might activities best be arranged so as to motivate, channel and support learners' efforts to learn? Let us explore this by returning again to Bruner.

6.2   Three types of general learning process

Bruner (1973) conceptualises learning in terms of three types of process:

1. acquisition (to refer to the processes of internalisation of new material);
2. transformation (to refer to the processes whereby the new material is adopted and deployed by learners for their own strategic purposes);
3. evaluation (to refer to any processes of review in the light of any internal and external criteria).

These processes can occur more or less simultaneously, and in many cases evaluation can operate before transformation has occurred.

Quote 6.1   Bruner on types of learning process

First there is acquisition of new information – often information that runs counter to or is a replacement for what the person has previously known implicitly or explicitly. At the very least it is a refinement of previous knowledge. Thus one teaches a student Newton's laws of motion, which violate the testimony of the senses. Or in teaching a student about wave mechanics, one violates the student's belief in mechanical impact as the sole source of real-energy transfer. Or one bucks the language and its built-in way of thinking in terms of wasting energy by introducing the student to the conservation theorem in physics which asserts that no energy is lost. More often the situation is less drastic, as when one teaches the details of the circulatory system to a student who already knows vaguely or intuitively that blood circulates.

A second aspect of learning may be called transformation – the process of manipulating knowledge to make it fit new tasks. We learn to unmask or analyze information, to order it in a way that permits extrapolation or interpolation or conversion into another form. Transformation comprises the ways we deal with information in order to go beyond it.

A third aspect of learning is evaluation, checking whether the way we have manipulated information is adequate to the task. Is the generalization fitting, have we extrapolated appropriately, are we operating properly? Often a teacher is crucial in helping with evaluation, but much of it takes place by judgments of plausibility without our actually being able to check rigorously in our efforts.'
(Bruner, 1973: 421–2)

Now let us relate this more specifically to second language learning. Bruner's 'acquisition' can be related to the processes whereby aspects of the language are perceived in terms of visual and acoustic forms, and in terms of the corresponding articulatory and graphic production plans, comprehended, and then internalised into the memory system, through processes of assimilation and accommodation. These processes involve what might be called *form* and *discourse*. By form we mean intonation, pronunciation – including the articulation of phonemes in the context of co-occurring words; grammar – referential, requiring users to have referents to refer to; discoursal aspects of tense, mood, aspect, modality, formulaic chunks and collocational sequences. The term 'discourse' can be used in different senses: we use it to refer to speech acts, including discoursal aspects of marking and phasing of speech acts; discourse structures, monologic, such as narrative, process, description, explanation; dialogic, such as conversation, debate, argument, instruction, interviewing, consultation, service encounters.

By transformation Bruner refers to the learners' personal strategic employment of the resources that are being acquired. In second language learning, transformation processes involve the personalisation of the language by the learner, part of what has been termed 'appropriation' by those working in a Vygotskyan perspective, as well as generalisation to new contexts. Evaluation refers to the processes of judging the match between the learners' use of language and target uses. We exemplify these three processes in more detail later, where we map each process onto the sample TIP task, and then explore what this could imply more broadly for the use of tasks as contexts for engaging second language learning.

6.3   Tasks as contexts for engaging learning processes

The case we have made thus far suggests that tasks are activities in and around which the processes of acquisition, transformation and evaluation can occur in contexts of holistic language use. Van Lier comments that second language learning

> can be accomplished by learners using a variety of different resources, including:
>
> a) assistance from more capable peers or adults
> b) interaction with equal peers
> c) interaction with less capable peers . . .
> d) inner resources. (1996: 193)

He also points out that feedback can have a more powerful effect on learning than interaction (1996: 192), and that one source of this can be the task itself. This suggests that in trying to understand the key ways in which tasks can relate to learning, we need to consider:

a) interaction with the task;
b) assistance from more capable peers;
c) assistance from the teacher before, during or after the task;
d) interaction with equal peers;
e) interaction with less capable peers;
f) inner resources;
g) other resources (e.g. printed, electronic).

This is presented diagrammatically in Figure 6.1.

Now let us see relate these factors to the TIP task we introduced as an example at the beginning of this chapter:

- *Teacher purpose*: to engage the learners in an activity which would raise awareness of the semantic area of epistemic modality (i.e. ways of expressing degrees of certainty).

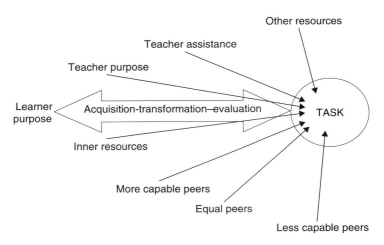

Figure 6.1   Key factors in understanding ways in which tasks can relate to second language learning

- *Teacher assistance*: pre-task: brief the learners orally on the purpose; underline and help learners achieve the purpose during the task as need arises and review their findings at the end of the task; post-task: draw on learners' joint experience as a basis for targeting expressions of epistemic modality.
- *Task design*: to engage learners in a series of processes, notably observation and interpretation of the objects, and prediction of their likely owner.

In line with our previous discussion of possible differences between the 'official' and the 'private' task, we are more speculative about the learner-related considerations.

- Learners' purposes could include: to manage relevant participation in a group task; to participate in organising or evaluating comments; to develop aspects of lexico-grammatical repertoire; to experiment with current resources; to play.
- Learner's inner resources: might or might not suffice to enable her to locate the nature of problem, and to assess her current resources for dealing with it.
- More capable peers and teacher: might help clarify the nature of the problem, and offer some resources to deal with it.

• Less capable peers: might lead her to articulate her own understanding of the problem, and how to deal with it.

Now let us relate these considerations to Bruner's three types of learning process: *acquisition*, *transformation* and *evaluation*, outlined in section 6.1.

During the task a learner might:

a) In terms of acquisition
  • notice relevant concepts for which resources were lacking, alone, or with the aid of the teacher, or a peer;
  • perceive the need for missing resources;
  • notice resources used by other students to handle the conceptual problem;
  • notice functional and possibly formal similarities between some of the resources being used;
  • notice aspects of the use of certain resources which she was already somewhat familiar with (for instance the structural regularities of modal verb groups);
  • discover the possibility of extending familiar resources to handle the conceptual area;
  • improve accuracy in using own or others' relevant available resources.

b) In terms of transformation
  • simplify or complexify the conceptual demand of the task – e.g. simplifying by shifting the problem of expressing degrees of certainty to verbs of opinion; or complexifying by using a range of expressions of modality;
  • find and use familiar linguistic resources for dealing with the conceptual content, either from her own memory store, or from the talk of others during the task;
  • embed familiar resources into a more extended (e.g. explanatory) routine;
  • increase fluency in using relevant available resources.

c) In terms of evaluation
  • appraise the extent of lack of resources;
  • appraise the adequacy of existing resources;
  • appraise the relevance of other people's resources and advice;
  • appraise the appropriateness of their or of others' use of new or available resources;

- appraise the extent to which the task and follow-up work helped her to understand and handle the problem area.

In short, all these resources can be seen as interacting with the learner's purpose in engaging in the task. All can feed into Bruner's three processes of acquisition, transformation and evaluation. The questions we will be pursuing in the rest of this volume cluster around the role of features of tasks in generating work and outcomes, and the ways in which tasks can be exploited by teachers and learners so as to promote the kinds of processes which we have outlined above.

6.4   Tasks in second language pedagogy: a summary

Rather than thinking in terms of concepts such as an all-embracing teaching method or approach, or theory of language acquisition, our focus is on the ways in which the task can be used to mediate language use, language processing and, through this, learning. This is illustrated in Figure 6.2.

Figure 6.2 suggests that varying an aspect of a task is simultaneously an issue of design, of pedagogy and of language use and learning. This interaction shapes and is shaped by the classroom ecology. For instance, in the case of the TIP task, changing the number and type of objects would be a design issue, and this could change the pedagogy and the learners' language. If the teacher decides to describe the various objects before the students start the task, then this would affect the nature of the input and could affect the learners' language. That is, any change in the task-as-plan corresponds at the same time to a pedagogic decision and

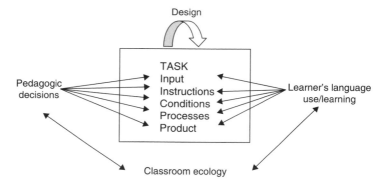

Figure 6.2   How a task can be used to mediate language use, language processing and, through this, learning

to learners' language use. Learners' language use is engaged at two points: in understanding the input, the instructions and the conditions; and in acting on this to engage the processes and achieve the target outcome.

What this amounts to is an analysis of the relationships between what might be called the 'task-as-tool' or instrument, and those who are using it – the teacher and the students. Similar relationships can be found in other areas of human activity. For instance, there is a comparable relationship between the rules of a game and those who play it: changing the size of a tennis racket, the height of the net or the nature of the ball will affect how the players perform. Similarly, in medicine changing the type of scanning devices that are available changes the behaviour both of doctors and of patients.

These relationships can be mapped broadly in terms of the following aspects:

1. Task	Characteristics (input; instructions; intended outcomes) Implementation (task conditions: preparation, briefing, monitoring, timing, familiarity)
2. Language	Task and language product
3. Processes	Task and processing
4. Learning	Task, language processes, task conditions and learning Task, language products, task conditions, and learning
5. Participants	Task and learner/teacher differences Task and learner/teacher strategies
6. Exploitation	Teaching processes (e.g. pre-/while/post-; $+/-$ explicit) Task purpose (e.g. role in the teaching cycle)
7. Ecology	Task and class ethos Task and learner identity

This may look complicated. However, the richness of a holistic approach to language teaching is bound to lead to a richness of issues for exploration. We return to these issues in the following chapters.

7
Researching Second Language Pedagogic Tasks

We turn now to some of the key issues and challenges in researching second language pedagogic tasks. We consider studies undertaken in terms of their potential to inform users and designers of tasks in pedagogically useful ways – that is, in terms of their pedagogical relevance. To be of use, empirical research, like pedagogy, needs to focus on practice and to describe and explain what happens and why. So if tasks are aimed at developing holistic language abilities, a key priority is to explore how far tasks achieve this, in what ways, under what conditions and why. Answers to questions such as these are important in practical terms and to further our understanding about the conditions and processes of classroom language learning.

Although tasks are devised and used for pedagogical purposes, the kinds of research that can be undertaken extend well beyond the theories and practices of classroom users. This is hardly surprising since it is not unusual for research to approach phenomena from many angles, with some being more closely related than others to users' concerns. This is partly due to the fact that all phenomena can be conceptualised from a wide range of distinct perspectives. For instance, meals can be studied in terms of gastronomy, culinary arts, diet, economy, psychology, chemistry, anthropology or language, among others, not all of them relevant to the family cook. All these potential perspectives generate distinct theories, which in turn are all normally open to verification and development. And although research is subject to budgetary constraints, there is nothing to stop a line of research being developed if there are people determined to do it and participants willing to cooperate.

It is no surprise then that research into tasks has been undertaken from a range of perspectives and distinct theoretical positions in ways which are not necessarily clearly related to pedagogical practices and theories.

7.1   Approaches to researching second language pedagogic tasks

It can be useful to distinguish between two aspects of research – the focus of study and the research paradigm. Both are theoretically shaped in the light of theories the researchers are interested in, whether these are derived from the classroom or from other sources. The focus is shaped by an idea of what categories or phenomena the researcher considers to be relevant; the paradigm by the research theories and practices which they consider most relevant and reliable. We can illustrate this in relation to the TIP task discussed in Chapter 1.

In the TIP task, students are given objects which they are told come from someone's pocket, and their task is to decide about who the owner is likely to be. Hence researching the task can involve any of the following:

- input information;
- aims;
- discussion process;
- outcome.

In addition, we know that tasks have to be enacted by teachers and by learners. We also know that what happens will be influenced by the participants' perceptions and understandings; that tasks are intended to contribute in some way to learning; that there are differences among learners and among teachers; and that they are used in the context of lessons, and of courses and curricula.

So a researcher studying a task such as this one could focus on a number of features, as illustrated in Table 7.1. Essentially, each feature is considered in interaction with one or more tasks. The aim is to understand tasks in the light of empirical data about how learners, teachers, materials designers and others interact with tasks, for better or for worse. This means that the research will simultaneously provide information about the people involved in it. Sometimes this may result in information which says more about the people than about the tasks – see Foster's (2001) study of the impact of planning on use of formulaic language, in Box 7.21.

Table 7.1 could be expanded in many ways and could also be elaborated. Bruner, Goodnow and Austin (1956/1972) raised a series of more detailed questions about tasks which at the time had been devised for investigating learning (see Example 7.1). Their concern was to examine how tasks can be used to explore one aspect of learning – concept attainment – and to raise three sets of questions: focus on the learning process; questions

Table 7.1   Potential elements of focus in researching second language pedagogic tasks

---

Teachers' procedures and processes
Teacher's pre-task preparation
Teacher's post-task follow-up

Learners' procedures and processes
Learners' talk; phases of task; outcomes

Impact of elements of task design
Complexity of the task
Demands of the discourse type
Prototypically of task structure
Types of roles required by the task

Impact of conditions of implementation
Familiarity with the task
Planning time
Repetition of the task
Distribution of roles

Dynamics around the task
Negotiation for meaning
Processes of talk construction
Kinds of learning generated through task involvement

Construals
Learners' interpretations of the task
Learners' evaluations of the task
Teachers' perceptions of the task

Individual differences
Learner differences: motivation, style, cultural background, age proficiency
Teacher differences: e.g. style, background, experience.

Task, lesson and curriculum
Relationship between tasks and schemes of work/course plan
Relationship between tasks and target tests
Relationship between tasks and overall curriculum goals

---

about the internal effectiveness of the activity; and questions about what we now might call the ecology of the activity.

Example 7.1 illustrates that our list of items to focus on can not only be extended, it can also be redefined, and the various parts of it can be elaborated in greater detail.

At the least, these options indicate aspects of the topic which are likely to be worth exploring. They reflect thought around the topic and

---

Example 7.1

Focus on the learning process

a. How do people achieve the information necessary for isolating and learning a concept?
b. How do they retain the information gained from encounters with possibly relevant events so that it may be useful later?
c. How is retained information transformed so that it may be rendered useful for testing a hypothesis still unborn at the moment of first encountering new information?

Internal effectiveness of the activity

a. What concepts (i.e. repertoires and skills) do the tasks enable learners to attain?
b. Using tasks, how speedily do learners achieve concept attainment (i.e. with as low a number of encounters as possible)?
c. How reliably do learners achieve concept attainment?
d. How comfortably do learners achieve concept attainment (i.e. without undue strain)?
e. How directly do learners achieve concept attainment (i.e. without excessive error or false directions)?
f. How far are learners helped to know when they have achieved their goals?

Ecology of the activity

a. What are learners' intentions and objectives?
b. What is the internal structure and focus of the activity?
c. How available is the feedback, and what is its quality?

(Bruner, Goodnow and Austin, 1956/1972: 132ff)

---

offer different directions depending on one's theoretical assumptions about what is relevant, and why further study could be informative.

7.2 Dimensions of task research

Whichever topic one chooses, however, there are a number of decisions to be made about the research methods to be used. Most of the topics outlined in Example 7.1 have to be approached along three sets of dimensions, each of which offers the researchers a choice. These are:

- systemic vs. process;
- macro vs. micro;

- quantitative vs. qualitative.

To clarify these distinctions, let us briefly consider each dimension in turn.

7.2.1   Dimension 1: systemic vs. process

Systemic studies

A systemic approach is particularly interested in obtaining a picture of one or more students at a given point in time. This might be in terms of their performance or what is inferred to be their internalised language system and might give rise to questions such as these: 'What speech acts do speakers use on a particular task?' 'What kinds of verb or noun systems are used at a given/different levels of proficiency?' 'And with what fluency or accuracy?' An interest in motivation, strategies or perceptions would attempt to derive a picture of a student's strategic repertoire, motivational disposition or overall perceptions in relation to a task, asking: 'What range of strategies do they seem to know about and/or employ in relation to a particular task?' 'What are their motivational attitudes towards the task?' 'What is the student's perception of a give task?'

A systemic study tends to seek out information from one or more teachers or learners such as:

- the range of language features used on a task or under particular conditions;
- the set of attitudes to and perceptions of a task or set of tasks, or of the experience(s) of using them;
- changes in language knowledge, language use or attitudes and perceptions after using one or more tasks;
- how tasks relate systematically to the broader curriculum.

That is, systemic studies seek to uncover systems of knowledge or understanding, often in order to make comparisons across tasks, groups or time. Systemic studies have difficulty in dealing with change processes as they tend to focus more on the differences between systems at two points in time than on the ways in which particular events between the two points might have contributed to the perceived changes.

Overall this approach can be seen as trying to get a snapshot or summative view of the learner. Even if studies are longitudinal, the researcher's target is an interlinked series of summative views. It is analogous to the cartographer's attempt to map a territory, the chemist's molecular view of the world or the attempt in the creative arts to summarise a work or performance. However, it has two main weaknesses. The first is that snapshots generally rely heavily on inference for interpretation, because the findings tend to become disembodied from the context which yielded the data. The second weakness is related to the first, namely that snapshot data are very difficult to understand in terms of the local processes which make sense to teachers and students. This is significant because it is important to know how outcomes relate to classroom processes, for both theoretical and practical purposes.

Process studies

In contrast, process studies attempt to address the problem encountered by systemic approaches by focusing on what one or more learners or teachers do prior to, while engaged on or after doing one or more tasks. Process studies aim to understand how learners and/or teachers use particular activities in order to complete them, and to promote learning. Process studies therefore concentrate on tracking learners' individual and joint behaviours moment by moment, in order to derive a picture of how tasks are accomplished. The primacy of this focus means that process studies are often carried out without reference to systemic data: such studies generate understanding of the dynamics of tasks, but may pay less attention to relating the processes to participants' existing or subsequent understandings.

This approach opens up other avenues for studying teaching and learning processes. An important strength is that teachers and learners can relate the findings to activities and episodes occurring within their classrooms, and the findings can therefore inform their use of materials.

The approach does, however, have important limitations. One is that observations made in the context of particular activities are open to multiple interpretations. A question from a student may not be what it appears: the student may know, or have a strong hunch about, the answer, but wish simply to launch the discussion. Alternatively, the student may have temporarily forgotten the answer or misunderstood the issue. Equally, apparent discoveries in the context of an activity may hide misunderstandings, be only partially understood or be understood but not yet have reached the point where they can be functionally applied. The point is that the complexities of the situation make uncontroversial interpretation from outside extremely difficult. Hence the danger with process studies is that without data which adequately sample the student's functional control it is not possible to interpret adequately what was known and what was learnt. Given their respective strengths, it makes sense to consider both options as potentially important allies in task research.

7.2.2   Dimension 2: macro vs. micro

'Macro' studies refer to group studies, while 'micro' studies refer to case studies. We separate this dimension from the systemic/process distinction because it is possible to undertake a systemic study on a single case (common in child language studies and in language pathology, among other domains). It is also possible to undertake a process-oriented study involving many participants (Lynch and Maclean, 2000, 2001, discussed below, are of this kind). The key point about the macro/micro distinction is that macro studies generally seek to generalise across cases, obliging the research to omit more details than a micro study. In contrast, micro studies offer more space to the researcher to explore idiosyncrasies within the data, although it is mistaken to imagine that micro studies usually enable the researcher to avoid having to make any omissions at all, because all research is necessarily selective. It is worth noting that studies can use both macro and micro procedures, one being used to cross-check the other (Bygate and Samuda, 2005, is a recent example).

7.2.3   Dimension 3: qualitative vs. quantitative

The final dimension is qualitative/quantitative. This concerns whether or not to handle the data numerically. We separate this from the other two because it is possible for a process-oriented study to check frequencies (see Swain and Lapkin, 2000, 2001). Furthermore, case study data can be handled either without attending to frequencies (as in Donato 1994) or with an analysis of frequencies (as is often the case in child language studies, language pathology studies and in task-related research such as Duff, 1993).

The dimensions taken together offer four main research paradigms, as illustrated in Table 7.2. Examples of studies for each subtype appear in the appropriate quadrant.

Most of the systemic research into pedagogic tasks has been through macro quantitative studies, while most (though by no means all) of the process research has been undertaken through micro qualitative studies. Some methodologies have been scarcely exploited at all in the study of tasks (e.g. personal construct theory, an approach to research which uses a micro-oriented methodology to investigate personal understandings has not been attempted in this field). Yet all approaches have an important contribution to make, and there are grounds for believing that all reflect some aspect of most teachers' thinking. If our concern is whether

Table 7.2 The four main research paradigms

	Systemic	Process
Micro		
Quantitative	Studies of how individuals personally construe tasks, or their use.	Studies of how individuals or small groups negotiate their way through a particular task.
Qualitative	Studies of how an individual's inter-language or motivation might change after experiencing one or more tasks.	Studies of how a teacher uses a task with a particular class.
Macro		
Quantitative	Studies of how students' fluency or accuracy, or motivation are generally affected by different tasks, or task conditions.	Studies of the extent to which students engage in particular discourse sequences in order to complete a task.
Qualitative	Interview-based studies of students' motivation before and after using a particular type of task or task condition.	Studies of designers' processes in task design.

tasks are a viable teaching instrument, then teachers, testers and materials designers all need to know how particular types of task generally work and whether their use has sufficiently consistent types of impact for them to be worth using. This implies a role for systemic studies. At the same time, it is important for teachers and designers to understand how individuals work through activities, and what kinds of language processes they engage in and why, since this too may be part of what tasks are being used to activate. General patterns reflecting the processes engaged in typically by groups of students are also of interest to teachers. Further, if one's concern is with the ways tasks are perceived and utilised, both a systemic perspective and the use of process-oriented methods will reflect some aspects of teachers' thinking.

However, it is also often important for findings from each approach to be related to analyses from other approaches. Thus, it can be important for systemic studies to be able to show how their findings relate to the processes learners engage in, while process analysts are sometimes likely to want to explore the extent to which their findings are typical/atypical in relation to a certain number of learners. In the same way, while it is important for teachers and testers to know what general processes or patterning occur under different conditions in different contexts, without studying individual cases we cannot know the kinds of experience that different learners have, and – just as important – it is impossible for us to take account of differences between learners.

We review some of the main directions of research from these perspectives next.

7.3   Overview of approaches to the study of tasks

7.3.1   Systemic studies of tasks: some examples

Systemic studies are interested in identifying representative patterning in data from students, individually or in groups. The aim is to understand the phenomenon being investigated in terms of a system – whether of knowledge, of proficiency, of attitudes and motivations, or of strategies. This means sampling enough to obtain information which is sufficiently thorough for the researcher to be able to conclude that the picture gained is stable, representative, not a chance occurrence, and therefore could be expected to appear again under comparable circumstances. Systemic studies can focus on a single individual or on groups. This approach is typical of many researchers (see Long, 1996; Loschky and Bley-Vroman, 1993; VanPatten, 1996; Skehan 1998; and in summary form Ellis, 2000).

Example 7.2   Long, 1981

Long's approach to the study of the use of tasks was based on a theory of learning significantly influenced by the work of Krashen. Long (1981) assumed that language is best acquired in the context of use, for two reasons. First, he argued that contexts of use help acquisition because they contain information about the language which is essential if the learner is to be able to relate the grammatical details of the language to their discourse meanings. That is, through talk language features can be simultaneously mapped onto both the grammatical system and the discourse system. Second, he held that since it is really only language which the learner is exposed to face to face that can be properly adjusted to the learner's level of acquisition, with problems being negotiated at source, tasks therefore offer a potentially valuable context for a learner to learn within the classroom. This means that the most effective learning is individualised, with the learner being able to identify new needed language, whether in an interlocutor's discourse or her own and at the point of need, obtain relevant clarification. This procedure Long termed 'negotiation for meaning'. Tasks clearly provide an opportunity for learning of this type, principally because they are centred on meaningful use of language. Deriving from Long's main concern, researchers have studied tasks in order to assess the extent to which tasks lead learners to negotiate for meaning.

This view is most succinctly expressed in the form of the 'interaction hypothesis'.

Long's interaction hypothesis

[N]egotiation of meaning, and especially negotiation work that triggers interactional adjustments by the NS or more competent interlocutor, facilitates acquisition because it connects input, internal learner capacities, particularly selective attention, and output in productive ways.
(Long, 1996: 451)

Loschky and Bley-Vroman (1993) also adopt a systemic approach to tasks: tasks are conceptualised in terms of traits which have consistent relationships to patterns of language use.

Example 7.3   Loschky and Bley-Vroman,1993

Loschky and Bley-Vroman (1993) propose that tasks can be designed to target more or less precisely the use of particular features of language. They suggest that the most precise targeting involves tasks for which a particular language feature is *essential* to task completion. A less focused task would be one in which the targeted language feature would be *useful* in the execution of the task. The least motivated level of focus is one in which the features would be *natural* in the execution of the task.

Loschky and Bley-Vroman underpin their discussion by highlighting the importance for all learners of the processes of automatisation (whereby new knowledge is made rapidly accessible) and restructuring (whereby old knowledge is reorganised to take account of new understanding).

Clearly the underlying learning processes and the qualities of task design are seen as being applicable to everyone: hence macro studies should be appropriate for exploring issues such as these since we should be looking for major effects, not distinct differences between learners. VanPatten (1996) considers a general effect on learning of the relative meaningfulness/lack of meaning of elements of the language.

Example 7.4   VanPatten, 1996

VanPatten (1996) focuses on a central process which he argues affects all communication-based learning, namely that language which is not essential to communication in some way will be perceived as redundant, and hence hard to learn. This is another form of the 'essentialness' debate, which can be traced back to the seminal work of George (1972). VanPatten, like George, therefore designs listening tasks to require the learner to attend to the target features to achieve the goals. VanPatten's approach to using listening to provide optimal input has given rise to a line of studies which essentially demonstrate that specially designed tasks can effectively draw learners' attention to pre-selected language features while at the same time they attend to the meanings of what they hear.

Skehan 1998 offers another example of a researcher seeking systemic effects. Skehan essentially acknowledges the role of redundancy and the need to deal with it, but believes that rather than reduce redundancy, it is better to work with it. Hence he incorporates this insight into a larger scheme of language learning, which he too proposes as essentially universal, although his scheme allows for different aspects to be emphasised more by some learners than others.

Example 7.5   Skehan, 1998

For Skehan, learning proceeds by a process of 1) lexicalisation (i.e. item-learning); 2) grammaticisation; and 3) re-lexicalisation. In proceeding through the different phases, Skehan sees the learner as having to pay attention to three processes – fluency, accuracy and complexity. For every learner he conceives of these processes as competing with each other for attention. However, each is important. Skehan characterises them as operating within communication as follows: 1) an essentially conservative approach, which prioritises accuracy; 2) an essentially strategic approach which emphasises fluency; and 3) a fundamentally progressive approach, which focuses on complexification. Skehan proposes that all three are essential to successful language learning, but that different people will lean more readily than one than another. Teaching therefore needs somehow to manoeuvre learners into exercising all three emphases at different times. Tasks can be used to do this.

Skehan's approach differs from VanPatten's in that whereas VanPatten believes in biasing the content of the tasks to direct learners' attention to the redundant grammatical features, Skehan believes that biasing should be avoided, to allow students normal task demands, using the conditions of the task rather than the task itself to influence the learner's processing.

Thus like the other authors exemplified here, Skehan proposes a universal set of processes, although he presents them in such a way as to allow for differences between learners and for them to follow different learning trajectories depending on the preferences they bring with them. Systemic approaches then agree that learning involves similar processes for everyone, although Skehan's position is distinctive in making explicit the need to allow for differences between learners, albeit in terms of the same three universal processes. Ellis (2000) summarises the various macro approaches under the heading 'psycholinguistic perspectives'.

Theories such as these give rise to studies that seek to establish whether their predictions about how tasks can work are generally justified. It is useful to note that explanations for any results are generally a matter of informed debate, though studies often attempt to structure the data collection and analysis so that if results are consistent with the theory, interpretation and discussion are assumed to be unnecessary. Null or negative results simply fail to support any proposed underlying theory, though these clearly can give rise to considerable debate over why. Findings so far generally but not always confirm the thinking that the use or type of tasks is indeed fairly predictably related to students' use of language. Features that have been studied are the degree of structuring of tasks; the propensity of different tasks to engage particular areas of language; incidence of negotiation for meaning; the impact of implementation options such as allowing students planning time, providing teacher feedback and using familiar or repeated tasks. For most of those who have undertaken systemic studies, tasks have been of interest more because of the kinds of learning process that they were interested in promoting than because of an interest in the qualities of particular tasks (though we will also see below that in this respect process-oriented studies often approach tasks in a similar way).

7.3.2 Process studies of tasks

Process-oriented research has generally studied talk on tasks with the intention of revealing detailed aspects of language use by particular students. While it can seem as though systemic researchers have been mainly motivated to study tasks in order to explore their suitability for engaging particular types of learning, those undertaking process-oriented studies have often been especially concerned to demonstrate the power and richness of their research methods. Process-oriented researchers have sought first to explore the range of collaborative processes used by learners, and second to demonstrate the sensitivity of their research methodology to the particularities of different learning encounters.

Many process studies have been inspired by socio-constructivist perspectives. This is understandable because socio-constructivists are particularly interested in how learners make sense of, structure and negotiate their way through an activity towards its completion. Because of this interest they have naturally tended to use a micro study approach. Micro-analytic approaches have also been used by researchers who are interested in the finer details of language use, albeit not from a socio-constructivist perspective, such as those working from a conversation analysis approach.

Socio-constructivist studies have highlighted a number of important themes: Duff (1993) and Coughlan and Duff (1994) have shown how student and teacher, or pairs of students, have come to reinterpret tasks from their initial design. Aljaafreh and Lantolf (1998) and Swain and Lapkin (2001) have studied student–student and student–teacher dialogue as a way to generate hypotheses and feedback for the learning process. Swain and Lapkin (2001) and Ohta (2001) have focused on interactive processes in the monitoring of lexico-grammatical accuracy. (We discuss these studies I more detail below.)

Process studies have also been undertaken within a conversation analysis (CA) framework. CA is an approach to the analysis of talk which studies in detail the chaining of utterances in order to grasp the ways in which coherence, mutual understanding and repair are locally managed, turn by turn. This enables a fine-grained account of the different types of talk. In line with Duff, Mori (2002) demonstrates that a task – here a loosely structured interaction task in which a native speaker was interviewed by a whole class – fails to materialise in the ways in which the teacher had anticipated. In another study using CA techniques, Nakahama, Tyler and van Lier (2001) undertook a qualitative analysis that shows clear differences in the talk occurring in a three-way conversation compared with an information gap task involving the same learners. They argue that on the basis of their analysis the conversation offers a richer learning context than the information gap task.

The socio-constructivist and CA-based studies mentioned above have generally adopted a set of analytical procedures to explore task-generated language data, sometimes with a pedagogically generated question (e.g. Swain and Lapkin, 2001; Ohta, 2001). However, other kinds of process-oriented studies are possible. Samuda (2001) adopted a case study approach to examine how a task was used by teacher and students in a single classroom. Her intention was to track how the participants used the task at an early stage of a lesson to provide a basis for work in the ensuing phases, with the focus on the extent to which students' group work contributed to the intended teaching dynamic. This is an example of a process-oriented study which is not situated explicitly in a particular paradigm, other than the concern to track the teaching–learning process through a task and into the following phases of the lesson. The study itself is unusual in addressing the issue of how a task can be used by teacher and learners to further an overall language learning goal. (We return to this study in Chapter 8.)

7.3.3   Reconciling the paradigms

The systemic/process and macro/micro dimensions tend to be mutually exclusive. This is partly because, as we have seen, process and system can be very difficult to interrelate. Similarly, handling data from large groups and from individual cases involves sufficiently different technologies for it to be a challenge for a single study to incorporate both types of analysis.

Yet if a phenomenon has an impact across large groups, it must be equally amenable to investigation with individual learners (though the reverse may not be the case). Lynch and Maclean (2000, 2001) have applied this assumption to the study of the impact of task repetition. Both studies adopted the procedure of examining in detail a series of individual cases, each in its own terms, but with the aim of exploring how far the individual patterns exemplified a general trend. In each case, the analysis involved detailed comparison of the grammar, choice of vocabulary and phrasing in the different versions of talk of each individual speaker, and identified many significant changes which would not have been spotted without a case-by-case comparison. Yet the individual changes, although different for each speaker, all reflected a similar trend across the data. By presenting the analysis of a series of individual cases, Bygate and Samuda (2005) similarly showed that individual case studies can usefully contribute to understanding the qualitative discourse processes hidden behind group statistics.

Similarly we find a parallel problem across types of micro study. Whereas personal construct theory (PCT) and neo-Vygotskyan approaches both assume the importance of detecting the individuals' own systems of understanding and processes in learning, PCT can tend to lose track of the overt processes which contribute to the development of people's internal systems of knowing, while neo-Vygotskyan approaches analyse closely individuals' processes of learning, but seem not to come to grips with the learners' underlying systems of knowledge. Reconciling the individual and the group, and reconciling the overt and observable with people's invisible states of knowing, are the dual challenge for our field in general, and for understanding language learning tasks.

Systemic approaches: an assessment

To the extent that the key aspects of language processing are the same for all learners – an assumption that is probably shared by teachers, researchers and learners – macro studies that focus on these processes can have an important contribution to make. For instance, most would agree that, all key things being equal, different types of planning, repetition, familiarity, task structuring and task type are each likely to have a consistent effect on speakers whoever they are and whatever their learning context. We would also probably agree that many of the effects studied are likely to be relevant in stimulating language development. Furthermore, some of the results shed an interesting light on the ways in which different tasks interact differently with different conditions. Skehan and Foster (1997) and Foster and Skehan (1996) found that planning affected a simple familiar task mainly in terms of fluency, whereas on the more complex decision-making kind of task, planning resulted in greater linguistic complexity. (We discuss such studies more fully below.)

In addition, although it is often said that case studies are more appropriate than macro studies for generating hypotheses, a macro study with a sufficiently rich design can be very thought-provoking. Skehan and Foster's series of studies (1996–9) eventually incorporated at least three distinct types of task, each with a more and a less structured version, each recorded with and without planning, and the whole data-set analysed in terms of the same measures of fluency, accuracy and complexity. A study of this kind is big enough for any emerging patterns to be fairly convincing, while at the same time leaving space for interesting distinct sub-patterns to appear. Ellis's series of studies (discussed below) illustrates how macro studies can be designed so that each study provides the basis for the next, creating a series of linked investigations. In other words, both micro and macro studies can be hypothesis-creating.

There are, however, limitations in the systemic studies undertaken to date. Generally because of the large amount of data to be analysed, they all have to abandon detailed study of the sequences of discourse moves through which learners deal with the tasks. For instance, in general they are not able to analyse the distinct phases of task performance or differences in the language strategies used. They also tend to neglect participants' perceptions, and few of the systemic studies have addressed the issue of how tasks are interpreted (Garrett and Shortall, 2002, is an exception), or how they are used by teachers within the context of lessons or schemes of work. Only two sets of systemic studies have attempted to address the issue of learning – Ellis's (e.g. Ellis, 1987; Fotos and Ellis, 1991) and Mackey's (e.g. Mackey, 1999; Mackey and McDonough 1998) – and these are also rare in exploring learning outcomes. A major problem with the systemic paradigm then is that it allows less detailed analysis of the data and less attention to the perceptions and processes engaged in by the participants.

A further apparent limitation is that studies from this perspective seem to operate with a relatively impoverished construct of what tasks are. For example, most macro studies tend to treat the learners' processes – and hence the language they use – as essentially the same throughout the task. Many of the studies analyse only relatively small – though supposedly 'representative' – extracts of the recordings, the implication seeming to be that it makes little difference which part of the task the data are taken from. In addition, a lack of attention to teaching and learning is reflected in the fact that many studies fail to focus on particular aspects of language that could be being targeted for use or learning. Finally, a significant weakness is the lack of pedagogical grounding for the studies: few of the systemic studies report professional ratifications of the design and implementation, and the data are rarely reported as being part of a pedagogical scheme of work.

Process studies: an assessment

While most systemic studies have adopted a macro approach, most process studies have been micro in orientation. Hence when we consider the strengths and weaknesses of work in the process paradigm we get something of a reverse picture from that of the systemic studies. The process paradigm is especially effective in studying particular phases, processes and trajectories of task performance for individual learners or particular groups of learners. Hence studies from this perspective get closer to tracking the ways in which the execution of tasks diverges from the intentions or expectations of the teacher and/or learners. Such a focus takes seriously the question of the kinds of processes learners can engage in in response to a task, and this can inform issues of task design and implementation. Process studies also track the ways in which pairs and groups of students help each other to identify and understand new language, or scaffold each other in selecting and manipulating familiar language accurately. In a similar vein, this type of study can track the ways in which a teacher presents a task and exploits the students' experience of a given task in her subsequent teaching. Hence this type of focus can illuminate the ways in which what students do on a task is connected to their learning before and after the task itself.

There are, however, limitations with work carried out from this perspective. One is that although a single case may be illuminating, we need to know whether it is representative or idiosyncratic. In research terms it may be revealing to discover how a given learner works on a particular task, but for both theoretical and practical purposes we need to know not just one learner's approach, but the main types of approach of learners in general.

Further, just as with systemic approaches, some of the process studies seem to adopt a fairly impoverished model of pedagogical tasks. As with many of the systemic studies, the design and implementation of some of the tasks are often only very superficially presented. In particular they generally fail to reflect explicitly the qualitative thinking of designer or teacher about what the tasks are intended to do, why they are structured the way they are and why the implementation followed the pattern it did. Hence although the learners' processes can be studied, it is impossible to generalise from this to the subsequent use of similar tasks.

A further potential problem with process studies can be a failure to tri-angulate analyses emerging from the data with the perceptions and interpretations of other judges. While there is a clear danger in systemic studies of the analyst imposing categories prior to the collection and analy-sis of the data, the opposite danger is for the data to be used to generate authentic categories which only the analyst(s) have recognised. Finally, given the general lack of attention to selecting tasks for study whose design and use were grounded in pedagogic contexts, the reader can eas-ily conclude that the main aim of the study is either to test a method of data analysis and interpretation, or (conceivably) to undermine argu-ments in favour of systematic use of tasks in the language classroom. That is, if the object of the research is the function, use and development of pedagogical tasks, then it is essential for the study to focus on features of tasks that have pedagogical credibility. However, as we have seen, this is a limitation which is also found in certain of the systemic studies.

7.4   Research into second language pedagogic tasks: main findings

In this section we look more closely at the main findings of the research that has been carried out to date in relation to a number of salient themes. Six main themes are listed in Table 7.3 (these are similar to the themes in Table 7.1).

Table 7.3   Main themes in task research to date

Task content
- the language focus of tasks
- task phases

Impact of elements of task design
- the impact of task complexity
- the impact of discourse type
- task structure

Impact of conditions of implementation
- task familiarity
- implementation effects
- participant roles

Task dynamics
- negotiation for meaning
- co-construction
- acquisition

We now review the major research studies to date in terms of these themes. The chapter concludes with a brief balance sheet, reviewing how much research seems to have achieved in relation to the potential aims outlined at the start of this chapter.

7.4.1   Task content

Language focus

An important concern for language teachers and learners is how tasks help the learning and teaching of particular aspects of language. As we have seen, while some (e.g. Long, 1996; Willis, 1996; Skehan, 1998) argue that this is not the principal contribution of tasks, but rather to engage communicative processing of language, most would agree with McDonough and Mackey that a main challenge is 'to create tasks that provide learners with opportunities to engage in meaningful interaction and to direct their attention to linguistic form (2000: 83). The question is, can particular areas of the language system be targeted? Long, Skehan and Willis, among others, believe that either it cannot or it should not. Others, like Loschky and Bley-Vroman (1993), argue that although it may not be possible to predict the occurrence of particular language features with certainty, most tasks are likely to be associated with the use of some language features with at least a reasonable degree of probability (e.g. Newton and Kennedy, 1996; Bygate, 1999; Mackey, 1999; Dufficy, 2004).

Quote 7.1   Newton and Kennedy on the predictability of the language used in tasks

As with written genre, we would argue that the discourse produced through a task is given its identifiable shape and structure by the communicative purpose of the task. Given this, it is possible to predict the likelihood of the linguistic and discourse features in the ensuing interaction.
(Newton and Kennedy, 1996: 312)

Empirically there is evidence that this is the case.

Example 7.6   Targeted information-processing in listening tasks

VanPatten (1996) reports studies in which learners' attention can be drawn to particular grammatical features in the context of communicative listening tasks. This is achieved by ensuring that the only source of the required information is found in the target morphemes, so that students are unable to complete the task without noticing and interpreting those morphemes.

Unfortunately, it is harder to do this in oral production tasks simply because in such tasks students are generally able to convey the key information by using other linguistic features. Nonetheless, some studies have shown that tasks can be used to draw students into particular areas of the language system, as illustrated in Examples 7.7–7.11.

Example 7.7   Bygate – question forms and lexical sets

Bygate (1988) found that a 20-Questions card game, carried out by eight groups of adult learners of English, was associated with the use of questions, although in many cases students avoided the use of a main verb, often but not always using intonation to mark the question. In addition, card games such as this clearly targeted particular lexical sets or domains (as could other tasks in other ways). This study provided early indications that tasks could be used to target grammar as well as lexis.

Example 7.8   Newton and Kennedy – prepositions and conjunctions

Newton and Kennedy (1996) found that tasks concerned with the layout of a zoo were significantly more likely to motivate the use of prepositions; more prepositions were used on the zoo topic where information was split rather than shared between students, presumably because the split information had first to be pooled, and this led to an increase in the amount of description of locations. On the other hand where information was shared at the outset, and students had to focus on arguing a case rather than transferring information to each other, there was greater use of conjunctions.

Example 7.9   Mackey – different types of question formation

Mackey (1999) studied learner performance on a series of tasks:

- Story completion task, in which students were to work out a story by asking questions.
- Picture sequencing task, in which students asked questions to discover the order of a picture story.
- Picture differences, where students identified differences between similar pictures.
- Picture drawing, which required students to describe or draw a picture.

In each case the students were required by the design of the task to gather the information they needed by asking questions.

Mackey found that various question forms could be effectively targeted by the four types of task, and demonstrated that performance on these tasks led to learners showing clear improvements in their production of questions as measured in pre-/post-tests.

McDonough and Mackey (2000), working with learners of Thai, similarly showed that tasks like those in the Mackey (1999) study could be used to target and promote learning of question forms.

Example 7.10   Samuda – epistemic modality

Samuda (2001) reported the use of the TIP task as a way of drawing students into expressing degrees of certainty. (For a detailed discussion of this study, see Chapter 8.)

Example 7.11   Bygate – discourse patterns

Bygate (1988), with a corpus of eight groups of adult learners working on five different oral tasks, reported a degree of patterning in the discourse structures that appeared on different tasks (e.g. in terms of the occurrence of IRF sequences, short and long turns, use of non-finite structures in card games, and the incidence of collaborative utterance building, particularly in a detailed and hence quite demanding map-completion task).

Furthermore, some tasks resulted in less varied discourse patterns than others. Card games seemed to give rise to relatively uniform discourse patterns across groups, while on the other hand, picture differences tasks and distributed picture-story tasks seemed to allow students option of negotiating the task, whether through a series of short turns (often where lower proficiency students seemed to be involved) or alternatively through fewer quite lengthy turns.

Studying the language of children in a multilingual classroom, Dufficy (2004) reports a notably regularity of language on a given task across different groups of children. He concluded:

Quote 7.2   Dufficy on regularity of language in task performance

Given the design constraints ... of the communicative task described in this paper it may not come as a surprise to see the way the task predisposed children to choose particular patterns of language which were relatively consistent across groups.
(Dufficy, 2004: 259)

The main limitations with studies in this area are that only a limited range of features have been studied and few have been replicated. Furthermore, apart from Mackey (1999) and McDonough and Mackey (2000), few longitudinal or pre-/post-designs have been undertaken so that we have little evidence so far of acquisitional processes around the target features. It is certain that without appropriate exploitation, the more redundant the features, the less likely students are to use them. The results to date, however, give no reason to doubt that judicious selection of topic areas and of task structures can draw learners into engaging with systemic areas of a target language.

To conclude this section, Dufficy (2004) considers that 'a valuable goal to pursue for teachers in linguistically diverse classrooms might be the development of a kind of inventory describing the relationship between task types and the varied language work that accompanies them' (2004: 259).

Task phases

As we saw at the beginning of Chapter 1, tasks by definition have their own internal phases, in contrast to mono-operational pedagogic procedures like drills or translation exercises. It makes little sense to ask of a drill or a translation task 'Were the data collected at the beginning, the middle or the end of the activity?' unless one is interested in factors such as the impact of fatigue, priming or internal practice effects. However, this is a highly relevant question where tasks are concerned, since these can often give rise to quite different kinds of interaction in different phases. For instance, many tasks require students at the beginning to work out how to use the input material, then to use it to achieve the target outcomes and finally to decide when these have been reached. In addition, during the task, there are likely to be procedural or communicational problems which need sorting out. As we saw in Chapter 2, Barnes (1976) and Barnes and Todd (1977) both provide data from L1 subject classrooms which illustrate the fact that groups need to deal with these aspects of tasks, and that in doing so, their thinking and use of language are differentially engaged. Curiously, however, little research has been devoted to this aspect of L2 tasks. One exception (Bygate, 1988) is shown in Example 7.12.

Example 7.12   Bygate – task phases

Bygate (1988) found that the five tasks in his study contrasted in terms of the types of phases they seemed to give rise to. For example, picture stories strikingly consisted of three basic phases:

Phase 1: Description of each picture

> Phase 2: Sequencing of the set of pictures
> Phase 3: Review to check the sequence
>
> Occasionally phase 1 turned into a question-and-answer sequence; phases 2 and 3 were sometimes negotiated and sometimes enacted by one speaker; and sometimes phase 2 involved significant checking moves to ensure that the various pictures had been correctly understood and remembered. Sometimes there was a fourth phase involving a telling of the full story, which might be done individually or jointly.

As can be seen, analysis of the phases of a task help us to understand more clearly what the speakers are typically doing and why. It also helps to distinguish between tasks – picture differences tasks and card game-based tasks, for instance, each resulted in quite different phases.

Three theoretical and practical issues arise here:

1. Evidence of the existence of different phases in tasks suggests that any analysis of transcripts needs to sample from across the different phases, and not from a single phase. Taking data from a single phase could easily give a highly misleading impression of the language work that the students are engaged in.
2. The analysis of phases helps to shed light on how a given task might be made easier or harder, and with what effects (e.g. in terms of negotiation of meaning, communication strategies, etc.).
3. Recognition of the existence of distinct phases might enable us to shed more light on the kinds of work that learners are doing through a task, and on the ways in which in particular they come to internalise the conceptual demands, and then to find ways of formulating the material. Studying phases might, for instance, reveal how learners engage with different aspects of the task, which could be valuable information for teachers.

A final point is that analyses such as this are avowedly *post hoc*: they explore what learners actually do, not what they are supposed to do. As a result, the phases are seen as a creation of the students in response to the materials. Different groups might phase tasks differently, and it is an empirical question how far differences are a matter of social, cognitive or cultural factors, or simply of language proficiency, and how far they diverge from – or indeed converge with – the phases mapped out by the original workplan.

Not surprisingly, given the lack of attention to this topic, there have been no studies so far of issues such as changes in phasing over time or of the impact of phasing to the learning of particular aspects of language, or of learner differences.

7.4.2   Impact of elements of task design

In this section we review some of main studies that have focused on the impact of selected elements of the design of tasks.

Complexity of task design

Language focus is not the only area of pedagogical interest. As we saw in Chapter 1, the use of any pedagogical activity raises the issue of task complexity and the possibility of sequencing tasks in terms of their relative simplicity or complexity. The reasoning behind this is that we do not want to place too heavy a load on learners by asking them to manage too many things at the same time. So the question is, can we distinguish between tasks in terms of their complexity, in order to select better tasks for our learners' levels of proficiency? This leads us to consider more closely the nature of different tasks and what it is that distinguishes one from another. However, as with many areas of pedagogic interest, little research has been undertaken so far. The kinds of empirical work carried out so far in this area are illustrated in Example 7.13.

Example 7.13   Brown and Yule; Brown et al. – design features and complexity of task

Brown and Yule (1983) and Brown et al. (1984) proposed using the number and distinctiveness of different referential information features present in a task as a basis for distinguishing between tasks. For example:

- A task based on a story involving two characters, a single location and a single time-frame would be less complex than one involving six characters, three locations and two or more time-frames.
- Tasks based on describing or giving instructions would be less demanding if they involved objects or arrays with a small number of distinctive elements; requiring students to take account of a lot of features in order to complete the task would be more demanding.

Brown et al. (1984) found that the ability to use referential language was consistently affected by variations in task complexity.

Robinson (2001) developed an expanded framework to account for the complexity of tasks. He distinguished between task complexity, task conditions and task difficulty. He found that task complexity was influenced by two cognitive dimensions:

1. resource-directing – amount of information, whether here-and-now or distant in time and space, and whether reasoning demands were included;
2. resource-depleting – presence or absence of planning, whether one or more distinct subtasks were involved in the task, and the amount of prior knowledge students had.

Robinson theorised that resource-directing factors would affect learners' focus of attention, whereas resource-depleting factors would impact on the amount of attention that students would have available. 'Task condition' covered *participation variables* (such as whether the task had an open or closed solution, whether it was one- or two-way, and whether participants' purposes were convergent or divergent) and *participant variables* (gender, familiarity of participants with each other, and power/solidarity factors). Robinson saw task difficulty as a perception of the students, which was influenced by their affective characteristics and by ability variables (e.g. aptitude and proficiency), as well as by the task itself, and the conditions under which it was used (see Examples 7.14a and b).

Example 7.14a   Robinson – Features of a task contributing to increased complexity

Using simple and complex versions of the same tasks, Robinson (2001) contrasted five versions of a map task, varying it on four dimensions:

- +/− planning time
- +/− single task (route already marked)
- +/− prior knowledge
- few or many elements

Robinson wanted to see whether varying the task along these dimensions could result in consistent difficulty effects for different students.

Example 7.14b   Findings

- *Task complexity affects speaker and hearer production*
  Task complexity significantly affects the lexical variety [more] and fluency [less] of speaker production, and amount of hearer interaction [more] in the predicted direction [ie. on the more complex versions].

Example 7.14b   (Continued)

- *Cognitive demands of tasks and ratings of their difficulty are related*
  Task complexity significantly affects ratings of overall difficulty, and stress in the predicted direction (i.e. more complex are perceived as more difficult). There is a trend to less confidence in ability on, and more interest in, the complex version.
- *Sequencing and ratings of difficulty are unrelated*
  Sequencing from simple to complex vs. the reverse sequence does not significantly affect ratings of the difficulty of the complex version.
- *Sequencing affects speaker production but not interaction*
  Sequencing tasks (from simple to complex vs. the reverse sequence) has significant effects on accuracy and fluency of speaker production, but has no effect on the amount of interaction.

The results suggest that the dimension can be used to influence the language, and that students' perceptions of the difficulty of the tasks will be congruent with these effects. That is, the results seem to provide an initial opening into the questions 'What causes task complexity?' 'What is the impact of task complexity on students?' 'What are the implications for sequencing?'

There are, however, issues relating to Robinson's study which remain unclear. Complexity is clearly seen in terms of several distinct factors, and we need to note that the study does not tell us whether all the factors are of equal importance, or whether some (e.g. planning time or the number of elements) are more important than others. In addition, it seems reasonable to point out that the model for analysing task complexity has to be read as a preliminary hypothesis, and hence is open to modification and refinement. For instance, it seems possible that some of Robinson's conditions could be defined as aspects of the task design, while the resource-depleting factors look rather like task conditions. Some might want to organise the concepts differently, as follows:

Task complexity

information load: number of elements; here-and-now; reasoning demands
Participation variables: open/closed; convergent/divergent; split/shared
One or more distinct sub-tasks

Task conditions

Implementation: +/− planning; +/− prior knowledge
Participant variables: gender, familiarity, power/solidarity

There are various other issues that need further exploration. For instance, the impact of the number of elements cannot be interpreted without reference to the number of elements that need to be referred to for the task to be completed. Furthermore, their impact is likely to be affected by the extent to which they form a more or less closely related set of elements and how far their similarity or distinctiveness is helpful or confusing so that similarity/distinctiveness of elements may need to be added to the framework. There are also questions to be asked about the importance of the match/lack of match between conceptual content and available language: in this framework the complexity and difficulty of tasks is being discussed without any reference to the language students would need or the language they actually know, which seems counter-intuitive. Robinson's work does, however, raise a number of fascinating questions for the exploration and development of repertoires of tasks.

Discourse type

Foster and Skehan (1996), Skehan and Foster (1997) and Skehan (2001) have proposed that the nature of a task may be partly reflected in the type of discourse they aim to generate (although note that in their early work they used the term 'task type' rather than 'discourse type'). (See Example 7.15.)

Since cognitive complexity was not controlled for across discourse type, Skehan and Foster were not able to locate a particular effect for discourse type. However, it is conceivable that keeping information content constant (which these studies did not attempt to do), different discourse types may vary in demand – consider, for instance, the possible differences between a task involving a pair of parallel descriptions of two objects on the one hand, and task requiring a comparison of the same two objects on the other. We discuss the issue of familiarity below, and both familiarity and cognitive complexity again in Chapter 8.

Example 7.15   Foster and Skehan; Skehan and Foster – impact of task on discourse type

Three types of task were selected as potentially distinct:

- personal
- narrative
- argumentation tasks

Skehan and Foster wanted to see whether each might have a different impact on the fluency, accuracy or complexity of the students' language.

Findings:

- Personal tasks generated more fluent, less complex language.

Example 7.15   (Continued)

- Narrative tasks and argumentation tasks were associated with more complex language.
- When performance was compared with and without pre-planning time, the opportunity to plan had different effects on performance on the three tasks, with complexity promoted on the narrative and argumentation tasks, while fluency and accuracy improved on the personal tasks.

This suggested:

- Personal tasks were already sufficiently familiar to the students, so that planning time made little difference to the way they performed the task, whereas planning time helped students perform more fluently on the less familiar content.
- Personal tasks seemed to involve less cognitively demanding material than the narrative and argumentation tasks, and hence gave rise to less complex use of language.

These conclusions suggested an effect for two factors: task familiarity and the cognitive complexity of the tasks, rather than the discourse type.

Task structure

A further dimension that affects the difficulty of tasks is the extent to which the content information given to the students at the beginning of the task is already structured (see Example 7.16).

Example 7.16   Studies undertaken by Skehan and Foster

In a series of studies carried out between 1996 and 1999, Skehan and Foster used a similar set of task types (personal, narrative and argumentation) and found differences in the linguistic complexity produced by students working on different narrative tasks:

- In the narrative task associated with less complex language students had received a picture story with the pictures already sequenced.
- In contrast, in the task which had generated more complex language, the students had to sequence the pictures themselves before producing the story.

Skehan and Foster (1999) found similar effects when comparing students' retelling of two video narratives. In the simpler one, the narrative followed a familiar restaurant scenario, whereas a far more unpredictable narrative was related to more complex language.

Skehan and Foster reasoned that in all cases where differences were found in the language across tasks with a similar genre (i.e. across narrative tasks) the less complex language was consistently associated with tasks in which the information was pre-structured, while tasks in which students had to work to provide a structure themselves to the narrative were associated with more complex talk.

Example 7.17   Song – structure of task and complexity of language produced

Song (2000) similarly found that where pictures for a picture story were not pre-sequenced, students tended to have difficulty working out the motivations of the characters, the connections between the events and sometimes even had difficulty working out from the pictures what the characters were actually doing. The result was that the parts of the talk in which the students verbalised the connections between pictures were linguistically more complex.

Skehan and Foster's argument, then, is that where the information given to the students is not already sequenced or organised into a fixed array before they start the task, the students will have a cognitively more complex task and will produce more complex talk. This is consistent with Robinson's (2001) model and makes sense. Skehan and Foster's results were also reflected in the differences in performance on tasks with a clear narrative thread as opposed to tasks with a random sequence of events. The notion of predictability suggests, however, that 'structuring' is often a product of the degree of match/mismatch between the knowledge or expectations of the students and the material they are given. That is, unpredictability is explained by a story sequence not fitting a schema with which viewers are likely to be familiar. This opens up the possibility that the structuring of a task will not be entirely intrinsic, but will depend on what is familiar to the participants.

So it appears that 'structuring' is partly a function of whether the input information is organised and partly of whether it is organised according to the learners' background knowledge and expectations. Some types of background knowledge may be widely if not universally shared across cultures, but others are less so, or more dependent on age and education.

Participant roles

In carrying out a task, participants have to do something if it is to be completed. This is partly influenced by the design of the task itself. Pica et al. (1993) propose that participant roles can be defined in terms of the following task typology.

Example 7.18   Pica et al. – task typology relating to participant role

- *Required exchange tasks*: tasks in which information has to be passed from one speaker to the other in order for the task to be completed –
  One-way tasks: one speaker has information to give to the other.

Example 7.18   (Continued)

Two-way tasks: both/all speakers have information to give and hence also have information to receive.
- *Optional exchange tasks*: tasks in which information can be passed from one speaker to the other, although this is not required, and the actual information to be exchanged may not be provided by the task.
- *Convergent tasks*: tasks in which all speakers are working to a joint agreed outcome.
- *Divergent tasks*: tasks in which speakers can all come to different conclusions or outcomes.

Note that Robinson's (2001) model defines these features as aspects of task conditions. In contrast, Pica et al. see these dimensions as a property of the design of the task. It is important to be aware that one of their principal interests was to define the properties of tasks which would lead or push learners to negotiate understandings. This led them to attempt to pin down ways in which tasks could define the roles of speakers.

Although research suggests that there are associations between these properties and the incidence of negotiated talk (e.g. Pica and Doughty, 1985; Doughty and Pica, 1986), it is also clear that participant roles are more complex than this account seems to allow for. For one thing, although 'convergent required exchange' tasks are likely to give rise to negotiation of understandings, the concept of one- and two-way tasks does not fully predict the roles of the participants. For example, it is possible for a one-way task to be managed by the more forceful of two students, whether or not they are the ones who initially have the information. The same is bound to hold for two-way tasks, with the more forceful student dominating for the information they hold, as well as for what they do not hold. Furthermore, some of the other categories are ambiguous: for example, a task can be convergent without all participants being a party to the eventual outcome. The implication is that our understanding of the impact of aspects of task design could probably benefit from a richer theoretical starting point than those we have been working with so far, one, for instance, which approaches the relationship between design features and student response in terms of relative probabilities of response from a likely range.

7.4.3   Impact of conditions of implementation

In the previous section we considered some of the ways in which the design of a task can affect what students do. In this section we now review some of the ways in which the teachers' *use* of tasks can affect what happens. Four main factors have been researched:

1. task familiarity;
2. planning;
3. task repetition;
4. attribution of roles.

Task familiarity

As we have seen, Robinson (2001) suggests that there is a good likelihood that familiarity with a task will affect performance. As with many aspects of the area, however, it is important first to clarify what is meant by 'task familiarity'. It could mean familiarity with the content of the task, but not with the task itself; familiarity with the *type* of task (i.e. the procedures to be used), but not with the content; or familiarity with both content and specific task. Furthermore, familiarity with the content can be broken down into content familiarity *per se*, and content familiarity in the context of a second language classroom activity. In addition, there is the question of the kind of impact that might be expected from task familiarity.

Intuitively, familiarity with a task should mean that some aspects of the work involved in doing a task can be taken for granted, hence facilitating task performance in some way. However, there are different ways in which this might happen. For instance, familiarity could enable increased fluency or increased accuracy. Equally, it could give rise to greater linguistic complexity or elaboration of the discourse. All things being kept constant, any or all of these are possible, although some theories, such as the limited capacity hypothesis (Levelt, 1978), predict that participants can normally not improve performance on all dimensions simultaneously. Little research has been done on this; hence the range of possible effects has not been investigated. One study which did explore the impact of task familiarity was Plough and Gass's.

Example 7.19 Plough and Gass – effects of task familiarity

Plough and Gass (1993) focused on the question of whether familiarity with a task influences the extent to which learners negotiate meanings when lacking a word, or when unsure of understanding their interlocutor or of being understood.

They operationalised familiarity as familiarity with a particular type of task rather than with the content. (Note that studies of task repetition discussed below have also distinguished between task type and task content.)

Example 7.19   (Continued)

Plough and Gass describe their results as 'uncertain' (1993: 51), with no statistically significant differences in frequencies. In one of two types of tasks studied, five of six measures were greater on the familiar task, and, on the unfamiliar type, three of six. The most consistent (though still not statistically significant) finding was that there were more interruptions in the unfamiliar condition.

From this the authors concluded that on the unfamiliar task there was 'a greater instance of involvement leading in [their] framework to greater negotiation'. Their conclusion was that novelty produces more negotiation of meaning than familiarity.

On the whole, given the lack of statistical significance, it would be wise to treat these findings as at most exploratory. The authors' conclusion does, however, raise several issues about how we think about the impact of familiarity. First, even if there had been significant results in favour of the unfamiliar task, both practical and theoretical reasons would still suggest that it is most unlikely that students work enthusiastically only on novel types of activities. The practical implications are impossible for any course or teacher to handle, but in addition, it is clear from experience that students often enjoy working with familiar types of activity. Second, the study raises the question of what we mean by novelty and how different degrees of novelty impact on task performance. Total novelty is presumably impossible, but it would be helpful to understand more about the impact of degrees of novelty. A third issue is that we have no account of whether familiarity of the content is helpful, and if so, what kind of content familiarity. Fourth, even if one accepted the authors' interpretation, the frequency effects are far too slight for us to leave the matter there – further research is needed. Finally, it is important to note that the authors were only interested in the incidence of negotiation of meaning on two sample tasks. It was not their purpose to see whether familiarity with the tasks had any effect on the effectiveness of the students' completion of the task or on other aspects of their language (such as their use of vocabulary, grammar, or pronunciation, or their general fluency), or how familiarity influenced students on other types of task. However, these issues are clearly well within the scope of any attempt to understand how familiarity/novelty impacts on learning. So, in a sense, the most important contribution of a study such as this is the way in which it clarifies further questions and opens up the topic for deeper and more extensive investigation. Related studies have explored the impact of task repetition (see below) with positive results; clearly this topic offers much potential for further study.

Planning

The main studies of the impact of planning are Ellis (1987), Crookes (1989), Foster and Skehan (1996), Skehan and Foster (1997), Foster (2001) and Yuan and Ellis (2003).

Two kinds of planning have been distinguished: pre-task planning and on-line planning.

Pre-task planning has been widely shown to result in greater fluency and more complex language, although this depends to some extent on the nature of the task: tasks with a limited potential for complexification, such as giving instructions to get to one's house or talking about oneself, tend to result more in fluency and accuracy than to changes in complexity. Although in an early study Ellis (1987) found that accuracy increased by provision of planning time, this study used two kinds of planning: one derived from working with the same material on an earlier task, the other from the distinction between the on-line planning available in oral and written tasks respectively. Written tasks clearly allow more on-line planning than do oral tasks, and this may have explained why they were performed more accurately. More recent studies of the effects of different types of planning on different aspects of task performance are briefly illustrated in Examples 7.20 and 7.21.

Example 7.20   Yuan and Ellis, 2003 – the impact of pre- and on-line planning

Yuan and Ellis (2003) explored the impact of pre- and on-line planning by allowing speakers in one condition to operate without any time constraints, while placing others under relatively severe time limits.

Findings:

- Students receiving pre-task planning time produced more complex and more fluent language.
- Students provided with on-task planning produced significantly more accurate language.

The conclusion, then, is that pre-task planning impacts on fluency and complexity, but only on accuracy in the context of less complex and familiar tasks; on-line planning, in contrast, tends to give rise to greater accuracy and to less fluency. However, Bygate and Samuda (2005) suggest that these differences are mainly attributable to the capacity of working memory under the two conditions: content planning is more likely to be associated with pre-task planning, and formulation planning (i.e. planning focusing on wording and grammar) is more likely to be within the scope of on-line planning.

Questions remain. In particular, studies have not so far explored the extent to which planning influences different aspects of language performance, such as discourse structure, lexical selection and range, grammatical selection and range, the performance of speech acts or students' pronunciation. Of all the studies on the impact of planning to date, only one (Foster, 2001) has focused on how planning affects a particular aspect of language.

Example 7.21   Foster – effects of planning on the use of formulaic language

Foster (2001) found that planning has a different impact on the use of formulaic language by native and non-native speakers. Interestingly, she found that whereas planning appears to lead native speakers to *reduce* their use of formulaic language, this is not at all the case with non-native speakers, who use roughly similar proportions of formulaic language both in planned and unplanned talk.

Studies such as Foster's shed fascinating light on the relationship between presence and absence of planning time and the way learners focus attention on language.

Task repetition

The main interest in planning is to explore whether it can be used to lead learners to direct more attention to aspects of their talk than they might otherwise do. An interest has developed in task repetition for a similar reason. Compared with written discourse, talk is ephemeral. Yet we frequently repeat discourses in everyday life, and this has been associated with language development in children (e.g. Bruner, 1983; Peters, 1983), and at least anecdotally for adults. This may be because repeating whole discourses enables linguistic features of talk to recur. Hence task repetition has been proposed as an opportunity for learners to rework their language when producing the same or similar talk on a second occasion. Indeed, many tasks are structured to give rise to repetition. And in order to complete some tasks, repetition may be extremely helpful.

Example 7.22   Bygate; Bygate and Samuda – effects of repeating the same task

In a case study, Bygate (1996) showed how repetition of the same task can result in increased idiomaticity and increased accuracy.

A follow-up study (Bygate, 2001) found that repetition of a specific task resulted in increased complexity and fluency, though not accuracy, while familiarity with a task type (as opposed to particular content) seemed to have no particular effect.

Bygate and Samuda (2005) found that, in a subset of the 2001 data, speakers produced significantly more elaborate talk when narrating a familiar story compared with an unfamiliar story. Familiarity established through prior engagement with the content material in the target language seems to affect people's subsequent use of the language on the same task.

Example 7.23   Lynch and Maclean – effects of task repetition

Lynch and Maclean (2000, 2001) showed that tasks structured to ensure that interaction demands required students to retell their material to a series of different interlocutors had the effect of leading speakers to rework aspects of their talk, whether in terms of their pronunciation, vocabulary, or grammar, with individual speakers altering and improving different aspects of their own talk. (We discuss their 2001 study in Chapter 3.)

These studies show reasonably convincingly that fluency, accuracy and complexity can all be affected by some form of task repetition. Questions remain, however, over the different types of repetition, on the ways in which working with the same content can help speakers work on their language, and on the ways in which tasks can be designed and used to exploit this parameter. Little research has been done to study the effects of planning and task repetition over time.

Distribution of roles

Does it matter which student does what in a given task? Yule and McDonald (1990) neatly illustrated some of the ways in which the roles participants adopt can be influenced by the way the teacher chooses to implement the task.

Example 7.24   Yule and McDonald – effect of differences in proficiency levels of participants

Yule and McDonald (1990) started from the assumption that to some extent participant role can be designed into the task, but they explored the extent to which participants' relative level of proficiency might influence their interaction according to the role they were allotted.

Example 7.24   (Continued)

They studied mixed pairs with one high and one low proficiency (HP and LP) student in each pair; pairs were given a one-way map task.

In half the groups the high proficiency student started with the information that was to be imparted, and in the other half this was given to the low proficiency student.

The results were unequivocal: information was negotiated far more successfully when it was entrusted to the low proficiency student. When problems arose, the LP students were more committed to resolving the problem, and the HP student more supportive, than when it was the HP student who was holding the material to be communicated.

Results such as this suggest that task design is only one influence on how participants fulfil their roles: relative proficiency and quite probably relative confidence and forcefulness as well are just as likely to influence what happens.

Finally, Skehan and Foster have noted the possible differences in the quality of talk in monologic and dialogic tasks, with the latter tending to lead to greater complexity. The vast range of potential task types falling under each of these two headings suggests that this distinction is a direction for further enquiry.

7.4.4   Task dynamics

In this section we consider features that have been studied in the dynamics of task enactment.

Negotiation for meaning

'Negotiation for meaning' has come to be used to refer to turns of talk in which speakers check the clarity and understanding of their own and each others' messages, particularly at points when there appears to be a breakdown or misfire in communication. These are sometimes referred to (especially in conversation analysis) as 'repair sequences'.

Several SLA researchers (Long, 1981; Gass and Varonis, 1985; Pica and Doughty, 1985) have been interested in the extent to which tasks generate 'negotiation for meaning' during task talk, focusing on a core set of moves believed to maximise opportunities for inter-language restructuring and development:

- confirmation checks;
- clarification requests;
- comprehension checks.

Unlike some of the researchers in studies reviewed above, these researchers were not primarily interested in the kinds of discourse that different tasks might give rise to or in the ways in which tasks might lead learners to attend to different aspects of language (e.g. grammar, vocabulary, pragmatics or pronunciation). Rather, the focus was on investigating whether tasks could be designed to stimulate those negotiations for meaning sequences hypothesised as both fundamental and effective in promoting language development. The implication seemed to be that if tasks did not to lead to negotiation for meaning sequences, or if negotiation for meaning failed to lead to acquisition, they would not support the pedagogic use of tasks.

Various studies were carried out to explore which tasks were most likely to lead to negotiation for meaning sequences. We have already seen an example of this in Pica et al.'s (1993) task typology (see Example 7.18). Although it appears that certain task types do result in more negotiation for meaning than others, none of the studies was designed to find out whether negotiation for meaning resulted in learning. In addition, there are a number of problems with the definition of the moves that constitute 'negotiation for meaning' as construed by this group of SLA researchers. In particular, distinctions between the functions of apparently similar moves (e.g. confirmation check/clarification request/comprehension check) can be motivated by many concerns and not just the need to check accurate and effective use of the code.

A strong association can be found between the rather narrow focus of 'negotiation for meaning' studies of SLA and recommendations for the use of tasks in second language pedagogy and in particular, the development of a pedagogy driven by tasks (see the discussion of TBLT in Chapter 9). In our view, it is unfortunate that so much early empirical attention to tasks was devoted to the study of negotiation for meaning when it is very clear that tasks generate considerable amounts of valuable talk *other* than the limited range of moves focused on in negotiation for meaning studies, and that exploratory talk is realised in a range of ways not captured by those moves. As we argued in Chapter 1, the rationale for using tasks extends well beyond their potential to stimulate negotiation for meaning sequences (see Foster and Ohta, 2005, for a similar view).

Constructivist processes

In this book we use the term 'constructivist processes' to refer to all those processes whereby individuals work together to develop and clarify their own and each others' understandings, whether of background knowledge, of previous and current situations or of their intentions.

Some of these processes overlap with the kinds of negotiation for meaning moves discussed in previous paragraphs. But the scope of constructivist concerns goes well beyond negotiation sequences to include the moment-by-moment prompting, eliciting, responding, questioning and elaborating which, as Barnes (1976) showed, characterise joint exploratory talk (see Chapter 2).

Socio-constructivists have been significantly involved in studying this in relation to tasks – see Examples 7.25 and 7.26.

Example 7.25   Donato – co-construction of meaning in tasks

Donato (1994) focused on the ways in which students learning French as a foreign language helped each other to recover grammatical rules from memory and to apply them in the context of new vocabulary items.

Donato's data were collected from students engaged in a one-hour planning session in which their task was to work out the conclusion for a dramatic scenario which they were to enact in a subsequent lesson (1994: 40).

His analyses highlight the role of peers jointly 'scaffolding' each other's talk – providing prompts, directions, reminders, evaluations including corrections, as well as additional contributions.

Example 7.26   Swain and Lapkin – collaborative talk on tasks

In a series of studies, Swain and Lapkin (2000, 2001) examined how students of French work jointly on dicto-gloss activities (activities in which students first hear a short piece of talk and then work orally in pairs to reproduce in writing what they heard).

They used micro-analysis on different types of 'episodes' occurring during task enactment to show how students help each other to recover language, negotiating for meaning and for form, that they had both heard and with appropriate grammatical features.

Studies like Donato's and Swain and Lapkin's highlight the productive role of collaborative talk among peers and illustrate how students seem to help each other by providing support, structure and focus to each other's talk. Blake and Zyzik (2003) apply a similar analysis to web-based peer tutoring between learners of Spanish. Ohta (2000) also adopted a socio-cultural approach to study classroom processes in the learning of Japanese as a second language.

Example 7.27   Ohta – the classroom processes of learners of Japanese as a foreign language

In a longitudinal study, Ohta identified a number of positive features of productive interaction. These included:

- creative use of the L2 to perform tasks;
- active resolution of problems that emerge through the use of the L2;
- peer assistance, which enables them to respond to challenges they might otherwise be unable to handle;
- use of L2, and minimal use of L1;
- taking risks and trying new language forms;
- a sense of flow, involving movement and development with learners helping each other and calling on the teacher when necessary.

In Ohta's data, tasks, among other types of activity, provided a context for important types of peer interaction to occur. Yet Ohta argues that these features were impacted by task design and the manner of task implementation, as well as by the individual learners. Furthermore if a task lacks clarity, is not well integrated into the lesson or is at an inappropriate level, this seems to lead to increased use of the L1.

In other words, Ohta proposes that there is an important relationship between the design, selection and use of tasks on the one hand, and the interactive processes that they can give rise to on the other. From this perspective, tasks offer a tool for mediating students' collaborative engagement and use of language.

In many ways the work exemplified here echoes the earlier extensive studies by Barnes (1976) on mother-tongue subject classrooms in the UK, and Wells (1981, 1985) of the adult-child interaction involving children in their pre-school years. Both Barnes and Wells argued that the interaction could be relatively productive or unproductive, depending partly on how interactants collaborate, and partly on the nature of the activities they are engaged in: the activity provides a context for the joint construction of talk. Without the activity, collaborative talk would not be possible, yet the quality of the talk itself depends on the interactive involvement of the participants.

Given this, socio-cultural studies can understandably choose to focus more centrally on the work of the students than the nature of the task. Indeed, a second group of socio-cultural studies (e.g. Duff, 1993; Coughlan and Duff, 1994; Mori, 2002) are more concerned to explore the ways in which language interaction is individualised, and suggest that tasks have little influence on what happens in classrooms. Hence, if any constructivist processes occur during the enactment of a task, the interest is to interpret this in terms of the constructive actions of the participants. Duff (1993), for instance, shows how a student in a series of one-on-one tutorials does not follow a pre-arranged set of tasks. A more recent study is Mori's (2002).

Example 7.28   Mori, 2000

Mori (2002) set up a series of visits by native speaker guests to a Japanese as a second language classroom. These followed class work on a video and textbook. Students were briefed to prepare for a session, consisting of the following phases:

1. Explain to the guests the content of the video and the textbook.
2. Ask the guest what kind of person his/her father is and what kind of relationship s/he has had with his/her father.
3. Tell the guests what kind of person your father is and what kind of relationship he has had with you (2002: 328).

Mori presents this as a pedagogical task, with the session defined for the participants as *zadankai* – a meeting in which 'several people get together and discuss opinions on a certain issue. It aims at discussing matters without enforcing formal structures.'

However, there are two issues to consider in how this task was designed and set up:

1. The instructions were not shared with the guests, so that there was a conflict between what the students were supposed to be doing and what the guests thought they were doing. Given this, Mori's finding that the NS guests did not follow the instructions given to the students is not surprising.
2. The instructions given to the students conflict with the definition of the session as *zadankai*. Giving the students three phases to follow is at odds with the idea of an unstructured session. It is not clear whether the guests were told that the session was to be 'zadankai', but if they were, this would reinforce the problem for the students.

The central problem with both Duff (1993) and Mori (2002) concerns the implementation of the concept of 'task'. In the first case, the student followed a different activity from the one that had been planned and the teacher allowed this to happen. In the second case, not only were the students and guests not given the same briefing, but the students were provided with two conflicting briefings. Our point is that a study that aims among other things to reflect on what tasks do or do not do has to make clear to the participants what the task is, and participants need to work to it. Otherwise, it is stating the obvious to report that the students did not 'do' the task. The reason they did not was either because they were allowed to change it or they did not understand what they were supposed to be doing and were not helped to do it. Not surprisingly, the studies discovered that the tasks did not result in the expected patterns of talk.

Pedagogically, the implication of both Duff's and Mori's discussions seems to be that unless students do tightly determined activities (e.g. exercises and drills), there is little predictability to work with in the classroom other than the collaborative processes students will engage in when left to their own devices. This argument echoes the argument by extremes evoked by Dewey (see Chapter 1) whereby activities are either tightly predictable or totally unpredictable. No scope seems left within this reasoning to uncover types of activity which can generate broadly similarly patterned discourse, while offering some optional variations and allowing students freedom of lexico-grammatical expression.

A more general point arises. We noted earlier two kinds of constructivist theory: the PCT and neo-Vygotskyan socio-cultural approaches (see section 7.3.3), with the former essentially a systemic theory and the latter a process theory. These orientations can cause problems: whereas PCT makes a virtue of the delicate detection of the particular perceptions of individuals, enabling follow-up studies of how these differ across time, it has difficulty in identifying how the surface behaviours of learners and teachers impinge on their underlying systems. In contrast, neo-Vygotskyan approaches are particularly adept at charting the surface behaviours, but seem to be less successful in relating these to underlying changes in learners' personal linguistic systems and thinking. In particular, neo-Vygotskyan studies tend to rely on the analyst's interpretation to identify whether surface moves in the discourse represent helpful talk or constitute evidence of learning, without consulting the students. In contrast, studies such as those reported in the following sub-section carry out pre- and post-tests, sometimes with multiple post-tests at different points. The purpose is to try to capture the students' systems of knowledge after the event. This kind of concern is rare in current neo-Vygotskyan work.

However, these limitations are not in principle irremediable. Meanwhile socio-cultural studies of tasks have the considerable merit of exploring the kinds of unscripted, exploratory processes of interaction between students which are a central reason for the use of pedagogical tasks and the kind of thing that teachers are concerned about. The major limitation in socio-cultural work lies in the fact that few socio-cultural specialists have as a principal objective to explore the ways in which the design and use of tasks can be improved.

Acquisition

Acquisition is the third and perhaps most crucial process which needs to be investigated in relation to tasks. Tasks are after all clearly intended to promote learning. Unfortunately, studies of learning generally require significantly more time for data collection than others. Furthermore, acquisition is hard to assess unless there is some expectation of what aspects of language the tasks will target, and we have seen that many researchers have doubted the ability or desirability of using tasks to target particular features of language. As a result, few studies have been carried out. However, two sets of studies have approached this issue, one by Mackey (1999), the other by Ellis and co-researchers (Ellis, Tanaka and Yamazaki, 1994; Ellis and Heimbach, 1997; Ellis and He 1999; all reported in Ellis, 2001). We have already sketched aspects of Mackey's study and her use of pre- and post-tests (see Example 7.9), and revisit it in Chapter 8, so in the following examples, we focus on Ellis and colleagues. Ellis and his co-researchers approached the issue of the role of tasks in promoting learning by exploring different types of oral input for language comprehension and acquisition. To do this they used a series of listening comprehension tasks and studied acquisition through the number of vocabulary items learnt.

Example 7.29   Ellis, Tanaka and Yamazaki; Ellis and Heimback; Ellis and He – vocabulary learning through listening tasks

These studies all used tasks in which students first listened to instructions and then numbered pictures of objects, or placed picture cards into a diagram in line with the instructions. The researchers were interested to see whether the form of the instructions might influence comprehension and acquisition.
   They compared four types of instruction:

1. unmodified instructions of the kind native speakers might give to each other (the 'baseline');
2. pre-modified instructions, simplified for comprehension by non-native speakers;
3. interactionally modified instructions, simplified in response to listeners' requests for clarification when they did not understand the baseline instructions;
4. modified output by fellow students, with listeners permitted to signal non-comprehension.

They first checked the impact of the types of input on comprehension and found that although modification seems to help comprehension, this is probably mainly due to the additional time created for the student to do the task.
   They then checked for the impact on acquisition in post-tests. They found that 'premodified and interactionally modified input facilitate acquisition' (Ellis, 2001: 61), but that the advantage for the latter 'largely reflects the additional time learners obtain for processing the input when they are given the opportunity to signal non-comprehension' (2001: 62).

> When time is controlled for, in some cases 'learners acquire new words more rapidly from premodified than from interactionally modified input' (2001: 62).
>   The authors checked the relationship between comprehension and acquisition, and found only similarly moderate correlations for the various forms of modified input, suggesting that input for comprehension and input for acquisition are not necessarily the same. In particular there is a distinction between understanding the directive and perceiving or understanding the particular vocabulary item.

Ellis (1995) investigated whether a relationship could be found between the frequency with which vocabulary items were acquired and aspects of the vocabulary items such as their length, prototypicality, frequency within the input, range of directives in which they were used and length of directives. He found that proto-typicality, frequency, range and length of directive were related to ease of acquisition, although length of directive operated positively in pre-modified input, and negatively in interactive input. Finally, Ellis and He (1999) studied the effect of involving the students themselves in using the new vocabulary items by giving the instructions to each other, working in pairs. The authors' findings here were clear-cut:

> The results were quite conclusive. Giving the learners the opportunity to produce and negotiate the directives in pairs resulted in significantly higher levels of comprehension than exposing them to premodified directives or giving them the opportunity to negotiate the teacher's baseline directives. . . . In short, the speaking task proved more effective than the listening tasks with regard to both comprehension and vocabulary acquisition. (Ellis, 2001: 67)

Ellis et al. then used tasks to explore the role of different types of input in comprehension and acquisition. This is a good example of how research can simultaneously investigate a particular theory (here Krashen's and Long's theories of the role of input in second language acquisition) and a set of pedagogical procedures, here a range of related tasks.

  Both the Mackey and Ellis studies successfully addressed the intuitively appealing issue of demonstrating that tasks can link to acquisition processes. Teachers are likely to need more of studies like these before they can feel that tasks are a reliable instrument for promoting development.

7.4.5   Teachers' use of tasks

We noted earlier that, like any artefact, what happens when tasks are used depends on two things: the characteristics of the task and the intentions of the users. The preceding subsections have discussed research which has largely explored characteristics of the task, rather than the impact of the intentions of the users. One user of tasks who can have considerable influence on how they are used is the teacher. A given task can be used at various points in a lesson, and for distinct purposes. Samuda (2001) is one study undertaken from a micro-perspective which reports on both process and outcome of the TIP task (see Chapter 1). Group or pair communication tasks are often used in the classroom as a main activity in their own right, or as a follow-up activity to engage learners' in using language they may have encountered earlier in the lesson in the context of some other activity. In contrast, Samuda's aim was to demonstrate what can happen when a communicative task such as the TIP task is used *at the start* of a lesson, before the teacher introduces the relevant language.

In Samuda (2001), students worked in groups to predict the likely owner of a set of objects they had been given. Following this phase, the teacher invited the groups to report on their findings for each object and for the set of objects as a whole. It is during this second phase that the teacher started to help students to form their judgements, providing words and phrases like 'may', 'might', 'could', 'is probably' and 'must', and using a percentage chart on the blackboard to indicate the corresponding level of probability (e.g. 100% probability = 'must'). Groups then returned to complete their accounts, using the new vocabulary.

There are three points to be made about this study. The first is that the teacher's use of the task fits into a broader perspective of how students learn and of how tasks can be used to promote learning. In this case, Samuda describes the task as 'preparing the conceptual ground' for any subsequent teaching, so that by the time the students interacted in plenary mode with the teacher they already had a clear conception of the *meanings* that they were aiming to convey. The task thus served to prepare the conceptual terrain and to provide a *need* for the language. The teacher was then in a position during the plenary phase to 'seed' the students with language elements which the task had primed them to look for.

The second point is that this study illustrates how a single micro-study can focus on both process and product, since Samuda implemented the activity within a pre-test/post-test design, enabling her to demonstrate learning gains, and hence to link the interactive processes of the lesson to systemic development. The fact that the pre-test/post-test design enabled the researcher to provide a statistical generalisation means that the study also sits astride the micro/macro distinction.

The final point is that the study illustrates more generally that by studying teachers' uses of tasks, it is possible to explore the ways in which tasks are integrated into lessons, and into more extended schemes of work. Little research of this kind has been done, yet from the perspective of teachers and teacher educators it looks a rich and valuable direction for future work.

7.4.6 Dimensions and processes of task design

Although *aspects* of task design are brought into focus through the studies outlined so far in this chapter, task design has not been generally treated as an area of empirical inquiry in its own right in the task research literature. An exception is Johnson's (2003) study of the working practices of task designers.

Example 7.30   Johnson

In a procedural study of second language pedagogic task design expertise, Johnson (2000; 2003) studied how different designers responded to the same design brief. The designers differed in terms of background in task design: 'specialist' designers (with at least five years' experience of task design work, all were or had been published materials writers); 'non-specialist' designers (with at least five years' experience as classroom teachers, with occasional task design for own use). Analysis was based on concurrent verbalisations collected from each designer 'thinking aloud' while developing a task based on the design brief.

Adopting a cumulative case study approach, Johnson analysed each think-aloud protocol on a case-by-case basis, gradually building up comparisons across cases. From this, he was able to identify a number of differences in the ways that specialist and non-specialist designers approached the design process and developed their tasks, many of which are broadly in line with findings from studies of expertise in other domains; this suggests that second language pedagogic task design is a specialised activity. As a preliminary step towards understanding what this entails, Johnson frames his findings as a set of hypotheses about the characteristics of a 'good' task designer.

Samuda (2005) reports part of a follow-up study investigating whether the differences in the design process identified in Johnson (2003) are reflected in the tasks produced, and finds a number of differences in the kinds of design features deployed by specialist and non-specialist designers.

There are two points about this work to be briefly noted here. First is its research methodology; a cumulative case study approach is being increasingly adopted in task research (e.g. Lynch and Maclean, 2000, 2001; Samuda, 2005; Samuda and Bygate, 2005) and offers considerable promise for future work. (We return to this in Chapter 8, where we focus in more detail on the Lynch and Maclean studies.) The second point is that focusing on tasks from the perspective of the designer represents a significant broadening of the research focus of task studies to date. If indeed, as Johnson suggests, task design is a specialist skill, understanding what good designers do is of considerable interest in supporting the development of 'non-specialist' designers.

7.5   Researching pedagogic tasks: a balance sheet

At the start of this chapter we identified a number of opportunities for research into language learning tasks. Here we revisit those in light of the studies reported in the body of this chapter. Let us now look again at the issues that we brought together in Table 7.1. There we highlighted areas for potential research focus; in Table 7.4 we provide an amended version, showing the areas of potential research focus, along with an indication of which areas have and which have not been investigated to date. (Space has precluded discussion of all of these themes.)

At first sight Table 7.4 suggests a fair amount of work has been undertaken. However, in a field such as ours, the numbers of studies must be considered slight. Recall that in 1980 Brumfit appealed for large numbers of small-scale studies on the grounds that large groups tend to give rise to neutral results and make interpretations of the relationship

Table 7.4   Areas of potential research focus

Teachers' procedures and processes	
Teacher's pre-task preparation	Samuda (2001)
Teacher's post-task follow-up	Samuda (2001)
Impact of elements of design	
Complexity	Robinson (2001)
Discourse type	Skehan (2001)
Task structure	Skehan (2001)
Participant roles	Pica et al. (1993)
Impact of conditions of implementation	
Task familiarity	Plough and Gass (1993)
Planning time	Foster and Skehan (1996), Skehan and Foster (1997) Yuan and Ellis (2003)
Task repetition	Bygate (1996, 2001), Bygate and Samuda (2005)
Role distribution	Lynch and Maclean (2000, 2001) Yule and McDonald (1990)
Learners' procedures and processes **Learners' talk**	
Language	Bygate (1988, 1999), Mackey (1999)
Phases	Bygate (1988)
Outcomes	Ellis and He (1999), Ellis (2001)

Table 7.4   (Continued)

Dynamics	
Negotiation for meaning	Doughty and Pica (1986), Pica and Doughty (1985)
Constructivist processes	Swain and Lapkin (2000, 2001), Donato (1994), Ohta (2000), Blake and Zyzik (2003)
Development	
Learning generated through task involvement	Mackey (1999) Ellis (2001), Izumi and Bigelow (2000)
Construals	
Students' interpretations of tasks	None
Students' evaluations of tasks	Garrett and Shortall (2002) Murphy (1993)
Teachers' perceptions of tasks	None
Designers' construals of tasks	Johnson (2000; 2003)
Individual differences	
Student differences	None
Student motivation	Kumaravadivelu, 1993;Dörnyei and Kormos (2000)
Teacher differences	Samuda, 2006
Task, lesson and curriculum	
tasks and schemes of work/course plan	None
tasks and target tests	None
tasks and overall curriculum goals	None

between context and performance almost impossible to track. Better, he argued, to work with smaller groups and to accumulate sufficiently large numbers of studies conducted along similar lines to gradually assemble a picture that would show general patterns as well as distinctive differences for different populations. From this perspective, we have to conclude that the research undertaken so far is both slight, and unsystematic. We need far more replication and cross examination of findings, so that errors in the systematicity of sampling and design can be gradually reduced.

Further, if we look again at the agenda proposed in 1956 by Bruner, Goodnow and Austin (see Example 7.1), it is clear that research into tasks for second language teaching has yet to get to the heart of the matter – learning on tasks within classroom contexts. Indeed, looked at from the perspectives highlighted in Example 7.1, it is clear that much more systematic and probing research is needed before we can confidently claim to understand how tasks work in pedagogical contexts or hope to be able to exploit research results within language pedagogy.

Part 2
Interactions between Research and Practice

Introduction

Having traced the historical and conceptual background from which tasks have emerged and sketched the current research state of play, we turn now to a critical exploration of a number of empirical studies and pedagogical developments. In doing this, we hope to bring together relationships between research and practice, and highlight the motivations of developments – both in pedagogical practice and in theory-driven research, as well as their theoretical and practical implications. In Chapter 8 we examine closely a representative sample of empirical studies into tasks. Chapter 9 then explores the ways in which tasks have been incorporated into curricula and materials.

8
Task Research from a Pedagogical Perspective

Chapters 1–7 have sought to highlight the educational richness of using tasks in the language classroom. As we saw in Chapter 7, what has been achieved is, however (as always), less than what might be. Yet research builds on previous work, and for development to be possible much can be learned and gained. The aim of this chapter is to explore methods of researching pedagogical tasks through a small sample of studies. In an empirically informed field, individual studies are crucial: they illustrate the ideas, as well as testing them and informing their potential development. The chapter considers each study in turn, examining its rationale and design, as well as the practical and theoretical implications. We focus on eight:

1. Samuda (2001)
2. Donato (1994)
3. Yule and Macdonald (1990)
4. Mackey (1999)
5. Yuan and Ellis (2003)
6. Ortega (2005)
7. Skehan and Foster (1999)
8. Lynch and Maclean (2001)

We have selected these, from among many possible candidates, on the basis that they illustrate a range of task-related issues that researchers have focused on, and used a variety of methods in researching them. They are summarised in Table 8.1.

All eight studies address how tasks can promote learning through communication. The first four are concerned with the nature and impact of interactional processes on language use or development, exploring issues

Table 8.1 Overview of the eight studies

Author	The problem	Context	Research purpose	Theoretical base
Samuda 2001	How can designers design, and teachers use, tasks to introduce students to new language?	ESL lesson for adult learners on a pre-academic intensive programme at an American university	To track the impact of task and student–student and teacher–student interaction on students' learning	Tasks may help learning of form where semantically complex aspects of language first need to be understood
Donato 1994	Does a dialogue preparation task lead students to help each other to resolve language problems?	A lesson from a French BA course for students at an American university	To investigate incidence of scaffolding moves in group work	Learning scaffolded by the students via tasks may be more effective than transmission-based teaching
Yule and Macdonald 1990	Does the relative proficiency of students in the roles of speaker and listener affect their performance of referential communication tasks?	An experiment involving NNS students at an American university	To investigate the impact of task role and relative proficiency on pairs' success in negotiating referential problems	Reference involves each speaker allowing for others' perspectives, and needs negotiation; can be effectively developed and tested through interactional tasks
Mackey 1999	Does participation in negotiation for meaning promote the development of certain structures?	A longitudinal experiment with NNS students in a sequence of activities at an Australian language	To investigate impact of task-based interaction on development of learners' questions	Involvement in negotiation for meaning may help acquisition of aspects of language

Yuan and Ellis 2003	What difference does pre- and on-task planning time make to students' talk?	An experiment involving EFL students at a Chinese university	To investigate impact of on-line and pre-task planning time on language processing through output	Tasks may provide essential language practice, but varying planning conditions may help optimise their use.
Ortega 2005	What do learners focus on during pre-task planning, and why?	An experimental study of planning involving NNS students at an American university	To investigate students strategies and perceptions of pre-task planning	Learners' planning processes and focus of attention may relate to style and proficiency
Skehan and Foster 1999	What is the impact on learners' talk of: content structure; prior content summary; or talking while/after watching?	An experiment involving NNS students at a British university	To investigate impact of story structure and processing load on language processing through output	Learning implies a balance between fluency, accuracy and complexity; varying story structure and task conditions may promote this
Lynch and Maclean 2001	How can designers design tasks to encourage repetition of talk, and does it affect learners' talk?	A lesson from an English language for Medical Conferences course at a Scottish university	To explore the effect in a normal class of a repetition element built into the task	Tasks lead to repeated attempts to formulate the same content, which may lead to improved formulation

such as how interaction can be influenced by the task or the conditions and how interaction can promote learning; The second four share an interest in processing capacity and task demand. They all focus on how varying some aspect of task conditions (planning, task structure, simultaneous or delayed narration, and task repetition) can affect learners' processing capacity.

The studies represent different types of research design. Four (Samuda, Donato, Lynch and Maclean, and Ortega) are case studies, exploring a one-off event through transcript analysis (Samuda, Donato), interviews (Ortega) or a combination of the two (Lynch and Maclean). In one case (Samuda) the study also incorporates a pre-/post-test. Three of the case studies also use some quantification – a reminder that statistics are not incompatible with case study designs. The other four studies are all experimental, quantitative designs.

The choice of research paradigm – case study as opposed to an experimental study – has implications for the choice and structure of the dataset. The case studies tend to use detailed transcript analysis to track changes in perception and formulation through the course of the activity, although Ortega's study is structured around data collected from a semi-structured interview. In contrast, the experimental studies all use some kind of statistical cross-group analysis, with the participants divided into two or more subgroups and given different tasks or conditions. The researcher compares the language of the task (Yule and Macdonald, Skehan and Foster), or studies possible differences in pre-/post-test results (Mackey). Effective statistical analysis depends crucially on the choice of appropriate categories for computing. Whereas quantification is an option for case studies (see Samuda, Lynch and Maclean, and Ortega), it is essential for experimental studies. The latter also have the option of providing illustrative examples of their data.

The choice of research methodology can also have implications for the ecological validity of the study. This may be because case studies can easily research activities that are already scheduled, whereas experimental studies tend to investigate a hunch which starts independently of any existing teaching programme. Hence three of the four case studies are from a single scheduled lesson within a programme of studies with the students' normal class teacher. The other four studies occurred in experimentally designed contexts, as one-off data elicitation events. Hence they were not part of the students' study programme, although Mackey's groups, while randomly grouped, were treated to experimental lessons over a three-week period. Ortega's is the only case study not located in a taught programme, her research exploring the individual reports of students who were participating in an experimental study she was running.

Table 8.2 Research methods of the studies

Author	Design
Samuda, 2001	Case study of a single class, analysing transcripts *and* interviews *and* statistical (pre-/post-) analysis
Lynch and Maclean, 2001	Case study of individual students, using detailed transcript analysis, statistical analysis and interviews
Donato, 1994	Case study of one small group, using detailed transcript analysis of group talk
Yule and Macdonald, 1990	Experimental cross-group statistical design, comparing high proficiency > low proficiency and low proficiency > high proficiency pairings, analysing transcripts to assess students' success in identifying and resolving problems.
Yuan and Ellis, 2003	Experimental cross-group statistical study of impact of planning conditions (three, including control), on fluency, accuracy, complexity of talk
Skehan and Foster, 1999	Experimental cross-group study of impact of task structure (two) and different performance conditions (four) on fluency, accuracy and complexity
Mackey, 1999	Experimental pre-/post- (one)/post- (two) study of impact on learning of 3 types of task, in relation to proficiency.
Ortega, 2005	Case study design, through semi-structured interviews

The implication of this is that the studies that were collected from students working on a normal classroom activity as part of a scheduled course (Samuda, Lynch and Maclean, Donato) are able to show the functioning and use of tasks in pedagogical contexts. The others are not in a position to do this. However, their strength is their ability to establish whether there are underlying parameters or principles which teachers and testers could use systematically to influence either the nature of the interaction or of the language processing, which students engage in on tasks.

The eight studies relate in different ways to the themes explored in Chapter 7:

- *Ecological issues*: studies implemented in a scheduled lesson – Lynch and Maclean, Samuda, Donato; as opposed to studies occurring outside of a taught programme – Yule and Macdonald, Mackey, Yuan and Ellis, Skehan and Foster.
- *Language focus issues*: designing tasks to engage learners with expressions of modality (Samuda); with question forms (Mackey); or in terms

of fluency, accuracy and complexity (Yuan and Ellis, Skehan and Foster, Lynch and Maclean).

- *Process issues*: notably creating a learning space for meaning and form (Samuda, Donato); engaging relevant interaction (Donato, Mackey, Samuda, Yule and Macdonald); planning (Yuan and Ellis; Ortega); task structure (Skehan and Foster); repetition (Lynch and Maclean).
- *Development issues*: via a pre-post-design (Samuda, Mackey) or via micro-analysis of short-term language changes (Donato, Lynch and Maclean).
- *Teacher–learner issues*: learners' perceptions of task planning (Ortega).

The selected studies are tabulated in relation to these dimensions in Table 8.3.

In considering these studies, there are three underlying issues which regularly arise:

1. the relative value of case studies compared with group studies;
2. the relative value of comparative studies and longitudinal studies; and
3. the relative value of pedagogically and non-pedagogically situated research into tasks.

Case studies can provide the most complete picture of processes and outcomes; group studies are best able to open a window on variation and representativeness. There is no doubt that teachers and other educationists need both. Comparative studies can offer a perspective on the differences between tasks-in-action, task conditions and between groups, but say nothing about learning outcomes; longitudinal designs can help to reveal changes over time, but without a comparative element, say nothing about the relative contribution of different types of activity. Again, teachers and educationists need both. Finally, there is pedagogically and non-pedagogically situated research: here too, both are needed. Much has been written on the need for pedagogically situated studies (e.g. Ellis, 2003), but studies situated in non-pedagogical contexts are also needed: a teacher is unlikely to feel comfortable using procedures that have never been trialled before, and more generally, in seeking to understand pedagogical activities, we need to know whether they are robust enough to work both inside and outside the classrooms.

In the following sections, each study is presented separately, starting with a factual account of the nature of the study, its rationale, aims, setting and participants, a description of the task and of how the data were analysed. The results are reported, with sample data presented where possible, and the study as a whole is then briefly discussed.

Table 8.3 The relationship of the selected studies to six variables

Study	Ecological context	Task variable	Special conditions	Language	Process	Development	Teachers and learners
Samuda	Scheduled lesson with intact class	Focus on predicting – meaning > form	Student–student and Teacher–student negotiation	Modality	Individual and joint exploration	Use of modality expressions	
Donato	Scheduled lesson with intact class	Interaction process			Joint exploration	Negotiated micro-changes	
Yule and Macdonald	Dyads in non-class context		HP or LP 'sender' + LP or HP 'receiver'		Extent of problem resolution		
Mackey	Randomly selected LP students, each paired with a different NS	+/– interactive task structure		Question forms		Use of question forms	
Yuan and Ellis	Dyads in non-class context		Pre-task/on-line planning	Fluency, accuracy, complexity			
Ortega	Non-class context, with intact classes		Pre-task planning				Sts' views on planning
Skehan and Foster	Students from different classes, conditions randomly assigned	+/– provision of structured content	Different processing loads	Fluency, accuracy, complexity			
Lynch and Maclean	Scheduled lesson with intact class	Repeated interactions on same topic				Individual micro-changes	Students' perceptions of the activity

8.1   Samuda

Samuda (2001) studied an implementation of the TIP task introduced in Chapter 1. It is a case study of a task being used in a lesson to work on aspects of epistemic modality (used to signal the degree of certainty of our speech acts). It tracks successive steps in the lesson and focuses on how the teacher negotiates meaning and form with the class. It also considers how far the task leads the learners to focus on the target features language, and explores the impact of the lesson on the learners' knowledge through a pre-test/post-test design.

8.1.1   Rationale

Samuda makes a distinction between language activating tasks, which are used primarily to activate, refine and stretch learners' existing IL resources, and processing and knowledge constructing tasks, which are used to enable learners make 'new' form–meaning connections. In this study, the TIP task was as a knowledge-constructing task. The task design was based on three components – *input data*, *operations on data*, *outcomes* – which are intended to underpin a meaning → form → meaning progression 'to manage shifts in attentional focus as the task unfolds [with] opportunities for focusing attention on novel form/meaning connections' (2001: 121). This progression was targeted partly in the belief that highlighting meaning in task input (2001: 122), helps to introduce forms once meanings are in mind, rather than relying on a progression from form to meaning which 'risks dislocating language form from language use'. The intention is for the forms to be encountered when the meanings are 'in the process of being expressed', rather than before the task has begun and the need perceived, or after it has been completed and the need has passed. This meaning → form progression may be more appropriate where the meanings are complex and the forms simpler, whereas where the forms are complex and the meanings relatively simple the linguistic environment is likely to require more attention. The rationale, design and participants of the study are presented below:

Aims

To explore empirically how a teacher can work with a given task 'to complement its essential meaning → form → meaning progression', and with what effect.

Setting

Programme: a pre-academic intensive ESL programme at a North American university. *The class*: the lowest of a five-level programme.

The lesson: a grammar/communication class, scheduled for 10–25 hours per week.

Participants: students, teacher and researcher

Nine students, mainly Japanese and Korean, with an average age of 22, studying for a wide range of purposes, from academic, to basic language improvement. Mean pre-tested scores on target features: 3.73/26.
Teacher: eight years' experience with similar students.
Researcher: spent one morning a week in the class over the course of a term; was familiar to the students as observer and co-teacher, and this could 'develop tasks around topics of interest to the students' (2001: 125).

Task design

Designed to target epistemic modality, but without including the forms in the input data, or prescribing use of the target forms.
   Piloting with NS and higher proficiency NNS groups showed that the target features were used to do the task as well as other forms of epistemic modality.

Task phases

```
┌──────────────────────┐
│ Input data           │
│  •  Rubric           │
│  •  Objects          │
│  •  Chart*           │
└──────────────────────┘
```

```
┌──────────────────────────────────────────┐
│ Operations on data                         │
│  •  Groups:                                 │
│        –  Form initial hypotheses           │
│        –  Complete charts                   │
│        –  Make preliminary presentations    │
└──────────────────────────────────────────┘
```

```
┌──────────────────────────────────────────┐
│ Language focus                              │
│ Teacher:                                    │
│  •  Builds on learner-initiated  meaning    │
│       to introduce new language data        │
└──────────────────────────────────────────┘
```

```
┌──────────────────────────────┐
│ Operations on data            │
│ Groups:                       │
│  •  Prepare posters           │
└──────────────────────────────┘
```

```
┌──────────────────────────────┐
│ Outcomes                      │
│ Groups:                       │
│  •  Poster presentations      │
└──────────────────────────────┘
```

*The chart which the groups worked to complete is shown in Example 1.1, pp. 9–10.

8.1.2   Analysis

The analysis adopted both a process and product perspective, that is, it aimed to link how the students and teacher worked through the task and how the students' knowledge changed. In order to follow a process dimension, the data for each of the three phases were analysed separately: the pre-focus phase, when the students worked in groups; the language focus phase, a plenary reporting phase, in which the teacher participated; the post-focus phase, in which students returned to group mode to prepare a poster. At a finer grain of analysis, the task processes were represented through extracts taken from transcripts of the lesson. The analysis distinguishes between 'mined' items (that is, expressions of modality that the students – as well as the teacher – appropriated from the task input material), and expressions of modality that students drew on from their own existing knowledge. The analysis also distinguishes between two types of language focus – *implicit* and *explicit* – occurring as two different sub-phases while the students were reporting their initial findings to the whole class. In the first, implicit language focus, the teacher responded to the meanings expressed by the learners by conversationally 'interweaving' expressions of epistemic modality into her responses without drawing overt attention to them. In the second, explicit language focus, the teacher briefly focussed attention to the form of the modals as they arose in her responses.

In addition, the study reflected the students' systemic language development by reporting pre- and post-test results, as well as by quantifying the changes in students' use of modal forms at the pre- and post-focus phases.

8.1.3   Results

Process results

Samples of extracts from the pre-focus, language focus and post-focus phases are shown in the box below. 'Mined' forms (that is, appropriated from the task input material by the students and the teacher) are underlined; forms provided by the students from their own knowledge appear in bold, and target forms introduced by the teacher (and subsequently used by the students) are shown in italics.

Samples of task language: Samuda (2001)

Pre-language focus*
A: Is this hobby or job? **May be** it's hobby, but
N: **Maybe.**
A: **Maybe** it's job.

C: Both.
A: Both.
C: It's <u>possible</u>.
N: <u>Possible</u> or <u>90 per cent</u>?
Y: <u>90 per cent</u> I think.

Language focus
Implicit
T: Hmmm, but you're <u>not certain</u> if he smokes, huh? (looking at matchbox)
A: Look (opens matchbox). Many matches so **maybe** he just keep for friend, not for him. (laughter)
T: Mmmm I – I guess <u>It's possible</u> he *might* smoke. It's hard to tell just from this.

Explicit
T: Did you have anything here you thought was '<u>probable</u>'? Like <u>90 per cent</u>?
Y: Businessman.
T: Businessman? <u>90 per cent</u>? OK. So you're <u>90 per cent</u> certain he's a businessman, right? Here's another way to say this. You think it's <u>90 per cent certain</u>, so you think he *must* be a businessman. He *must* be a businessmen (writes on board). So this (points to *must be* on board) is showing how <u>CERTAIN</u> how SURE you are. Not <u>100 per cent</u>, but almost <u>100 per cent. 90 per cent</u>.
A: So <u>100 per cent</u> is 'be' or '*must*'?

Post-language focus
Y: He likes
N: Golf
A: Tennis
C: Art
N: Mmm (looking at chart) are just <u>probable</u> and chess
C: <u>So probable</u>?
A: <u>Probable</u>.
N: (writing) He *must* like chess?
A: And art

---

* A more extended sample or pre-language focus talk can be found in Example 1.2, pp. 11–13.

Quantitative results

Results reflecting use of forms at the pre-focus and post-focus phases are presented in Table 8.4. Note how, although there is only a fairly small increase in the total proportion non-mined forms at the post-focus phase, four target forms appear in use, while the range of mined language expressions falls sharply.

Table 8.4   Mined forms pre- and post-focus

	Pre-focus	Post-focus
Mined:		
Total	27%	24%
(It's) possible	10.5	7.3
(It's) probable	5.6	9.7
90%	4.8	7.3
Certain	4.0	0
50%	1.6	0
Non-mined:		
Total	73%	76%
Maybe	53.2	36.5
(I'm) sure	11.3	0
(I'm) not sure	8.9	0
Must	0	17.0
May	0	12.1
Might	0	7.3
Could	0	2.4

Table 8.5   Pre- and post-test results

	Pre-test (mean)	Post-test (mean) ten days later
Maximum 26	3.73	19.01

Table 8.5 presents the results of the pre- and post-tests. Note that standard deviations were not presented, and nor were the precise test methods that were used.

8.1.4   Discussion

The study presents both process and product data relating to each phase in a three-phase lesson and a snapshot of the students' language knowledge through pre- and post-tests. It is conceivable that it is only transcript (or in writing, draft) data that are capable of presenting evidence of the nature of the surface processes which students and teacher engage in through tasks, but that statistical data give a perspective on the changing profiles of the students' language in both use and test contexts. The study also illustrates how teachers can engage with students' autonomous work on tasks and use the tasks as a means of focusing attention on target language features. Whereas teachers have generally focused on form before students need to use it (as in PPP approaches) or after the need has passed (in post-task feedback and practice materials), this approach specifically times the teacher's input so that it occurs at a mid-point during the task, before the task has been completed. Methodologically, this is fairly close to the idea of teachers using recasts in their oral responses to student talk, to implicitly feed in language features which students appear to lack at the point of need. However, recasts are provided on an ad hoc basis according to students' moment-by-moment need, so that there can be little opportunity for the teacher to return to the same language point with a given student. In contrast, the approach illustrated through this study suggests using tasks systematically to target particular areas of language. The study also highlights differences in types of talk occurring in different phases of the task.

Aspects of the study suggest unfinished business, however. First, although the pre- and post-tests are very suggestive, more thorough testing, especially for the post-test, and more information about the standard deviations in the scores would give a more reliable picture. Second, some written or oral self-report data from the teacher and especially from the students would help to illuminate their own assessments of the procedures being used. While to an outsider the lesson seems to work well, we should not assume that this is the students' view. Third, a more extended longitudinal time-frame would be valuable in helping to show the ways in which phases in the teaching–learning process contribute to longer-term learning. Finally there is a danger that the report might be taken to suggest that tasks play a peripheral role compared to the teacher's own intervention, and that in larger classes, and with less time, this use of tasks is a luxury which most teachers can easily dispense with. However, our interpretation is that this study suggests that tasks can play a powerful role in knowledge construction. Whether this proves to be the case is an empirical question, and hence we argue that what is needed is more research evidence: such decisions should not be made purely in terms of teachers' or researchers' instincts, but on the basis of empirical documentation.

8.2   Donato

One aspect of Samuda's study is its interest in how interaction – first between students, then between teacher and students – could lead them to work on the meanings and to integrate new forms which would they would perceive as relevant to the meanings they wanted to express. Student–student interaction is seen as an important exploratory forum for learning. Student–student interaction has widely been seen as an important space for learners to encounter relevant language. This theme has been of particular interest to interactionists or socio-constructivists (see Chapter 7) who believe that overt interaction is a key means by which learners acquire new language and construct new understandings, and for whom the major value of tasks is their ability to generate this type of interaction. Donato (1994) is one of a number of 'watershed' papers written from this perspective. The paper studies the talk of a group of three students in a French class, planning a dialogue to be acted out in the following lesson. The analysis investigates how far the students help each other in the selection and production of accurate language.

Aims

'… to discover if, during open-ended collaborative tasks, second language learners *mutually construct* a scaffold out of the discursive process of negotiating contexts of shared understanding' (1994: 42).

'[to seek] to answer the question of whether learners can exert a developmental influence on each other's interlanguage system in observable ways' (1994: 39).

Task

A one-hour planning session for an oral activity, to take place in the next class, in which a wife discovers that her husband has purchased a fur coat for another woman (1994: 40). (The activity was a scenario from DiPietro, 1987.)

Participants

Third term students of French at an American university; they had been together for ten weeks, working on a range of small-group projects. Reportedly, knew each other well, enjoyed working on projects together and assumed 'a collective orientation to problem-solving' (1994: 39–40).

Analysis

Adopts a 'micro-genetic analysis' (i.e. close study) of the way in which the talk develops utterance by utterance, aiming to 'observe directly how students help each other during the overt planning of L2 utterances and the outcome of these multiple forces of help as they come into contact, and interact, with each other (1994: 42).

Uses concept of 'scaffolding' to analyse interaction:

1. *recruiting* interest in the task
2. *simplifying* the task
3. *maintaining* pursuit of the goal

4. *marking* critical features and discrepancies between what has been produced and ideal solution
5. *controlling* frustration during problem solving, and
6. *demonstrating* an idealized version of the act to be performed
7. 'Additionally, the metaphor implies the expert's active stance toward continual revisions of the scaffold in response to the emerging capabilities of the novice.'

Definitions from Wood, Bruner and Ross (1976) and Rogoff (1990) (1994: 41).

Results

Sample transcript of group sorting out how to say 'you remembered' in French

A1	Speaker 1	... and then I'll say ... *tu as souvenu notre anniversaire de marriage* [*sic*] ... or should I say *mon anniversaire*?
A2	Speaker 2	*Tu as ...*
A3	Speaker 3	*Tu as ...*
A4	Speaker 1	*Tu as souvenu* ... 'you remembered?" ' [*sic*]
A5	Speaker 3	Yeah, but isn't that reflexive? *Tu t'as ...*
A6	Speaker 1	Ah, *tu t'as souvenu.*
A7	Speaker 2	Oh, it's *tu es.*
A8	Speaker 1	*Tu es.*
A9	Speaker 3	*tu es, tu es, tu ...*
A10	Speaker 1	*T'es, tu t'es*
A11	Speaker 3	*tu t'es*
A12	Speaker 1	*Tu t'es souvenu.*

Interpretation of students' problem

[This] is an attempt to render 'you remembered' into French. The compound past tense formation of reflective [*sic*: more commonly referred to as 'reflexive'] verbs in French presents complex linguistic processing, since students are required to choose the auxiliary *être* instead of *avoir*, select the correct reflexive pronoun to agree with the subject, form the past participle, which in this case is an unpredictable form, and decide if, and how, the past participle will be marked for agreement with the subject (Donato, 1994: 44).

Representation of the scaffolding

The data are represented through the use of a chart to display the relationship between the chronological dimension of the interaction, which is shown on the horizontal axis, and the accumulating clarification of information, which is set out along the vertical axis:

The order of linguistic elements on the vertical axis matches that observed in the group members and reflects the structure of the interaction as it occurred in real time.

The numbers 1, 2, and 3 refer to the three participants themselves. Next to each number is a positive or negative sign. The positive sign represents correct, but not necessarily complete knowledge: the negative sign reflects incomplete or incorrect knowledge. The sequence of number is faithful to the [order] in which utterances appeared in the conversation. (1994: 42-3)

Representation of scaffolded help for 'you remembered'*

subj-pro-aux-pp			1−		1+
subj-aux-pp	1−				
subj-pro-aux			3−		1+ 3+
subj-aux		2−3−		1+ 2+ 3+	

interactional time

* The numbers represent each of the three speakers; the ' +/− ' symbols indicate presence or absence of understanding of the target feature.

Description of the interactions in terms of scaffolding

… Speaker 3 sets the goal, or more specifically one of several sub-goals of the total task by questioning the accuracy of the utterance [of Speaker 1 in line 4]. The need to verify the accuracy of the utterance appears quite spontaneously and is attended to jointly by the other two students. …

That the students collaboratively attend to Speaker 1's initial phrase, and Speaker 3's questioning of its legitimacy, is clearly shown. Remarkably, however, no student alone possesses the ability to construct the French past compound tense of the reflexive verb 'to remember'. Each student appears to control only a specific aspect of the desired construction. Speaker 1, for example, produces the correct past participle (A1) but the incorrect auxiliary verb. Speaker 2 recognises the verb as reflexive (A5) but fails to select the appropriate auxiliary *être*. Speaker 3, on the other hand, understands the choice of the auxiliary for reflexive compound past tense forms but does not include the correct reflexive pronoun into his version of the utterance (A7). At this point in the interaction Speakers 1 and 2 synthesise the prior knowledge that has been externalised during the interaction and simultaneously arrive at the correct construction (A9–12).

8.2.1   Analysis of the interaction in terms of Wood et al.'s scaffolding features

Key categories are underlined and numbered in terms of Wood et al.'s list (see above).

Analysis of scaffolded help

'The interesting point here is that these three learners are able to construct collectively a scaffold for each other's performance. Following the definition of Wood, Bruner, and Ross (1976), they <u>jointly manage</u> (3) components of the problem, <u>mark critical features of discrepancies between what has been produced and the perceived ideal solution</u> (4) (A5, A7, A10), and <u>minimize frustration and risk</u> (5) by relying on the collective resources of the group. ...

'The affective markers in this interaction, "Oh", "Ah", and "Yea", <u>reveal ... task and information management</u> (3). They are also indicators of <u>orientation to the task</u> ... thus signifying the point at which <u>joint focus of the attention</u> [sic] (1) has been achieved. ... Their collectivity is also exhibited by their ability to <u>establish intersubjectivity</u> (1). ... The convergence of affective markers appears at the critical point in the interaction, when negative evidence is transformed into positive knowledge (A5, A6, A7), indicating a point of development for the participants.

'These students have constructed for each other a *collective scaffold*. During this interaction, the speakers are <u>at the same time individually novices and collectively experts</u>, sources of new orientations for each other, and guides through this complex linguistic problem solving. (Donato, 1994: 45–6).

This type of analysis involves a detailed study of the data to identify elements which can be interpreted in terms of the model under discussion. Utterances or parts of utterances ('ah', 'oh'), or whole utterances (such as A5, A7 and A10) are identified as examples of the phenomena which the analyst is seeking. The surface interaction is then interpreted in terms of how the learners signal problems, draw each other's attention to the problems, and propose and evaluate solutions, signalling as they go whether they understand each other and how far they have got. The analysts uses the surface utterances as evidence of what the speakers are trying to achieve and of what the speakers know at any point in time. In adopting this procedure, interaction processes are taken to be directly indicative of the students' interlanguage capacities. In this case, Donato uses the data to argue that the students' talk is an instantiation of joint learning in which students indicate what they do not know, and help each other to produce the correct form.

8.2.2   Discussion

Donato's is an interesting account of the surface dynamics of the interaction. A key contribution of analyses such as this is to demonstrate in detail the work learners engage in when collaborating on a task. It shows that group talk on tasks can be textured in such a way as to enable a level of personal involvement and focus on detail which would be hard to envisage in whole class interaction. In addition, such data have an immediate face validity, since they illustrate how the materials work in a way which can translate directly to the classroom. The possibility that such language work might contribute to learners' development will obviously be of interest to teachers and quite possibly to learners too (see Lynch and Maclean's comment on this).

There are, however, some points of caution. First, the study is not concerned with tasks as defined in Chapter 1 or as reflected in the studies discussed earlier in this chapter. That is, Donato's task does not involve learners in holistic uses of the target language, but simply in using the mother tongue to produce a target language script. This is not to say that there is no place for the use of such activities, but to note that the term 'task' is used by teachers and researchers in different ways. For instance, some researchers or teachers might consider Donato's 'task' an example of *pre*-task planning. We include it here because of the potential value of the analysis he uses, and because pre-task planning is relevant for our theme, rather than as an example of a type of 'task'.

Second, we need to be aware that Donato's description of the data is not simple, but involves significant interpretation. Consider, for example, turns A2, A3 and A4. It is possible to interpret A2 and A3 as either buying time to recall the correct forms or as simply indicating doubts on the parts of speakers 2 and 3. Similarly although in A7 Speaker 2 does not produce a fully correct phrase (it should be *tu t'es*), it is possible that s/he is aware of the correct phrase but needs time to access it. Hence when Donato says, 'each student appears to control only a specific aspect of the desired construction', he is interpreting what the students say as offering a direct window onto what they know. That is, their actual performance is taken to represent their systemic knowledge. This may not be a warranted assumption.

A similar point concerns Donato's interpretation of the scaffolding moves. For example, how justifiable is it to analyse utterances such as 'ah' and 'oh' as revealing 'task' and 'information management', and in addition as signalling 'the presence of distributed help and mutual orientation to the task' (1994: 46)? These interjections might have these values, but equally well might not. Presumably the terms 'task management' and 'information management' cannot be applied to *all* occurrences of 'ah' and 'oh' in talk. Similar questions can be asked of other aspects of the analysis: for instance, the suggestion that the interpersonal discourse gives rise to 'a discourse structure reminiscent of that of a single speaker', or that the talk reflects the speakers' 'ability to establish intersubjectivity'? The question is not whether these are plausible interpretations of the data, but rather whether they are accurate. To find out, we need a way of cross-checking our interpretations with the participants.

These points reflect a more general and interesting issue, namely the assumption that we can straightforwardly deduce what learners know of the target language directly from what they say. For one thing, performance cannot reflect competence directly (Chomsky, 1957). Indeed, it varies according to context (Labov, 1972) and needs to be carefully handled in attempting to identify the state of learners' interlanguage (Tarone, 1988). So performance data can be misleading. This has a pragmatic dimension too. Various researchers (e.g. Aston, 1986; Foster, 1998; Rampton, 1995) have pointed out that for both social and psychological reasons speakers often prefer convergence to divergence. Aston (1987) has been frequently cited to critique the analysis of 'negotiation for meaning' sequences: people might appear to negotiate meaning satisfactorily, but 'negotiation' may be concluded so as to avoid inconveniencing the self or others. That is, what speakers say may not always reflect what they know. Hence we could question conclusions such as that 'the convergence of affective markers appears at the critical point in the interaction, when negative evidence is transformed into positive knowledge (A5, A6, A7), indicating a point of development for the participants' (1994: 46). It is possible that this was a point of development for all the students, or for two of the students, or for just one; after all, it is equally possible that much of the talk was devoted to tactfully jogging each other's memories in order to enable one to work out the form. It is also possible that by the end of the exchange one or more of the students remained unsure of the correct form. We do not know. It is one thing then to report the data, and another to interpret it. We may need more evidence before deciding whether students have ended up with complete or incomplete knowledge.

Nevertheless, we do want to know how individual utterances in intragroup talk can contribute to learning, and in this respect Donato's study was a landmark paper, raising key questions about ways of representing and interpreting task data. It also suggests pedagogically enlightening ways in which interaction on second language tasks can be seen. The challenge though is how to analyse what we might call the 'systemic' importance of learning processes. We return to this issue in another guise in a later study: Mackey (1999).

8.3   Yule and Macdonald

Yule and Macdonald (1990) summarise their study as follows:

Quote 8.1   Abstract of study

Extending the research done on the effects of different types of task and different participant arrangements used to foster negotiated interaction among L2 learners, we developed a task that presents specific referential conflicts and analysed the solutions adopted within two different pairings of learners. Pairs in which the higher proficiency member had the dominant role engaged in little interactive cooperation and in some cases changed the task rather than negotiate a solution. Pairs in which the higher proficiency member had the nondominant role engaged in substantial negotiation work, sought each other's perspective and generally shared much more in the interactive turn-taking and the successful resolution of referential conflicts.

(Yule and Macdonald, 1990: 539).

Whereas Donato's paper explores the potential of a group *planning* activity to generate collaborative language work, Yule and Macdonald *design* an activity with in-built communication problems so as to study how far students resolve the problems.

Aims

To find out whether the effectiveness of SL students in negotiating referential meanings is influenced by how they interpret their own and each other's roles, with relative proficiency seen as a potentially significant factor.

Relevant concepts

Reference: the use of language to identify, locate, move or follow movement or changes in entities; seen as influenced by the ways in which speakers interpret their own and their interlocutors' respective roles and perspectives.

  Referential effectiveness: inevitably influenced by the relationship between the participants in any given discourse, and in particular by their ability to take account of each other's perspective. Speakers' effectiveness in doing this varies.

Theoretical motivation

To explore whether the design of a task can engage negotiation of reference, and how far this can be systematically affected by students' engagement in their respective roles. Secondary motivation is to see whether relative proficiency is a relevant factor.

Pedagogical motivation

To consider ways of focusing students on negotiation of reference; and since no class is homogeneous, and proficiency is relative, to explore the likely impact of giving higher or lower proficiency student the dominant role in information gap tasks.

Design

Aims to study effects of role and relative proficiency level on speakers' management of referential language. It analyses the frequencies of identification and resolution of problems, and surveys quantitative patterns across two types of pairing of students, making it a cross-group study.

Task

Each student in a pair had a slightly different version of the same map of a city, with buildings labelled. One student was required to tell their partner a route. The task was completed when the student who knew the route had communicated it to the student who didn't know it.

Referential problems built into the task design

Problem 1: the old map has a road through one block which in the new map is closed off.
Problem 2: the old map has one building labelled 'Hats', which in the new map (identical location) is labelled 'Bicycles'.
Problem 3: the old map has one 'Office' building marked in an area whereas the new map marks that 'Office', plus another two 'Office' buildings.
Problem 4: the old map has a 'Dentist' next to a 'Motel' in one area whereas the new map has 'Shirts' and 'Doctor'. …

Those in the 'sender' role will encounter places where their reference points differ from those of their receivers. To achieve successful communication, there has to be some form of negotiation.

Task instructions

'*To Speaker A ("the sender")*: You have a map with a delivery route marked on it, showing where ten packages have to be delivered. Your partner has a similar map, but does not know the delivery route. Describe the route so that your partner can draw the delivery route on his/her map.
To Speaker B ("the receiver"): You have to draw the delivery route on your map. You can ask questions any time you want.
To both speakers: The two maps are similar, but one is older than the other, so you will find that some parts of your maps are different' (1990: 543).
The sender was given the older version of the map, and the receiver the newer one, though neither knew who had which.

(Continued)

Participants and procedures

Participants: 40 volunteer international graduate students at a North American university, from 16 different language backgrounds, with an English language proficiency described as 'high intermediate to advanced (TOEFL 500+)'.

Pairing: students paired with colleagues from a different L1 background, one ('H') with a mean TOEFL score of 625, and the other ('L') a lower mean of 562. In ten pairs H was given the sender role, and L was the receiver (H > L); in the other ten pairs, the roles were reversed (L > H).

Task procedures: 'In performing the tasks, the students could not see each other's maps, but could face each other, allowing gestures to be used (though infrequently). The spoken interactions . . . all took place in separate rooms, without investigators present' (1990: 544).

Analysis

The authors sought 'evidence in the L2 performance of students that they did, or did not, comprehend each other', and aimed to 'recognize when comprehension of specifically referential information was being appropriately signalled or not'.

To do this, they 'looked at those points in the task in which a referential conflict existed and determined whether the interactants resolved the conflict by arriving at a mutual understanding of their referential worlds or not' (1990: 542). This led them to analyse the transcripts in terms of the following criteria:

- Students failed to identify the problem
- Students identified the problem but ignored it or gave it up
- Students identified the problem and solved it by mandate
- Students identified the problem and solved it by negotiation

Results

Summary: 'The difference in performances elicited under the two conditions was so marked that it seems unnecessary to apply standard quantifying measures to characterize them' (1990: 545).

Overview:

Effectiveness in dealing with problems	H > L	L > H
Did not identify problem	11 (27.5%)	5 (12.5%)
Identified but ignored or gave up	11 (27.5%)	3 (7.5%)
Identified, and solved by mandate	11 (27.5%)	5 (12.5%)
Identified and solved by negotiation	7 (17.5%)	27 (67.5%)

To see the pattern, it is necessary to read the table *as a whole*, rather than line by line. That is, 67.5% of the problems were successfully resolved in the L > H condition, while in the H > L condition, 55% were simply not resolved (lines 1 and 2), and a further 27.5% were not satisfactorily resolved. This is a massive difference in effectiveness, in favour of the L > H condition.

Detailed results, problem by problem, and by pair type

	Identified the problem?							
	Not at all		Yes, and Ignored or gave up		Yes, and solved by mandate		Yes, and solved by negotiation	
	H > L	L > H	H > L	L > H	H > L	L > H	H > L	L > H
Problem 1	6	2	4	2	–	–	–	6
Problem 2	–	–	6	1	1	1	3	8
Problem 3	1	–	1	–	6	3	2	7
Problem 4	4	3	–	–	4	1	2	6
	11	5	11	3	11	5	7	27
Totals %	27.5	12.5	27.5	7.5	27.5	12.5	17.5	67.5

Interpretation

H > L pairings: although meanings are apparently being negotiated, often agreement is no more than superficial, with problems of comprehension and expression not being resolved. When LP receiver signals problems, HP sender often ignores them; and even where discrepancies between the maps are noticed, HP sender tends to mandate solutions without negotiation. Sometimes HP sender simply abandons his/her role.

L > H pairings: in contrast:

'there is a lot of evidence to show that negotiation of meaning, the discovery of the other's perspective and a more balanced sharing of interactive turn-taking are the result. In its simplest form, the higher proficiency participant's contribution as receiver (H-R) is to respond more actively to the directions received' (1990: 549). The result is far more frequent use of features like clarification requests, suggesting 'greater cooperative negotiation of their joint goal' (1990: 551).

Advantages for both LP and HP students:

'[W]e find the sender's role gives the less proficient students greater opportunity (or even the necessity) to use the language productively, to create messages that

(Continued)

take account of their own world of reference and also what their interactive partner has told them. It also places them in a type of spoken interaction in which, instead of only responding with passive backchannels, they participate in the joint creation of linguistic structures, across turns . . .' (1990: 552).

'To appreciate the benefits [for the higher proficiency speaker], one has to accept that taking part in the cooperative, negotiated resolutions of referential conflicts does develop communication skills that are missed when the higher proficiency speaker, as in the H > L pairings, only produces one-way talk, with little feedback. The L > H interactions force the higher proficiency speaker to listen (as well as speak), to take one's interlocutor's perspective into account (rather than ignore it), and to tailor one's contributions to fit a particular interactive partner's knowledge (instead of only displaying one's own knowledge). These are the kinds of L2 skills that are not typically addressed in the language classroom, yet which are required skills if our advanced learners are to become effective participants in a range of L2 interactions' (1990: 553).

8.3.1   Discussion

Like Samuda (2001), this study is relatively unusual in using a task design to target a particular area of language, and one of relatively few studies to investigate how differences between students can impact on the processes and outcomes of a task. The study demonstrates once again that it is possible to build particular communication problems into the design of a task which can be used to raise awareness, in this case to assess the effectiveness of learners' ability to use particular aspects of language. It is unusual for the key elements of task performance to be broken down into four levels of achievement as here. The analysis seems unproblematic, in that because of the design, surface features can be interpreted directly in terms of whether information has been shared and problems jointly resolved. However, we are not told how reliability of the analysis was checked. In practical terms, the issue of how to pair students in the classroom and what roles to give them is one that is rarely considered in the literature, and which would be hard for teachers to address in a principled way without research data such as this. It would be of interest to see how far speaker role relates to proficiency on other types of task and at other levels of proficiency. The study may also have interesting implications for the teacher talk in teacher–student interaction.

There could be questions surrounding the claim that communicating reference successfully is more of a pragmatic interpersonal problem than other uses of language. While it is true that it is essential for speakers to assess their interlocutors' perspectives, this is probably also the case for most areas of the grammar of the language. In addition, building connections between task, pragmatics and language is theoretically tricky, though it seems to work here. However, one of the reasons why this seems a particularly valuable study is because of the way in which it illustrates two key dimensions of tasks: 1), the dimension of the particular challenge they are designed to present learners, which teachers and designers (among others) can evaluate as more or less effective; and 2) the dimension of interpersonal role, which without the use of tasks would seem to be pedagogically unmanageable.

8.4   Mackey

8.4.1   The study

Mackey (1999) explores the impact of interactive participation on students' ability to use different question forms. Thus the study researches an aspect of the interaction hypothesis – 'that taking part in interaction can facilitate second language development' (1999: 565). The hypothesis here is that two-way interaction between students is potentially more productive than non-interactive learning activities in which meaning negotiation is unnecessary. The focus, then, is how far the interactive dimension of tasks can contribute to the learning of targeted language structures.

Aims

To see if students assessed as having reached a certain stage of development in question formation could be led, through task use, to produce question forms typical of more advanced stages of development. Stages of question-form development assessed via an adaptation of Pienemann's stage model (Pienemann and Johnston, 1987). Mackey wished to see if students could progress from Stage 3 (fronting, such as 'Where the cats are?') to Stages 4 ('pseudo-inversion', e.g. 'Have you got a dog?') and 5 (do-auxiliary in second position, e.g. 'What do you have?' 'Where does your cat sit?')

Research questions

'a) Does conversational interaction facilitate second language development?
 b) Are the developmental outcomes related to the nature of the conversational interaction and the level of learner involvement?' (1999: 565).

Design

Participants randomly assigned to four groups: three treatment, one control, while the 'beginner group' joined the lower-intermediate group of 'interactors'.

(Continued)

1. The *'interactors'*: Students interacted with a NS interlocutor to complete the task. NS interlocutors were briefed about the target language features. Two groups of students followed this condition – a lower-intermediate group, and a beginners' group. This enabled a comparison of the impact of interaction on different levels of developmental 'readiness'.
2. The *'scripteds'*: The NS followed pre-scripted input to give information to the student. If students did not understand, the scripted input could be repeated, but if they still did not understand, the interlocutor would move on to the next point. The scripting was 'so detailed that communication breakdowns and negotiation of meaning were rendered highly unlikely' (1999: 570).
3. The *'observers'*: Students observed a video recording of students with a NS doing each of the tasks, and completed the task sheets from watching the video.

A *control group* did the pre- and post-tests, but none of the treatment tasks, enabling the study to check for general learning processes taking place outside the treatments.
   For all groups, each task took from 15–25 minutes.

Theoretical motivation

The key issue is whether the three treatment conditions have different impacts on the learners, with particular interest in condition 1, the interactive condition. The reasoning is as follows:

1. *The interactors*: In this condition, students would share responsibility for completing the task, and would therefore be able to generate as much negotiation of meaning (i.e. as many repetitions, clarifications, comprehension checks and clarification requests) as needed to ensure task completion. The question is whether a high incidence of negotiation of meaning gives rise to more repetition of question forms, leading to more development.
2. *The scripteds*: In this condition, the native speaker will be less open to negotiation moves from the student, and therefore fewer questions would be used or reworked. If so, this condition should lead to less development.
3. *The observers*: Here the students are not personally responsible for managing the interaction; hence although they could have the same exposure as students in the interactive condition, they will not be pushed into processing the language so fully themselves. Less development is expected.
4. The *control group*: this group is not expected to have the relevant experiences, hence less development is expected.

Participants

Thirty-four adult ESL learners from a private English language school in Sydney, Australia; randomly selected, from lower proficiency programmes and from a range of language backgrounds.

Tasks

Four 'treatment' tasks were used, designed to engage learners in using questions:

- a story completion task: 'working out a story by asking questions'
- a picture sequencing task: discovering the order of a picture story
- a picture drawing task: 'describing or drawing a picture' (1999: 568)
- picture differences: 'identifying the differences between similar pictures' for the tests.

Procedures

Students were tested once before, and three times after, the treatment. For these tests, the picture differences task was used so that students' performance would not be influenced by familiarity with the test type.

The pre-test: used to provide a basis for comparison with the post-tests.
The three post-tests: the first the day after the last treatment day, the second a week later, and the third three weeks after the second, enabled the researcher to check on longer term retention and possible delayed development following the treatment.
Dyads: For all tasks, including tests, students were paired with a NS interlocutor.
Administration: Participants did one of each of the three types of treatment task on three consecutive days (i.e. one of each on day 1, one of each on day 2, and one of each on day 3).

Analysis

Data were analysed using two measures:

- the numbers of students per group who improved their stage of questions (the 'developmental stage increase');
- the number of advanced stage questions per group ('developmentally more advanced questions').

A student was judged to have improved their stage 'if they produced at least two different higher level question forms in at least two of the post-tests' (1999: 571).

Table 8.6   Numbers of students showing developmental change

	Interactors n = 7	Controls n = 7	Interactors (beginners) n = 7	Scripteds n = 6	Observers n = 7
Percentage	71	14	86	16	57
Ratio	(5/7)	(1/7)	(6/7)	(1/6)	(4/7)

Table 8.7   Increase in number of questions at stages 4 and 5 produced by each group in the post-tests

	Interactors n = 7	Controls n = 7	Interactors (beginners) n = 7	Scripteds n = 6	Observers n = 7
Post-test 1	2.3	1.8	1.6	1.4	1.6
Post-test 2	4.0	0.5	2.9	2.2	1.0
Post-test 3	4.8	2.0	7.0	2.4	0.9

Figures are approximate, based on a graph in Mackey, 1999.

Results

The increase in questions at stages 4 and 5 was studied by calculating the mean numbers of questions at those levels on the three post tests (see Tables 8.6 and 8.7).

Table 8.6 shows that the two interactor groups benefited most, and the controls and scripteds benefited least. The observers were close to the two interactor groups.

In Table 8.7 (showing the mean number of stage 4 and 5 question types per group), the interactors outperform the other groups, with the observers performing weakest.

These data are interpreted as showing that the interactor condition was more helpful for development in the use of questions thanthe other conditions, with the beginners showing most improvement. That is, the 'negotiation for meaning' condition seems to have helped development.

An ANOVA test was run on the gains for each group (the post-test scores per group minus the group's pre-test scores). Statistically significant differences were found only for the two interactor groups (post-elementary group: $p = .018$; beginner group: $p = .048$), with post-test 2, and post-test 3 respectively being the point of significant gains). So comparison of the pre-test and the three post-tests showed that the interactor groups scored higher on each successive post-test.

8.4.2   Interpretation

Mackey interprets the results as showing that negotiation for meaning in the context of tasks is positively associated with development of the ability to use question forms:

Quote 8.2 Negotiation for meaning and the opportunity to develop use of question forms

By taking part in interaction, [a sample] learner received examples of advanced structures. Through interactional modifications that arose through negotiation of meaning, some of those structures were repeated or rephrased. The learner also had the opportunity to produce questions and receive feedback through the answers. Structures that were more developmentally advanced were produced after treatment. This pattern was true for the two groups of learners who took part in interaction.
(Mackey, 1999: 577)

That is, the group study shows a common pattern in the ways in which learners respond to tasks, and by the same token, types of task interaction have a recurrent quality. Mackey concludes that tasks are a valuable context for promoting learning.

Quote 8.3 Tasks as a context for language development

This study suggests that one of the features that best interacts with the learner-internal factors to facilitate subsequent language development is learner participation in interaction that offers opportunities for the negotiation of meaning to take place. This interaction is effectively obtained through the use of tasks.
(Mackey, 1999: 583–4)

8.4.3   Discussion

Quote 8.3 suggests that in this study the most important aspect of tasks is their capacity to engender negotiation for meaning – that is, their role in mobilising peer group talk with the target interactive qualities. In other words, achieving this purpose is a matter of appropriate task design. However it is not only a matter of design, since in order for the tasks to function appropriately the NS interlocutors needed careful briefing. So, one implication of the study is that for the interactive design to function, it needs to be complemented by appropriate engagement by at least one of the interlocutors.

In successfully influencing the learners' ability to use question forms, the study also provides evidence that tasks can be designed to target particular aspects of language over and above the general nature of the learners' language processing, such as the relative fluency, accuracy or complexity being encouraged. This, then, is a second aspect of language use that task design can be reasonably expected to activate.

In terms of the impact of the tasks, this is one of the rare studies successfully to have shown a learning effect through a pre-/post-design (note, though, the series of studies of listening comprehension tasks reported in Ellis, 2001, as well as Samuda, 2001). We might wish to have more detailed information in order to study how far the tasks in fact made a qualitative difference to students' use of questions, and whether speedier progress could have been made with more explicit teacher intervention in the context of the use of such tasks. In the future we hope to get a fuller picture of the learners' emerging control of the language features under study. Yet overall, the broad impact of the study is robust.

Mackey's study also carries other pedagogically significant implications. One is that tasks need to be selected to target areas of language which are relevant to the learners in terms of their current level of development. One can also reasonably anticipate that it would be helpful if learners themselves perceive the need to improve their mastery of the language feature, and are aware of the value of the selected tasks for achieving this aim. There is no indication of whether the learners were aware of the focus of the experiment – the implication is that they probably were not informed, to avoid any bias. In pedagogical contexts, however, there are obvious reasons for not withholding this kind of information – if the tasks work under these experimental circumstances, then from this perspective presumably they have just as good a chance of working in the classroom. From this we can argue for further work in exploring learners' perceptions of tasks (see Ortega, 2005, discussed below).

The question of classroom effectiveness returns us to the issue of ecological validity. Although the study was pedagogically oriented in the sense that the sequence of tasks was carefully selected in light of the students' phase of language development at the time – quite possibly even more carefully than a teacher would normally be able to manage (a significant point when we consider the relationship between teaching and research) – aspects of the implementation diverged fairly significantly from most pedagogical practices: each student had their own NS interlocutor; the NS interlocutors were carefully briefed; and a series of pre- and post-tests was used to monitor development carefully. To build on studies such as this, we will obviously need further work cataloguing how tasks of this kind function in normal classroom contexts.

Nevertheless, this study provides empirical support for the view that there are four important aspects of tasks: 1) their design; 2) their relevance for the learners; 3) the way they are used; and 4) their impact on development.

8.5   Yuan and Ellis

8.5.1   The study

With Yuan and Ellis (2003) we shift from studies focusing on interaction to those researching task demand. This is one of a series studying the impact of planning time on oral performance (see also Ellis, 1987; Skehan and Foster 1997 1999, 2005; Ellis, 2005).

Aims

To find out how students' performance on oral tasks is affected by a) allowing them pre-task-planning time, b) on-line planning time, and c) no planning time.

Theoretical motivation

Previous studies suggest that *pre-task* planning influences speakers' fluency and complexity, and sometimes their accuracy. *On-line* planning had not been explicitly studied, but theorising (e.g. Johnson, 1996; Skehan, 1998) and empirical studies (e.g. Ellis, 1987) suggested that having more time during performance can affect performance, especially accuracy (e.g. where SL users are able to speak more slowly, or write without time pressures).

Pedagogical motivation

Most communicative approaches to language teaching emphasise the importance of communication *per se*. However, there has long been concern that communicative activities can encourage communicative effectiveness at the cost of accuracy (Skehan, 1998), leading users to neglect formal details in comprehension (VanPatten, 1996) and in production, redundancy reduction (or 'stem form' English; George, 1972). If planning time can shift learners' attention to language, this might usefully offset any neglect of form.

Participants

Forty-two full-time UG English major students in the International Business Department of a Chinese university; homogeneous in terms of age (18–20 years), learning history (eight years' schooling, no visits to an English-speaking country) and proficiency (marks between 100 and 120 on the Higher Education Bureau Examination, and in terms of scores on a pre-test taken from the TOEFL).

Task and procedures

Monologic narration of a picture story comprising six images, from Heaton (1975), carried out individually in a language laboratory booth, during a listening and speaking class. The task was selected to enable comparability with other studies (cf. Skehan, 2001; Ellis, 2005). The story was chosen to require some interpretation on the part of the learners, and to make the task reasonably demanding. Instructions were given in Chinese.

Task conditions

Three groups:

- *No-planning* (NP) group (no pre-task planning time and a five-minute time-limit for telling the story).
- *Pre-task planning* (PTP) group (ten minutes' pre-task planning and a five-minute time-limit for telling the story).
- *On-line planning* (OLP) group (no pre-task planning time and no time-limit for telling the story).

The design aimed to lead the OLP group to plan more while telling the story, and the PTP group to do their planning before speaking.

Research design

Table 8.8

	NP	PTP	OLP
Preparation	0.5 mins	10 mins	0.5 mins
Target output		Four sentences per picture	
Task time limit	5 minutes	5 minutes	None
Other instructions	None	Planning to focus on content, organisation and language. They could write notes, but not use them while speaking	None

Categories of analysis (measures)

Independent variables

To check that the conditions worked, the authors counted the following:

1. Length of time: total number of seconds on task
2. Syllables A: the number of syllables produced to reflect productivity.
3. Syllables B: the number of syllables produced, minus all syllables repeated, reformulated or replaced, to reflect meaningful productivity.

Dependent variables (calculated per student and averaged per group)

Fluency:

1. Rate A: number of syllables per minute
2. Rate B: number of productive syllables per minute

Complexity:

1. Syntactic complexity: ration of clauses to T-units
2. Syntactic variety: total number of different verb forms
3. Lexical variety: mean segmental type-token ratio, calculated for each segment of 40 words, by dividing total number of different words by the total number of words in the segment (i.e. by 40).

Accuracy:

1. Error-free clauses (including lexical errors) – as a percentage of all clauses
2. Correct verb forms – as a percentage of all verb forms.

Analysis and results

An analysis of variance (ANOVA) was conducted to test for statistical significance of differences between the groups' scores.

General impact of conditions

Table 8.9

	NP	PTP	OLP	F-value	Sig	Locations of significance		
						NP-PTP	NP-OLP	PTP-OLP
Time	186.43	189.29	243.57	3.474	.041*	.993	.077	.098
Syll A	194.36	242.50	235.50	3.886	.029*	.046*	.101	.932
Syll B	173.71	227.00	210.36	5.585	.007**	.009**	.093	.598

These measures reflect the impact of the different conditions on the time spent talking and the amount of talk produced. The OLP group spent most time talking; the planning groups produced more than the NP group; and despite the greater time spent by the OLP group, they did not produce significantly more than the PTP group. To end up with a similar amount of talk produced with more time to produce it, the OLP group must have spoken more slowly. So the conditions seem to have the intended impact on the students' behaviour. The next question is how far this influenced the quality of their talk.

Table 8.10   Impact on quality of talk: fluency, complexity and accuracy

	F-value	Sig	NP-PTP	NP-OLP	PTP-OLP
Fluency					
Rate A	2.737	.077	.359	.690	.081
Rate B	3.412	.043*	.247	.691	.048*
Complexity					
Syntactic	7.480	.002**	.007**	.008**	.997
Syn. Variety	2.523	.093	.164	.164	1.00
Lexical variety	4.439	.018*	.103	.811	.025*
Accuracy					
Clauses	5.152	.010**	.256	.010**	.322
Verbs	4.45	.018*	.604	.020*	.170

Fluency

The results show that in terms of fluency, the only significant difference is between PTP and OLP in terms of meaningful output (checking the means we find that it is the PTP group that is the more productive). The NP group falls between the two.

Complexity

The non-planning group produces significantly less complex talk than the other two groups. The planning group once again falls between the two. However, it is only the PTP group which is significantly different in terms of lexical variety, as compared with the OLP group.

Accuracy

The OLP group is significantly more accurate than the NP group on both measures, this time with the PTP group falling between the two extremes.

8.5.2   Interpretation

We now need to consider how to interpret results such as these. They are complicated in two ways. First, the comparison between three groups is harder to conceptualise than if it had been between two groups: we tend to find differences between two groups, but not between all three pairs. Second, we need to note that when we have a significant difference, this could be produced by either of the two conditions, or by a combination of the two. For instance, the PTP and OLP groups differ significantly in terms of fluency. But this may be as much due to the conditions of the OLP group (slowing them down) as to the conditions of the PTP group (either the pre-planning in which they get organised, or the five-minute time limit which speeds them up, or perhaps both). Hence when we consider findings such as these, we have to bear in mind that comparisons often involve more than one factor.

8.5.3   Discussion

What are the practical implications of this study for the use of tasks in the classroom? First, it is clear that it is tricky to ask students to attend to accuracy and fluency at the same time. Either they will take longer in trying to be more accurate, or they will try to be more fluent at the cost of accuracy. In contrast, syntactic complexity could be promoted by getting students to attend to accuracy or by getting them to prepare the content of what they want to say. If they attend to the content, they may also produce a wider range of vocabulary. More generally, encouraging a particular focus generally: a) biases performance in a particular direction, and by implication away from the other; and b) carries with it at least one other consequence (syntactic complexity, and possibly lexical variety). So when we notice that students are continually dysfluent but accurate, or fluent but inaccurate, this is understandable; and we may want to do something using information from this study to 'balance them up'.

We might wonder whether this holds for all oral activities, or only for some. Similarly, does the same thing hold for reading and writing activities? And how does it affect memory? If people initially focus on accuracy, where does this leave them if they have to use their work again?

And what if people focus on content? This brings further questions into focus: is complexity necessarily a good thing, and are all kinds of complexity the same? For instance, do we simply want more embedding, or might we be interested in encouraging more complex types of complementation? And in the same vein, can on-line planning focus more on some aspects of the grammar than others?

In relation to the theoretical implications of this study, unresolved problems remain. First, we know that people took longer in the on-line planning condition, but do we know that they were actually doing more planning on-line? And do we know what they were actually attending to? Is it possible that they were doing the same kinds of on-line planning as the other groups, but simply spending longer on it? Also, is it possible that they were not attending more to accuracy *per se*, but were simply being more careful in the way they accessed their memory stores?

A second issue is whether the pre-task planning students were focusing only on content during their ten minutes' preparation, or whether they were also attending to language, as they were invited to. Research into this would be useful – we need to know what students do in response to what they are asked to do (see Ortega, 2005, discussed below for a study on this topic).

Third, planning prior to talk is fairly artificial in everyday, spontaneous talk. How do we justify the use of PTP in leading students towards greater competence? Here it would be useful to explore the impact of planning in relation to different levels of proficiency and especially useful to know how effective this is in normal class contexts.

Overall, then, this study is valuable in various ways. It shows that even a fairly simple pair of constructs (pre-planning and on-line planning) are not straightforward in terms of how they are implemented, or what we assume is happening when they are implemented, or indeed in terms of the actual results. Second, though, it shows fairly clearly that speaking tasks are not identical: the conditions might make quite a significant difference to how people do them. Third, the study leaves open interesting questions about student responses and perceptions, about planning in relation to levels of proficiency, and more generally about the use of student planning in normal classrooms. It also illustrates how, to be productive, research in the field needs to involve a cumulative series of attempts to solve intriguing puzzles: this study follows on a sequence of studies initiated originally by Ellis in 1987 (Crookes, 1989; Skehan and Foster, 1997), each using earlier findings to reconceptualise the problem, improve the design and refine the analysis. Yuan and Ellis themselves comment that the design used in Ellis (1987) contained problems it was worth attempting to resolve.

8.6   Ortega

8.6.1   The study

As we have seen, most studies of language learning tasks have concentrated on various types of performance data: Yuan and Ellis (above) is one example. Indeed, relatively few (notably Lynch and Maclean, 2000, 2001; see below) have investigated students' construals of work on tasks. In contrast Ortega (2005) investigated *students' perceptions* of the benefits of pre-task planning. As we noted in Chapter 7, the general purpose of such studies is to build up an understanding of the interface between pedagogical procedures and learner perception. It also provides an opportunity to open a window specifically on learners' rationales, preferences and strategies.

Aims

To study 'the benefits afforded by pre-task planning through . . . what learners say they do when they plan' (2005: 77)

Participants

Two groups of learners of Spanish as an FL in an American university: 14 'low intermediate' fourth term students; 32 'advanced' students from the fifth term and beyond.

Data

In the form of retrospective interviews collected in the context of a sequence of pre-task planning → narrative telling task:

Phase	Activities	Comments
Pre-task	Input: Picture strip; L1 recording Planning +/− in writing	To ensure comprehension Enables repeated measures study of planning *vis-à-vis* language
Task	Monologic oral narrative to peer listener	Authentic listener giving speaker a communicative purpose
Post-task	Listener: story retelling in writing Speaker: retrospective interview	Motivates listening and occupies listener during interview

Summary of results of pre-task planning study by group

Planning generally resulted in greater fluency and greater complexity, with the Advanced group also showing more accuracy. The main differences between the two groups were increased lexical complexity for the Low Intermediate group, and more accurate noun-modifier agreement in the Advanced group.

	Low Intermediate	**Advanced**
Fluency	More disfluency markers in unplanned narratives	Faster speech rate in planned narratives
Syntactic complexity	More words and propositions per utterance in planned talk	More words per utterance in planned narratives
Lexical complexity	Higher type-token ration in planned talk	No differences in type-token ratio
Accuracy	No differences in accuracy on definite article or subject–verb agreement	More accurate noun-modifier agreement

Findings from the interview data

a) Frequency of reported strategy use by type

Ortega first analysed the students' stated frequency of strategy use, in terms of strategy types, by group. No differences emerged.

Summary of mean frequencies of reported use of strategy types

	All strategies	**Metacognitive**	**Cognitive**	**Socio/affective**
All participants	12.11	5.20	5.91	1.00
Advanced	12.78	5.53	6.16	1.09
Low-intermediate	10.33	4.33	5.25	0.75

b) Frequencies of reported use of particular strategies

Next, Ortega considered the frequency of reported use of specific strategies, once again by group. Here the striking differences are in organisational planning, with the low intermediate students reporting very high use, and in rehearsing, with high frequency reported by the Advanced group, but not by the Low Intermediates.

Strategies reportedly used most frequently

Outlining/summarising	84%	(both groups equally)
Production monitoring	75%	(both groups equally)
Organisational planning	68%	(both groups, but low intermediates very high)
Lexical compensation	64%	(both groups equally)
Translating	57%	(both groups equally)
Empathising with listener	52%	(both groups equally)
Rehearsing	48%	(advanced 53%, low intermediates 33%)

c) Perceptions of benefits and limitations

Ortega's interview explored students' general perceptions of the benefits and limitations of pre-task planning. Most (59 per cent) saw planning as helpful, but a significant minority (41 per cent) found it *un*helpful. In itself this information is of limited value: more helpful is to know why. The perceived benefits and limitations are reported next.

Perceived benefits and limitations

Beneficial feature	*Function*
Extra time:	Organising thoughts; formulating thoughts; lexical solutions; practising/rehearsing
Writing notes:	Formulating thoughts; lexical and grammatical retrieval; improving lexical choice; improving content; practicing/rehearsing; monitoring grammar
Locus of limitation	*Limitation*
Performance conditions	1. Low task complexity
	2. Poverty of planning conditions
Language expertise	1. Ceiling to retrieval benefits
	2. Lack of transfer to on-line performance
Learner preferences	1. Added pressure with planning
	2. Extemporaneous performance feels good

Ortega summarises this as follows:

• The main advantages were in terms of retrieval and organisation; and rehearsal and monitoring.

- The main limitations were in terms of:
  - the conditions, the task was too simple, or the planning conditions did not allow access to enough sources of information;
  - expertise, lack of knowledge limited the value of planning time, and lack of capacity meant that what was planned didn't transfer; and
  - learner preferences, for some, planning time increased the sense of pressure by increasing the challenge; for others, planning detracted from the agreeable sense of spontaneity in improvising speech.

The key trend is a difference in language focus between communication and accuracy. These Ortega links to differences in level of language expertise.

Table 8.11   Individual differences in focus on communication vs focus on accuracy by group

	Low-intermediates	Advanced
Writing	For retrieval, none for recall, fewer (33%) rehearsed.	Balanced writing for retrieval, for recall; 50% used rehearsal; cycles of organising thoughts, retrieving appropriate words and rules, and rehearsing for performance.
Monitoring	Of production and impact on listener. Little monitoring of language.	Of production, impact on listener; auditory, visual, cross-language, style and 'double check' monitoring.

Listener sensitivity and orientation to the language

Under 'monitoring', there is a difference in how the two levels tended to allow for the listener. Low intermediates tended to prioritise their awareness of the impact of their talk on the listener, reducing their attention to language; in contrast advanced speakers used a far wider array of strategies for generating and monitoring the quality of their language, with the listener as a motivation for additional attention to accuracy.

Listener sensitivity and prioritization of communication

- Organising the content in listener-sensitive ways.
- Coming up with simple vocabulary or approximation good enough to ensure listener comprehension.

- Focusing away from language, keeping it simple.
- Reluctance to self-correct on-line, pressure to keep going.
- Slowing down during performance.
- Thinking of grammar that is essential for listener's understanding.

Explicit focus on form during planning

- Cross-language monitoring, translation, using meta-cognitive knowledge of self as learner, using meta-linguistic knowledge, attending to grammar of low communicative value.

In other words, it appears that in terms of attention to language, advanced learners were able to use planning time more constructively because they had more expertise to draw on, rehearsed more and had a wider range of strategies to draw on. Low intermediate learners focused more on retrieving what they knew (notably vocabulary) and reducing risks during performance, while occasionally seeking out grammatical features likely to be essential for listeners.

Summary of findings

1. Centrality of retrieval and rehearsal operations; attention to form through retrieval, monitoring and rehearsal.
2. Perceptions moderated by:
   - Individual differences, guiding effort in terms of what students view as important – communication or accuracy.
   - Differences in expertise: retrieval strategies of low-intermediate speakers leading to greater lexical complexity, balance of retrieval, rehearsal and self-monitoring, leading to greater accuracy.
3. Presence of listener, leading to prioritising communication, deterring some 'from engaging in propositional, lexical and/or syntactic complexity and … self-corrections', but also leading 'to a heightened process of meaning-form mapping by priming some learners to attend to certain aspects of grammar that were perceived as essential for the listener's understanding'.

8.6.2   Discussion

Clearly, Ortega's study is not particularly close to the ecology of classroom teaching: the design was experimental, involving students in non-classroom-based pair-work; and the procedures involved more intensive debriefing than teachers would normally be able to conduct in the context of a regular programme. The study seems not to start from a particular theoretical background, and of the various studies reported in this chapter, this one strikingly lacks any research questions. On the other hand, it has some rare virtues. One is that it is unique in the current literature in exploring in depth the perceptions and beliefs of students about a task-based procedure which they have just experienced. This is an informative line of enquiry, and provided it is conducted rigorously and impartially, as clearly Ortega's study does, will generate crucial information for the future use of tasks.

A second refreshing aspect of this study is the intuitively real-life complexity of the array of information generated. In this respect, the study is a challenge to the researcher not only to gather the data, but also to unpick the various strands of information in a careful and sensitive way. This is another important contribution of Ortega's study. It is also worth noting the way in which she adopts a careful, 'iterative' exploratory approach to the analysis of her data, involving what she calls 'a two-pronged approach' combining, on the one hand, 'content analysis of emergent themes and [on the other hand] application of a priori categories' (2005: 83). It is unusual for researchers deliberately to combine the use of prior theoretical analytical categories with categories emerging from the particular data set, and particularly starting from a theoretically informed experimental study.

Finally, an important strength is the way the closing discussion links back to one of the enduring major controversies in the field – the tension for learners between focusing on form or on meaning during communicative language use. Ortega's data suggest that the question may be resolved in terms of relative levels of proficiency: for low proficiency learners this may well be a tension that needs careful management; however, more advanced learners may have the capacity to integrate the two. Overall, Ortega's study illustrates how talking to learners may provide a wealth of valuable information for developing the field.

8.7   Skehan and Foster

8.7.1   The study

This study brings us back to a focus on performance effects. Like Yuan and Ellis, Skehan and Foster (1999) aim to understand how communicative processing demands can affect learners' attention to language. This study focuses on the relationship between the internal structure of tasks, their processing load and learners' fluency, accuracy and complexity.

Theoretical motivation

Basic assumptions: communication is a complex activity, placing three distinct types of demand on learners' language production: fluency, accuracy and complexity. Each needs to be developed, but each requires different types of attention.

Skehan and Foster's definition of the language processing demands

Fluency	the capacity to use language in real time, and emphasise meanings, possibly drawing on more lexicalised systems
Accuracy	the ability to avoid error in performance, possibly reflecting higher levels of control in the language, as well as a conservative orientation, that is, avoidance of challenging structure that might provoke error
Complexity	the capacity to use more advanced language, with the possibility that such language may not be controlled as effectively. This may also involve a greater willingness to take risks and use fewer controlled language subsystems. This area is also taken to correlate with a greater likelihood of restructuring, that is, change and development in the interlanguage system

The learner's problem: attention capacity is limited; so during communication learners lack the means to attend to all three demands simultaneously. They therefore tend to prioritise them differently, according to individual preference. Over-emphasis on one is likely to lead to skewed language development.

The dangers of over-emphasis of each language processing demand

- Consistent prioritisation of fluency may lead to over-lexicalised performance, and performance in which fossilised language is difficult to change.
- Consistent prioritisation of accuracy might lead to lack of fluency and avoidance of engagement with cutting-edge language, presumably as well as under-lexicalisation.
- Consistent prioritisation of complexity might lead to a wide range of structures but a failure to move toward accuracy and control.

So, given that communication is a prime context for language development, the authors are interested in exploring whether tasks can be used deliberately to promote fluency, accuracy and complexity. The study focuses on whether the internal structure and the processing load of a task might influence learners' fluency, accuracy and complexity: tasks with clearly structured content may be less linguistically demanding than one with relatively unstructured content. Processing load may have similar general effects.

Pedagogical motivation

The main pedagogical motivation is its potential use to teachers and designers. Finding ways in which task structure and processing conditions can affect students' language could help task designers to exploit the parameters in materials they write, and could enable teachers to adjust the difficulty of tasks.

Aims and hypotheses

The purpose of the present research is twofold: to explore how performance of a task can be affected by the degree of inherent structure within the task, and to explore how different processing conditions can influence performance. Drawing on the previous discussion [of earlier studies], four hypotheses were framed:

Hypothesis 1: Tasks with a clear inherent structure will lead to more fluent performance than tasks without such clear structure.
Hypothesis 2: Tasks with a clear inherent structure will lead to more accurate performance than tasks without such a clear structure.
Hypothesis 3: Task structure will have no effect on the complexity of performance.
Hypothesis 4: There will be an inverse relationship between the processing demands of the task conditions and the accuracy, fluency, and complexity of the language produced; that is, as the processing load decreases, complexity, accuracy, and fluency will increase.
(Skehan and Foster, 1999: 102)

The tasks: rationale and choice of video material

Monologic tasks: students retell a short comedy sketch shown on video. After piloting, two episodes of the TV series *Mr Bean* are selected because they are:

a. short (around 8 minutes);
b. highly visual and virtually dialogue-free (thus avoiding problems of comprehension);
c. proven to be appealing to an international audience;
d. easy to follow, without excessive cultural bias;
e. amusing and engaging (and hence more likely that participants will enjoy re-telling).

It is worth noting that 'task structure' is actualised through the structuring of the *content* of the two narratives, rather than in the nature of the processes students have to engage.

The two episodes

1) More predictable story structure: the 'restaurant' episode
'In this "restaurant" episode, Mr Bean goes alone to a restaurant, gets the menu, orders steak tartare, is served, and then spends some time desperately trying to hide the food (which he thinks is too disgusting to eat) in various places on and around the table. There is thus a predictable basic sequence to the narrative ... against which less predictable events are embroidered' (1999: 103).

2) Less predictable story structure: the 'golf' episode
'In this "golf" episode, Mr Bean is playing Crazy Golf and makes a very bad shot, hitting the ball outside the Crazy Golf area. At the outset, he was warned by the course owner that it is against the rules to touch the ball, and as a result of overzealously applying this rule, he hits the ball all over the town in a desperate effort to get the ball back on the course and into the hole. Inadvertently, the ball is hit onto a bus, into a shop, into a manhole, and so forth, with the problem being in each case how to retrieve it. The events have no predictable sequence and appear as a random series' (1999: 103–4).

Four processing conditions

Table 8.12

Condition	Description	Rationale
1 Watch and tell simultaneously	Participants shown the video and asked to describe the story as they watched.	Predicted to be the most cognitively demanding, because participants had to put words to an unknown story in real time.
2 Storyline given, watch and tell simultaneously	Participants briefly told the outline of the story before seeing the video, and then asked to describe the story while watching it.	Predicted to ease the processing burden somewhat by provision of prior knowledge. However, the outline necessarily only gave partial information and the real-time performance would have to deal with the considerable detail of the actual story.
3 Watch first, then watch and tell simultaneously	Participants allowed to watch the video first and then described the story as they watched it again.	Predicted to ease the processing load further because participants had full knowledge of what they were about to describe, both in terms of general story outline and the more detailed elements.

(Continued)

Table 8.12   (Continued)

Condition	Description	Rationale
4 Watch first, then tell	Participants watched the video, and afterwards retold the story in their own time.	Predicted to be the least cognitively demanding. Participants had knowledge of the story they had to tell and no time pressure. Although there was a memory element involved, there was much greater scope for control.

Combining each of the four conditions with each of the two stories produced eight combinations.

Participants and procedures

Forty-seven students of English as a foreign language from a range of L1 backgrounds at a British university, selected from six intermediate-level classes, to which they had been allocated following a standard internal placement test. (In fact, the authors report that a total of only 45 students were involved.) They were judged to have 'a broadly similar level of proficiency'.

Participants randomly assigned to re-tell one of the two episodes under one of the four conditions (suggesting seven conditions had six students each, and one condition had five).

Participants were recorded individually. Before starting, the nature of 'steak tartare' and the rule of not touching the golf ball were explained to the participants.

Relevant to the broader context of our discussion, in terms of ecological context, the activities being researched were not part of a normal programme, and were not carried out in normal classroom conditions.

Data analysis

Complexity: analysed in terms of *number of clauses per c-unit*. (*C-units* are 'a simple clause or an independent sub clausal unit, together with the subordinated clauses associated with them'.) Minimum value for this score is stated as 1.00, since every c-unit contains only one clause.

Accuracy: assessed in terms of the number of *error-free clauses*, as a percentage of the total number of clauses (implying that non-clausal elements were not included).

Fluency: analysed in terms of number of repetitions (immediate and verbatim), false starts (incomplete utterances), reformulations (repetition of clauses or phrases with some modification) and replacements (word substitutions). Pauses were not used because in the first three conditions 'pausing is more likely to be a reflection of the need to keep pace with the story as it unfolds'. The authors assess means and standard deviations of the different measures, and select one for statistical treatment.

Like all measures these are open to discussion, but we will limit ourselves to three comments. Regarding c-units, if these include phrases like 'yes', 'no', 'on the left', the minimum value could presumably dip below 1.00. The accuracy measure seems to leave out of consideration errors in non-clausal units (which in monologue may not matter). The authors ultimately selected false starts as their preferred measures, on the grounds that this correlated best with the other measures.

Results

Presentation of results: First, descriptive statistics (means and standard deviations) are shown, comparing performance on the two video stories, and on the four conditions. Tables then present ANOVA results, followed by a comparison of the accuracy results, by story and condition.

Table 8.13   Results: Task structure

Variable	Golf task (n = 21)		Restaurant task (n = 24)	
	M	SD	M	SD
False starts	29.5	16.2	15.5	8.1
Complexity	1.32	0.18	1.32	0.22
Accuracy	47	14	50	15

Table 8.14   Results: Mean fluency, complexity and accuracy scores

Variable	Watch and (n = 11)		Storyline, watch and tell (n = 12)		Watch, watch and tell (n = 12)		Watch, then tell (n = 11)	
	M	SD	M	SD	M	SD	M	SD
False starts	24.30	12.80	19.10	8.50	19.30	14.00	26.30	21.00
Complexity	1.25	0.13	1.28	0.16	1.25	0.09	1.54	0.26
Accuracy	41	16	52	13	47	9	54	18

Results for task structure suggest that the story structure may have influenced fluency, but not complexity or accuracy. The authors then compare mean fluency, complexity and accuracy scores across the four conditions.

Fluency scores: despite differences between the means, SDs are fairly high (up to 50 per cent or more of the mean), suggesting a lack of systematic patterning for fluency.

Complexity scores: although means are small (1–2 clauses per c-unit), SDs are tiny, so that a difference between any of the means may be systematic. In fact, the fourth mean is the only one to stand out from the rest.

Accuracy scores: vary between 41 and 54. However, three of the SDs come from 25–33 per cent of the means, hence the differences between the means may not be 'systematic'.

ANOVA tests are then run on the three measures, in relation to the two sets of independent variables (stories, and conditions), and any interactions between them.

Table 8.15   Two-way ANOVAs for false starts, accuracy and complexity

Source of variance	F	Significance of F
False starts		
Task	12.48	.001*
Condition	0.74	.530
Two-way interaction	0.24	.870
Complexity		
Task	0.23	.640
Condition	8.76	.001*
Two-way interaction	1.27	.300
Accuracy		
Task	0.91	.340
Condition	2.11	.120
Two-way interaction	3.2	.030*

NB: alpha levels at .05, so that *p* scores below .05 are judged to be statistically significant, i.e. are not chance patterns, so thought to be reasonably attributable to the conditions.

The significant results here suggest that:

- story affects fluency (restaurant task is associated with more fluency);
- processing condition affects complexity ('watch then tell' more complex);

- accuracy – there is an interaction – i.e. accuracy is affected differentially on the two story types under one or more type of processing conditions.

Table 8.16 Mean accuracy scores by task and condition

Variable	Watch and tell		Storyline, watch and tell		Watch, watch and tell		Watch, then tell	
Accuracy	.40	.42	.56	.47	.49	.45	.40	.64

Note: Pairs of scores are for the unstructured and structured stories respectively.

Table 8.16 shows how accuracy is influenced by 'task' and 'condition'.

For condition 1 there is little difference; for conditions 2 and 3, the unstructured story is performed more accurately than the structured one, but in condition 4 this is reversed – here the *structured* story is performed more accurately.

8.7.2 Interpretation

The authors interpret the results to show that:

- structuring has an overall (main) impact on fluency, but not on complexity or on accuracy;
- processing conditions have an overall impact on complexity, the fourth, 'watch, then tell', condition generating significantly more complexity than the others;
- accuracy is influenced by both condition and story structure, the 'watch, then tell' condition being the only one to result in significantly more accurate talk on the structured story.

Structuring is seen as making it easier for speakers to produce their talk smoothly. Complexity seems to be most strongly influenced by the 'watch, then tell' condition, giving rise to more complex talk than the other three. This may be because the other three conditions all require the speakers to speak while watching, setting a time pressure which perhaps makes more complex talk difficult. Accuracy seems unaffected by structuring or condition alone. For some reason it is the unstructured task that generates generally more accurate talk in all except the 'watch, then tell' condition, in which more accurate talk occurs on the *structured* task. This is not easily explained.

8.7.3   Discussion

Skehan and Foster are rare to have undertaken a sustained sequence of studies on the same topic. Furthermore, in doing so they have gradually expanded what is intuitively a theoretically and pedagogically interesting framework, and have used a mixture of theory-driven and *post hoc* thinking around their data. Bringing complexity, accuracy and fluency together reminds us that language is not simply content, but also has to be performed. The study, however, prompts a number of thoughts.

- *Structuring in stories:* Some readers would have welcomed more discussion of the nature of structuring in stories, how it can impact on talk and the pedagogical relevance of structuring for different task types. An issue related to this is that the variable represented by the tasks (structuring) may not be what actually affects the learners' performance: they could have been influenced by some other aspect of the film (the humour, or some distracting aspect of one of the stories). We do not know for sure in this design that the target variable (structuring) is the one that mattered.
- *Content familiarity:* related to this is that in their background section, the authors refer to the notion of 'content familiarity' as the focus of studies by Ellis (1987) and Bygate (1996). However, those studies focused on the impact of having already formulated the content during a previous task on students' subsequent performance. This type of familiarity is almost certainly different from the relative familiarity of the two story settings which they are studying here.
- *Choice of measures:* how far is it pedagogically useful to conceptualise fluency in terms of false starts? (In Skehan and Foster (2005) the authors review a wide range of fluency measures.) The definition of accuracy could be reformulated to extend beyond the limits of grammatical error, to include discourse features and conceptual aspects (such as pragmatic or semantic appropriacy), or pronunciation; and complexity/range could be extended to cover aspects of morphology, collocation, pragmatics and discourse structures.
- *Interpreting the measures:* one point here is to question the seemingly negative interpretation of accuracy as implying 'avoidance' of challenging structures and 'conservatism'; and attention to complexity as implying a willingness to take risks, use of fewer controlled subsystems and a greater probability that learners will restructure their knowledge. Presumably, a focus on accuracy could be associated with mastery of new language (for instance we may wish to adjust the accuracy of language we have roughly acquired by attending to our own and others'

language), while risk-taking, which Skehan and Foster see positively, could be little more than random recklessness.

- *Pedagogical relevance:* We cannot take for granted the pedagogical importance of the scores of relative accuracy, complexity and fluency. On the surface, the results suggest interestingly different effects on learners' processing. Below the surface, we have the problem of knowing what levels of complexity, accuracy or fluency are significant for classroom learning, and over what time-scale. In practical terms we also need to understand more about the kinds of relationship that exist between condition and performance. For instance, the impact of high task demand is unlikely to be entirely linear since we are all likely to respond variously to excessively high or low loads by reducing or increasing our levels of performance (see Levelt, 1978, on the varying impacts of high and low task demand).

Although these are problems, they are interesting ones. Furthermore, they illustrate how confronting initial hypotheses with actual data, and attempting to understand the data is a powerful way of refining one's thinking.

8.8 Lynch and Maclean

8.8.1 The study

This study (Lynch and Maclean, 2001) is one of two which the authors published (see also Lynch and Maclean, 2000), focusing on the language of different students working on a given task. Like Samuda's (see 8.1), this is a case study of a scheduled lesson. It explores potentially significant changes in students' language in relation to 'task repetition'.

8.8.2 Rationale

The aim was to examine a theoretical proposal (see Bygate, 1996, 2001) that repeating their discourse on different occasions leads learners to develop aspects of their talk. The reasoning is that having already attempted the task, students will be more familiar with its content, forms and pragmatic potential, and that this will affect their use of vocabulary, grammar, pronunciation and their discourse as a whole. Bygate's studies involved repetition of the task two days and ten weeks later respectively, with the students asked to re-tell their stories without prior warning. Complexity and fluency were greater when students were repeating precisely the same task. In contrast, Lynch and Maclean designed a task which required learners to re-run the same material with different interlocutors.

Hence this study implemented repetition in a pedagogically convincing way, and did so within a single lesson.

Aims

In light of previous experience of using task repetition:

a) as researchers, to explore the theory that students would improve aspects of their performance through repeated engagements with the material;
b) as teachers, to see how their learners worked with the task;
c) as materials designers, to explore how their material worked in practice.

Participants and setting

- A short course in English for use at international conferences, University of Edinburgh;
- Fourteen doctors from six countries, in their late twenties-mid-fifties, of different levels of proficiency;
- Focus on three students, with the following level on an in-house test:

	Susanna	Olga	Carla
Listening	36%	71%	74%
Grammar	12%	36%	44%
TOEFL equivalent	450	525	525

Task design and implementation

Out-of-class preparation: in pairs students summarise a medical research article (800–1,000 words) and represent it in poster form.

In class: Pairs display their posters.
Student A stays at poster to answer questions from visitors; student B visits the others posters in turn, having about three minutes to ask questions of each student A.
After student B has seen the full display, the pairs change roles.
Closing plenary discussion, the teacher giving general language feedback.

Aspects of task: Substantial reading input; planning focuses on preparing the poster, rather than on talk; no guidance given on procedures to follow; no rehearsal time; repetition is: dialogic, immediate (at three-minute intervals), and – since different visitors raise different points – involves 'recycling' rather than strict repetition.

Data
- Six conversations of three student A's with each of their six visiting students.
- Students' self-report questionnaire on their experience, prior to teachers' comments.

Analysis

The talk analysed for changes across the six recordings in terms of:

- phonological accuracy;
- syntactic accuracy;
- choice of vocabulary and expression;
- self-correction;
- fluency, as reflected in the amount of pausing, rephrasing and repetition;
- other features reported when considered significant.

Results (represented in the report in the form of extensive extracts from speakers, with key parts underlined).

Susanna	Olga	Carla
Changes in phonology: 'survival' cycles 1, 2, 3, 6, with errors at cycle 2.	*Changes in syntax*: 'the excluding three hundred twenty two woman' (cycle 1) 'the excluding of this number of women' (cycle 2) 'this exclusion of these patients' (cycle 3)	*Changes in fluency*: 'I think mastectomy probably versus less extensive tumourectomy and segmentectomy and things like that' (cycle 1)
Changes in syntax: 'I think so' cycles 1, 6 'I think that...' cycles 2, 5 'I think Ø + clause' cycles 2, 3.	*Self-correction*: 'this spare surgery' (cycle 1) 'spare eh sparing surgery' (cycle 6)	'um localised uh localised tumourectomy segmentectomy or radical mastectomy' (cycle 6)
Changes in ease of expression (cycles 1, 4, 6): 'All patients hadn't uh metastatic disease' 'we had only patients without metastasis' 'we had only patients + after operation and no reparation evidence of metastatic disease'	*More precise formulation*: 'to give a local control + the better rates of local control' (cycle 1) 'to have a local control + to have a proper local control' (cycle 4)	*General tendencies*: - to self-correct - to distance herself from the study and the authors' views - tendency to refuse to yield her turn
	General inaccuracy and hesitation	

Authors' conclusions on transcript analysis

Analysis confirms findings of their 2000 study of two students. Across both studies, the students 'selected and produced more accurate L2 forms in successive cycles. All '... whose conversations we have analysed improved in terms of phonology (segmental or stress) and vocabulary (access or selection); all but [one, in the 2000 study] increased the semantic precision of what they were saying; and three made improvements in syntax' (2001: 155). The task seems to provide 'an opportunity for different types of improvement from different learners across a wide proficiency range'.

Authors' analysis and discussion of student feedback

- Some participants report feeling more relaxed as the task continued.
- Lower level students (e.g. Susanna) report no planning or implementing changes to their talk; more advanced students report planned and/or unplanned changes (2001: 156). Hence students may benefit from activities without being aware of it; so authors propose use of post-task activities and task transcripts to help increase learners' awareness and ability to monitor their language.
- Data show learners learning from each other, but since they are unaware of this, or may not take advantage of the opportunity (e.g. Carla), it may be worth helping 'learners to appreciate what they stand to gain from conversations with other learners' (2001: 158).
- Repeating tasks with different partners may well provide a kind of interactive environment which can help push learners forward: 'successive cycles of classroom activity under varied conditions may have an important part to play in proceduralisation of the L2' (2001: 158–9).

8.8.3　Discussion

This is one of the rare studies – possibly unique in the field – able to make general claims about the talk of a group, while respecting the individuality of each student's development. Generalisations about the power of task repetition can be extrapolated from a series of careful case studies: that is, the case studies can be aggregated into the strength of a group study. A further point to notes is that, as with the Samuda study, Lynch and Maclean bring together the two concerns of teaching (through its study of design and pedagogy) on the one hand, and learning (with their close attention to what the learners do) on the other. In addition, learners' questionnaire responses enable them to make tentative connections between awareness and level of proficiency, and to consider pedagogical implications of the students' lack of awareness of processes they engage in. Hence as with Samuda, this study demonstrates clear connections between materials design, teacher implementation and language learning theory: the issues are simultaneously of both theoretical and practical interest. However, it should be noted that the lack of a pre-/post-test comparison makes impossible any claims about systemic changes in learners' proficiency. Also, as with the three preceding studies, this one does not address the problem of targeting particular features of language.

8.9 Summary and conclusion

The eight studies examined in this chapter used a range of types of methodology and worked in distinct paradigms. In Chapters 6 and 7, we drew attention to the *potential* scope for research into language learning tasks. We highlighted: task design; task selection; conditions of task implementation; teacher exploitation; language production in terms of: language content and language processing; language development; teachers' perceptions; learners' perceptions; teacher development. However these topics are addressed at best inconsistently by the studies that we have reviewed in this chapter, and we will return to examine the potential for further research into these topics in Chapter 10.

In the introduction to this chapter we noted three themes that recur through the studies: the choice between experimental and case study designs; the value of comparative and longitudinal studies; and the value of pedagogically and non-pedagogically situated research.

The choice between a case study and an experimental design

It is worth considering the implications of this distinction. A key element of a case study is the opportunity it offers to study the individual cases in their own terms. In contrast, an experimental design is typically structured around the hunch that there may be similarities in people's behaviours in given contexts. Case studies are therefore widely seen as tending to derive their categories and constructs from within, while experimental studies are commonly thought of as testing assumptions derived from outside the context of study. However, our sample shows that this distinction is inaccurate. For example, Samuda's study is based on the idea that a task can be used to focus learners' attention on a language feature. It also assumes that doing so will help most learners in the class, and that this can be demonstrated by comparing the marks for accuracy on pre- and post-tests. Lynch and Maclean's case study also works from externally derived beliefs. One is that communicative repetition will tend to promote changes in accuracy in most learners; another is the belief that the design of a task will have a similar impact on different learners. Yet Lynch and Maclean also demonstrate that it is possible to study data case by case in order to explore general patterns across a series of cases (here, patterns of changes in accuracy through repeated encounters with a task). Ortega too, while investigating individual students' perceptions of pre-task planning, one at a time, works with a number of external categories, notably borrowed from Oxford's 'strategy inventory'. Yet she also derives categories from the interviewees themselves. This enables two kinds of generalisation: a detailed check on the extent to which Oxford's strategy inventory works for individual cases (a form of validation); and, as with Lynch and Maclean's study, the opportunity to generalise across her two proficiency groups, working from the individual statements of her participants.

Ortega's use of a priori and emergent categories

This takes the form of a 'two-pronged attack including content analysis of emergent themes and application of a priori categories . . . evolved over three recursive phases' (2005: 83).

In other words, case studies can have both an exploratory orientation and a verificatory (or hypothesis-testing) function. At the same time, case studies offer the opportunity to study the internal logic of the processes of the event (as in Samuda, and Lynch and Maclean), and the rationale of the various participants through the conduct of interviews (such as those in Lynch and Maclean, and Ortega). The limitation of case studies is that their isolation impedes generalisation and broader validation. Here, though, the word 'isolation' is important: as Lynch and Maclean's study shows, an accumulation of case studies around a similar focus would be no impediment to development and testing of generalisations.

In contrast, experimental studies start precisely from an interest in developing or testing generalisations. This is not unreasonable, given that teachers and testers have to generalise – for instance, about what is and is not likely to work for their students, and how and why. Indeed, it is not unreasonable, given the pervasive evidence that language use is highly patterned at all levels, and that learning also is patterned. Hence Mackey, Skehan and Foster, Yuan and Ellis, and Yule and Macdonald all use their studies to explore the hunch that there is an association between certain conditions and patterns of behaviour. Their conclusions are inferential: assuming the soundness of the design, they implicitly argue that we are entitled to attribute the patterning of the results to the condition and to some hypothetical intervening human process. That is, their argument is based on the probability that on future occasions, given the same conditions, different people are likely to behave in the same way.

There is a double justification to this kind of approach: the research findings permit generalisation to other people in other contexts, and at the same time they contribute to the development of our understanding. In addition, the field is young and grounded results are few – hence it may be that, hitherto, research was more likely to be supported if informed by some externally acknowledged theory. It can be argued though that after carrying out experimental studies like these, we still do not know the significance of such patterns within the context of the language learning of an individual or a group over time, within normal lessons. That is, although these studies are hypothesis-testing, in terms of educational practice, they remain exploratory. This is no bad thing – indeed several experimental researchers use exploratory statistical analyses to study unsuspected patterning within the data, assuming that subsequent confirmatory studies will be needed. But it might be useful if the exploratory nature of these studies were recognised more often. It also has to be acknowledged that the inferential reasoning used by such studies often tends to jump over a lack of information about the detailed real-time individual classroom processes and uses of language needed to reach the macro-results that the studies yield. The problem then is how to obtain information about probabilities and the micro-events of real-time classroom learning, rather than where to generate the hypotheses and categories of analyses.

The second issue raised by the eight studies is the presence or absence of a longitudinal (or at least pre-post) time dimension. Although this is a fairly obvious consideration in pedagogical research, few studies address it. Of the eight, only Mackey's ran over a period of three weeks, and Samuda's was the only other one to use a pre-/post-test design. This may be partly a logistical problem: time-wise studies are inevitably more time-consuming and involve more data manipulation, and as a result, can be expensive. But here too the problem may be aggravated by the relative lack of previous research: early studies were perhaps right to concentrate mainly on analysing performance data and wait until an empirical picture emerged before attempting time-wise studies. Nevertheless, pedagogically oriented research needs to inform us on the impact of task work in real time – that is, in the course of a lesson, over the period of a scheme of work and through a syllabus. Which leads us to our third issue.

The contextualisation of the research

Throughout this book, we have been justifying the use of tasks for language education from a holistic educational and linguistic perspective (see Chapter 1). Our grounds for adopting this position are that tasks provide a structured space for a wide range of contextualised teaching and learning processes, involving all levels of language, whether pragmatic discourse structures or the details of grammar and phonology. It is therefore axiomatic that in terms of research, the heart of our domain is the task in pedagogical action. The kinds of problem we are trying to solve through research concerns how teachers and students can use tasks, and with what effects. From this perspective, studies such as Samuda's, Lynch and Maclean's and Donato's have a distinct advantage in that they all focus on the teachers' and students' use of the tasks in scheduled lessons. Furthermore, their case study designs enable the researcher to track classroom processes as well as outcomes. And although these studies might be seen as exploratory (compared with experimental studies), they can also be seen as hypothesis-testing or verificatory, in the sense that the results provide evidence of the extent to which the procedures work in classrooms.

The choice of context offers some important advantages. First, it means that any observed learning patterns are sufficiently robust to emerge in the context of teaching procedures and purposes. Second, it makes it possible to assess any problems that might arise in terms of the extent of the match between the task and the context, rather than simply in terms of the internal attributes of the task. Third, it generates the kinds of data which are likely to be essential for professional evaluation and subsequent dissemination. Finally, although Ortega's study is not situated in normally functioning classrooms, the fact that her investigation focuses on the learners' own construals of the task, of the preparatory planning activity and of how they managed them, it sheds light on issues of learner engagement and learner style, which speaks forcefully to any potential pedagogical concern.

There may well have been good reasons for the relative lack of classroom-based studies, similar perhaps to those adduced for the lack of longitudinal and case designs: teachers, who are probably best situated to carry out such studies, are generally not able to add this to their workload, whether in collaboration with outside researchers or, even less likely, on their own; researchers from outside the classroom are not well situated, and in any case depend on the collaboration of teachers; teachers working with researchers from outside their institution need to have a basis for collaboration if the research is to work; researchers need to be willing to negotiate with teachers and with students to carry out the research, and vice versa; and the tasks being researched need to be relevant to the teacher and the class. Apart from this, we can add the numerous contingent problems (absences, holidays, schedule changes) that can arise. In a word, such research is costly and labour-intensive. But undertaking it would ensure that the focus of research meets the needs and understandings of teachers and learners. However until classroom-based studies become a mainstream for research in this field, the pedagogical use of language learning tasks will never be properly researched, and we will have to make do with whatever researchers feel motivated to explore.

9
Pedagogic Perspectives on Second Language Tasks

We began this book by observing that even though tasks have been a familiar part of second language teaching for several decades – both as an element within CLT and as the centrepiece for various task-driven initiatives – their use remains highly controversial. Issues relating to when, why and how to use tasks, or indeed whether they should be used at all, continue to invite heated debate in both the research and practitioner literatures. In this chapter we attempt to tease apart issues contributing to this controversy.

Our concern in Chapters 7 and 8 has been with the study of tasks: how researchers have approached the construct of 'task', and what elements have emerged as relevant and interesting both for the purposes of study and as outcomes of study. The issues focused on there were inevitably filtered through the perspectives of the researchers studying them; in this chapter we explore the kinds of insight that are brought into focus through the perspectives of practitioners (teachers, designers, curriculum developers) working with tasks in light of four questions:

1. How do practitioners approach the construct of 'task'?
2. What elements of tasks emerge as relevant and interesting from a practitioner perspective?
3. What kinds of issues are brought into prominence through everyday classroom use of tasks?
4. How do these relate to topics and issues brought into prominence through task research?

In this chapter we explore these questions in light of controversies about the use of tasks that have emerged in recent years. These include:

- perceptions of task-based language teaching (TBLT) as a 'top-down' initiative (Van den Branden, 2006), imposed on teachers by researchers

with limited understanding of the demands of everyday pedagogy (Swan, 2005);
- conceptual unease among teachers about the potential pedagogic value of tasks and pedagogic approaches that make significant use of tasks (Littlewood, 2007);
- unrealistic demands and expectations placed on teachers in the implementation of task-based programmes of instruction (van den Branden, 2006).

9.1 Practitioner and researcher perspectives on tasks

Example 9.1 opens up a pedagogic perspective on a number of the issues raised in previous chapters. Column A presents a selection of topics pursued in the empirical studies reviewed in Chapters 7 and 8, and Column B, topics raised by teachers in on-line discussion lists at the time of writing this chapter.

Example 9.1   Issues of concern to researchers; issues of concern to teachers

A: Issues pursued by researchers

- Planning time
- Task familiarity
- Task repetition
- Interaction effects
- Interlocutor effects
- Discourse effects
- Attention capacity
- Task complexity
- Negotiation for meaning

B: Issues raised by teachers

- Using tasks in monolingual classes in FL settings
- Matching tasks with skill level
- Integrating tasks with a prescribed syllabus
- Viability of tasks for beginning level students
- Using tasks to introduce new language
- Giving feedback on task performance: how and when
- Fitting tasks with other kinds of activity
- Tasks and grammar learning
- Using tasks in mixed ability classes
- Motivating students to engage in tasks

As we might expect, there are differences in the ways that teachers orient themselves to the use of tasks: the issues in Column A are framed in relation to underlying constructs that researchers have used tasks to probe (attentional capacity, processing demands, negotiation, etc.), and in Column B, in relation to specific pedagogic phenomena that teachers see themselves as having to handle while using tasks (introducing new language, the role of grammar, giving feedback, etc.). This is not surprising – researchers and teachers obviously have different concerns, and as we have already seen in Chapters 7 and 8, in much of the empirical work associated with issues in Column A tasks have been viewed as a context in which to study different aspects of language use and processing rather than as a situated pedagogic instrument mediated by teachers. But as we also saw in previous chapters a substantial amount of that work has been carried out with a view to informing pedagogic decisions about task selection, sequencing and implementation, and a number of researchers associated with Column A issues would argue that aspects of their research can – or eventually could, given sufficient time – address questions raised in Column B. Thus although the orientation may be primarily towards 'task' as a research construct, there is an underlying assumption that task research has the potential to say something about task pedagogy – for example, 'implications for pedagogy' are often included among the closing sections of research reports.

In contrast, from a Column B perspective, 'task' is viewed primarily as a pedagogic instrument (albeit a potentially problematic one), and again not surprisingly, the focus is with how that instrument could be used, integrated within broader sequences of instruction and exploited in the light of everyday classroom demands. As Column B makes clear, an orientation towards 'task' as a pedagogic construct brings different concerns to the fore and offers a different lens through which to view the issues raised in Column A. A key problem here is that sets of mutual relevance across the respective sets of issues may not be readily apparent. From a Column A perspective, the kinds of questions raised by practitioners in Column B can be perceived as too broad to be answerable, too local to be generalisable or simply too 'pedagogic' to be theoretically interesting, while from a Column B perspective, the topics pursued by researchers are not readily recognisable *vis-à-vis* the day-to-day demands of working with tasks in different kinds of classrooms.

This contributes to the uneasy relationship between pedagogy and research noted at the end of Chapter 8, and to the perception of tasks and TBLT as a top-down initiative. From a pedagogic perspective, this relationship becomes particularly problematic when recommendations about the use of tasks are made, when curriculum guidelines are put in place or when specific procedures are advocated without apparent awareness of – or interest in – issues of everyday pedagogy. It is in this context that tasks have come to be perceived as part of an externally imposed top-down initiative.

9.2   Tasks in pedagogy

In recent years, the use of tasks has been vigorously promoted as part of language education policy at national, state and institutional levels worldwide. Nunan (2004), Leaver and Willis (2004), Edwards and Willis (2005), Pica (2005), Littlewood (2006) and van den Branden (2006a) attest to the breadth and scope of proposals advocated in various parts of Asia, Europe and North America. However, reports of the implementation of different task-based initiatives (Tinker Sachs et al., 2000; Carless, 2004; Hampshire and Aguarales Anoro, 2004; van den Branden, 2006a; Littlewood, 2006, among others) suggest considerably more unease among practitioners working with tasks 'on the ground' than is generally acknowledged in the literature.

Two broad factors may be feeding into this sense of unease. One is situation-specific and relates to the conditions in which certain curricular innovations involving tasks may have been implemented (or perceived to have been implemented). Later in the chapter we take a closer look at some contexts where tasks have been introduced as significant elements in state and regional curricula. The second is conceptual and relates to different perceptions of what is meant by 'task' and 'task-based' learning, and to different understandings of the pedagogic roles that tasks can play in an overall programme of instruction. Given the enormous inconsistency with which 'task', 'task-based' and their associated acronyms (TBLT, TBL, TBI) have been used, it is not surprising that many teachers charged with implementing task-based material report 'conceptual unease' (Littlewood, 2007) about what tasks are and what task-based teaching involves. Example 9.2 shows some of the different ways that 'task-based' has been used in teaching materials, curriculum proposals and teacher resource books in recent years:

Example 9.2   Different uses of the term 'task-based'

1. To designate an approach to syllabus design driven by target tasks that learners need to engage with outside the classroom and driven by pedagogic tasks carried out within the classroom.
2. To refer to specialised classroom procedures designed to respond to elements of task performance.
3. To describe programmes of instruction in which tasks play some role, but are not necessarily the central driving force.
4. To promote textbook materials containing tasks.
5. To characterise a general style of teaching that draws on tasks.
6. To denote a genre of meaning-focused classroom interaction.

Richards (2005) also has a number of examples of how 'task-based' has been used.

Some of these uses of 'task-based' are considerably more specialised than others – 1 and 2 versus 5 and 6, for example, and in Chapter 4 we suggested that one way round this problem might be to adopt a more careful use of terminology relating to the way that tasks are used. A solution offered by Bygate (2000), Ellis (2003) and Shehadeh (2005) is to distinguish between: *task-based learning and teaching* (to refer to contexts where tasks are the central focus for instruction); and *task-supported learning and teaching* (to refer to contexts where tasks may play a less central role).

To explore the usefulness of this distinction, we look at ways tasks are used in task-based and task-supported contexts, and what these imply for task pedagogy.

9.2.1   Task-based language learning and teaching

In Chapter 4, we outlined the key characteristics of task-based learning and teaching (TBLT) as follows:

- tasks define and drive the syllabus;
- task performance is a catalyst for focusing attention on form, and not vice versa;
- assessment is in terms of task performance;
- task selection is shaped by real-world activities of relevance to learners and their target needs;
- tasks play an essential role in engaging key processes of language acquisition.

Three widely cited examples are:

1. The Bangalore Communicational Teaching Project (Prabhu, 1987).
2. Task-based syllabus design (Long and Crookes, 1992; 1993).
3. A framework for the implementation of task-based learning (Willis, 1996).

Although commonly grouped together as examples of task-based learning and teaching, each is quite distinct and, so in light of misunderstandings about TBLT noted above, we trace the conceptual background of each one, with samples of representative tasks and pedagogic procedures.

The Bangalore Communicational Teaching Project

The Bangalore Communicational Teaching Project (widely known as The Bangalore Project) is an early example of a task-based pedagogic initiative put into action in a specific context at a certain period of time:

Example 9.3 The Bangalore Project (Prabhu, 1987)

Setting and context	Selected primary and secondary schools in southern India, 1979–85
Initial impetus	To explore alternatives to the prevailing 'Structural-Oral-Situational method' (structurally/lexically graded syllabuses, 'one at a time' presentation of discrete items, extensive controlled practice)
Theoretical motivation	A 'pedagogic intuition' that the necessary requirement for second language acquisition is 'the creation of conditions in which learners engage in an effort to cope with communication ... to the exclusion of any deliberate regulation of the development of grammatical competence or a mere simulation of language behaviour' (Prabhu, 1987: 1–2)

This was not intended as a formal experiment to prove/disprove one methodology over another, but as an exploratory, classroom-based initiative within which alternative methodologies could develop and through which pedagogic insights could be explored. The pedagogic procedures that evolved were referred to as 'task-based teaching'.

Example 9.4 The Bangalore Project: principal pedagogic procedures

- Task selection and sequencing on the basis of 'reasonable challenge' (Prabhu, 1987), not on the basis of a pre-set structurally/lexically defined syllabus.
- Focus on finding appropriate task solution, and not on the linguistic accuracy with which that solution might be expressed.
- Criterion for successful task completion: at least 50 per cent of the class with the correct solution.
- No pre-emptive focus on specific linguistic features at the beginning of a lesson/task sequence; use of a teacher-led 'pre-task' to clarify necessary concepts and rehearse task procedures.
- Incidental error correction within the context of communication, without interruption to the flow of meaning; teacher reformulation of error without explanation of grammatical rules/generalisations.

Lessons were built across sequences of tasks and followed a characteristic pattern, drawing on different task types:

Example 9.5   The Bangalore Project: components of a task-based lesson

Task 1 (pre-task)	Task performed as whole-class activity under teacher control and guidance, using a question-and-answer format to lead pupils step by step to the outcome
Task 2 (task)	Parallel to pre-task, performed by pupils independently, sometimes collaboratively, seeking help from teacher as necessary
Outcome assessment	Carried out by the teacher, based on *content*, not language; to give pupils feedback on degree of success in solving the problem posed by the task, and to provide teacher with input for task selection and planning for subsequent lessons.

Example 9.6   The Bangalore Project: task types

Information gap*	Involving transfer of given information from one form to another
Reasoning gap	Involving processes of deduction/inferencing to derive new information from some form of given information
Opinion gap	Involving identification/articulation of personal preferences, attitudes and/or responses to given information

*Since pair and group work were de-emphasised, 'gap' refers here to the nature of the cognitive challenge posed by the task, not to the collaborative 'gap principle' associated with CLT (e.g. Johnson, 1979).

Over time, through a process of trial and error, 'reasoning tasks' based on diagrams, calendars, timetables, itineraries, maps, distances, etc. were found to be most successful in sustaining pupils' engagement with meaning

---

Example 9.7   The Bangalore Project: sample task

Pre-task: The teacher asks questions about a railway timetable written on the blackboard:

	Madras	Katpedi	Jolarpet	Bangalore
Brindavan Express	Dep. 0725	Arr. 0915 Dep. 0920	Arr. 1028 Dep. 1030	Arr. 1300

Some example questions:
- When does the Brindavan Express leave Madras/arrive in Bangalore?
- How long does it stop at Jolarpet?
- How many stations does it stop at on the way?

Example 9.7   (Continued)

Task: Pupils work independently on following timetable and questions, with initial teacher guidance as necessary

	Madras	Arkonam	Katpedi	Jolarpet	Kolar	Bangalore
Bangalore Mail	Dep. 2140	Arr. 2250 Dep. 2305	Arr. 0005 Dep. 0015	Arr. 0155 Dep. 0210	Arr. 0340 Dep. 0350	Arr. 0550

Some example questions:
When does the Bangalore Mail leave Madras?
At what time does it reach Katpedi?
How long does it take to go from Kolar to Bangalore?

---

at an appropriate level of cognitive challenge. An example – the second in a sequence of five reasoning tasks on the topic of 'railway timetables' – is illustrated in Example 9.7 above.

Three key characteristics of the project are reflected in this example task:

1. a parallel increase in cognitive demand (i.e. degree of reasoning involved) within and across the pre-task and task (and, although not shown here, across sequences of tasks);
2. the language to be used in carrying out the task was not specified in the materials, but was to be negotiated in the classroom on the basis of teacher perception of pupil need/capacity and the intellectual challenge of the task;
3. success in task completion was marked by correctness of solution, not linguistic accuracy. A rough rule of thumb – 50 per cent of class with the correct answer – was used as the criterion for moving on to the next task.

The project was evaluated in different ways over a five-year span, as shown in Example 9.8.

Example 9.8   Evaluation of the Bangalore Project

Process evaluation   Developments documented, discussed and evaluated on an ongoing basis via:
- classroom observation
- regular newsletter bulletins
- review seminars with visiting specialists
- used as feedback for ongoing project development.

Example 9.8　(Continued)

Product evaluation
- Battery of proficiency and achievement tests administered to classes participating in the project and a control group
- tentative support for the project claim that 'grammar construction can take place through a focus on meaning alone' (Beretta and Davis, 1985) (although some qualification as to the validity of the instruments of assessment deployed are also noted).

A number of issues, both theoretical and practical, were brought into focus during the running of the project and were subject to considerable question and critique at the time and subsequently (e.g. Greenwood, 1985; Brumfit, 1984a). Some of the controversies to have surfaced are summarised here in Example 9.9.

Example 9.9　The Bangalore Project: Elements of the project brought into question

- The extent to which the pre-task was a 'rehearsal' for the task as intended or in fact comprised a form of covert teaching (see Prabhu, 1987, for a rebuttal).
- The extent to which the success of the project was carried by the enthusiasm and commitment of team members and participating teachers rather than the pedagogic procedures themselves (see Prabhu, 1987).
- The adequacy of 'rule of thumb' approaches to assessing task difficulty (Crookes and Long, 1993).
- Reliance on a narrow range of teacher-led, externally set problems, and a de-emphasis of open-ended, collaborative pair/group work (but see Prabhu, 1987, for an account of how these were conceived as local adaptations, and considered essential to operability in the context of southern India at the time).

Despite its limited time-span and specificity of setting, the Bangalore Project is still of considerable interest as an example of task-based principles in action. The conditions under which it was implemented – large classes, minimal resources beyond blackboard and chalk – and its radical commitment to a meaning-focused approach that went against prevailing cultural expectations of language teaching practices – also make it an interesting example of what can be achieved in so-called difficult circumstances (see also Coleman, 1987) in non-Western settings. However, the significance of the Bangalore Project is not just that it is an early example of TBLT, it is also one of the few examples of a systematic (though relatively short-lived) attempt to develop and explore task-based procedures in real classroom contexts and to seek different types of empirical evidence as to how they play out over time – an issue we take up again below.

Task-based syllabus design (Long and Crookes, 1992, 1993)

The second example – also widely cited as an example of task-based learning principles – is an approach to syllabus design/programme development in which 'task' is taken as the key unit of analysis at every phase of the process. The theoretical perspective and principles underlying it are closely associated with proposals developed in Long (1985, 1989; 1996), Long and Crookes (1992, 1993) and Long and Robinson (1998). In contrast to the Bangalore Project, which was initially driven by pedagogic intuition and evolved through pedagogic practice, Long and colleagues make the case for a psycho-linguistically grounded approach to task-based syllabus design compatible with evidence from SLA research, particularly the body of work associated with the interaction hypothesis, and negotiation for meaning studies. (See Chapters 7 and 8.)

Long and Crookes (1992, 1993) characterise the procedure for task-based syllabus design and development as a series of steps. Central to the whole procedure is an analysis of learner needs to identify real-world 'target tasks'. On the basis of these, appropriate 'pedagogic tasks' are selected/developed for classroom use. Initially less complex in focus and scope, pedagogic tasks are designed to increasingly approximate the kinds of demands ultimately made by target tasks. The overall design sequence is set out in Example 9.10.

Example 9.10   Steps in the design and development of a task-based syllabus

- A comprehensive needs analysis →
- Diagnosis of learner needs →
- Identification of *target tasks* learners are preparing to carry out + real-world performance criteria →
- Classification of target tasks into task types →
- Development/selection of *pedagogic tasks* for classroom use →
- Sequencing of pedagogic tasks to form a task-based syllabus →
- Implementation of syllabus via appropriate pedagogic procedures →
- Assessment through performance on tasks/task-based criterion referenced tests

(after Long and Crookes, 1992, 1993)

Learners' ultimate real-world needs are thus taken as the *sine qua non* of language instruction, and tasks are the pedagogic conduit for addressing those needs. Key pedagogic principles for implementing the syllabus are shown in Example 9.11.

Example 9.11   General pedagogic principles for enacting a task-based syllabus

- Elements of linguistic form are not pre-specified in the syllabus or at the beginning of a lesson
- Pedagogic tasks are not 'seeded' with pre-selected linguistic features, nor are they designed to target particular elements of form
- Attention to form emerges out of task performance on the basis of problems occurring in the context of meaningful communication. These may be identified (and resolved) by learners themselves during the task, and/or by the teacher after it has been carried out.

(after Long and Crookes, 1992, 1993)

Example 9.12 is a set of thematically linked tasks proposed in Long (1997) as a means of enacting a task-based syllabus, as an illustration of how a task-based syllabus could be realised.

Example 9.12   Sample task sequence within a task-based syllabus

An instructional sequence for a 'false beginner' class of young, adult, prospective tourists:

- *Intensive listening practice*: The task is to identify which of 40 telephone requests for reservations can be met, and which not, by looking at four charts showing the availability, dates and cost of hotel rooms, theatre and plane seats, and tables at a restaurant.
- *Role-playing*: The learners take the role of customers and airline reservation clerks in situations in which the airline seats required are available.
- *Role-playing*: The learners take roles in situations in which, due to unavailability, they must choose among progressively more complicated alternatives (seats in different sections of the plane, at different prices, on different flights or dates, via different routes, etc.).

(Long, 1997)

A number of characteristics from Long and Crookes' original proposal are present in this task sequence:

- task content reflects learners' target needs in carrying out real-world tasks (here, making tourist reservations);
- tasks are sequenced in terms of complexity of demand placed on learners as they carry them out;
- specific design details, for example, ways of fleshing out the above guidelines as fully developed tasks that would be operable in normal classroom conditions and consonant with relevant empirical findings, may be left open for the individual programme developer/teacher to carry forward in light of local/contexts;
- the use of role play to simulate real-time demands within the target domain.

Central to this perspective on task-based learning then is an interplay between two elements of the syllabus: one that is determined by real-world target need (a key characteristic of LSP programme development from the 1970s onward, as Long and Crookes observe), and another that is emergent, shaped by the needs of learners as they engage with meaning-focused pedagogic tasks (also a characteristic of the 'deep-end' approach' to CLT proposed in Brumfit, 1978, 1984b). However, a distinctive plank in the Long and Crookes proposal (and one also strongly argued in e.g. Long and Robinson, 1998; Long, 2005; Robinson, 2006) is that decisions about the selection of sequencing of pedagogic tasks should be compatible with, and underpinned by, evidence from current SLA research.

Various aspects of Long and Crookes's approach to task-based syllabus design have given rise to controversy. Some of this has focused on the theoretical underpinnings on which the work rests and the appropriacy of variables selected for study as we saw in Chapter 7. Issues more directly related to classroom pedagogy have been raised in Sheen, 1994; Bruton, 2002a and b; Swan, 2005, and these include concerns about:

- the overall workability of this approach to TBLT on a day-to-day basis over time;
- a lack of widely disseminated evidence from fully-fledged applications of the proposal in action (in the sense intended by Long and Crookes), and consequently little documented evidence to date of full-scale programme evaluations;
- the adequacy of current research findings for sustaining informed decisions about task design, selection and sequencing over extended periods of instruction and for guiding decisions about the timing of teacher interventions.

To this extent, the critics argue, the full scope of the approach to task-based learning associated with Long and Crookes's proposal for syllabus design and development remains hard to assess in light of real-world pedagogic demands.

Framework for task-based learning (Willis, 1996)

Willis (1996) offers a framework for task implementation at the level of the lesson/suite of lessons. As with our previous examples, it is presented as an explicit alternative to pedagogic progressions that isolate discrete elements of form and gradually build up opportunities to integrate them through controlled practice and free production (characterised by Willis in terms of the 'P, P, P' sequence). The framework, which grew out of the author's experience as a teacher educator, is based on a three-phase task cycle consisting of pre-, during and post-task stages, spanning a lesson/ sequence of lessons:

Example 9.13   A framework for task-based learning: Willis, 1996

- **Pre-task**
  - Teacher introduces topic and task
- **Task cycle**
- **Task**
  - Students carry out the task
- **Planning**
  - Students plan how to report on task outcome
- **Report**
  - Students report back to class
- **Language focus**
  - Analysis
  - Practice

(– Students may repeat same or similar task)
(based on Willis, 1996)

Central to this cycle is the positioning of the 'language focus' as a post-task activity arising out of task performance. Willis summarises this from a learner's perspective as: 'First experience the target language in use and then examine the language you have used and learn from it' (Willis, 2004: 35). A recurrent element in some task-based materials (e.g. Willis and Willis, 1988) is to begin the cycle with learners observing native speakers perform a task (e.g. giving instructions on a map) that they will later attempt to carry out themselves. This, it is argued, orients learners to the kinds of task-based language use that they will be engaging with themselves, and also provides baseline data that could be useful for guiding teacher interventions during the language focus stage. To this end, Willis also makes a case for the use of 'pedagogic corpora' based on performance on the same or similar tasks as those to be used in the classroom (Willis, 2004).

Throughout her work, Willis provides numerous task exemplars, sample lesson plans and practical tips for managing each phase of the cycle for different pedagogic purposes. An example based on a reading task used as an illustration in Willis (1996) is summarised in Example 9.14 and gives a flavour of the level of support and degree of micro-planning offered to help a teacher implement this type of task-based lesson.

Example 9.14   Plan for a task-based lesson – Spiders: a success story

Two task cycles leading into a newspaper report about woman with arachnophobia.

Pre-task *(2–3 minutes) Introduction to the topic.*

Task cycle 1 (speaking, 2–3 minutes)
Pairs brainstorm sequence of steps to help the woman overcome phobia of spiders.
Planning: (2–3 minutes) Pairs prepare how to present and justify ideas from above
Report and reading 1: (10 minutes) Pairs present their proposals, class discuss and vote on steps most likely to be in newspaper report.
Students read (incomplete) newspaper report in light of above, and compare this with their own proposals, nominating those most similar.

Task cycle 2 (reading, 4–5 minutes)
Students re-read text; pairs discuss probable position of missing part of text.
Planning and report 2: Students share opinions on position of missing part of text. Students check against complete text.

Language focus
Analysis and practice (20–35 minutes)

1. Main theme: Spiders: Students circle phrases in text relating to spiders, and draw lines to link phrases as lexical chains. Students compare (focus on lexical cohesion).
2. Time and sequence: Students select phrases expressing time (focus on structure of sequential narrative).
3. Place and position: Students select phrases expressing place and position, and subdivide into categories as given.
4. Grammar points:
   – Students find four phrases containing *was* and look for similarities in structure. (Focus on passive voice and adverbial placement.)

> **Example 9.14   (Continued)**
>
> *Either:*
> – Students find six phrases with *to*, note related verbs and categorise; note where *to* can be omitted.
>   *Or:*
> – From a concordance sample, students categorise different uses of *to*. (Focus on uses of *to*.) (Suggested homework activity.)
> – Students identify patterns in verb phrases in given set of examples. (Focus on passive and uses of to.)
>
> Students write useful language from the lesson in their books.
> (based on Willis, 1996)

As can be seen, Willis's approach differs from Long and Crookes's along a number of dimensions, notably in placing less emphasis on tasks derived from target needs (although more recent work - e.g. Willis, 2004 – reflects a greater concern with this), and considerably more emphasis on the micro-details of lesson planning. The lesson plan in Example 9.14 reflects many general principles central to her approach:

- a 'task' is characterised as a set of interlocking stages;
- there is a progression from the whole to the parts;
- there is a progression from meaning to form, and the integration of meaning and form;
- language skills can be integrated across a task cycle;
- there are opportunities for planning and rehearsal.

Further examples of materials following the task cycle proposed here can be found in Willis and Willis (1988) and more recently in Willis (2004) and Willis and Willis (2007).

One striking feature of Willis's framework is that it is presented as a pedagogically grounded, practitioner-friendly initiative. This has had widespread and immediate appeal for teachers seeking concrete guidance on how to work with tasks, and the task cycle has been widely used as a model – sometimes *the* model – of TBLT in pre- and in-service teacher education in the UK and elsewhere. However, despite extensive practitioner appeal, there has been little documentation of the framework being applied in fully-fledged task-based programmes in the sense presumably originally intended, and although Willis has increasingly drawn on selected aspects of existing SLA research as a rationale for elements of the task cycle (Willis, 2004, for example), the overall concern has been to present the framework as a set of accessible guidelines for practitioners to follow rather than to problematise underlying issues or to explore a psycholinguistically grounded rationale for instruction. Although seeking empirical evidence to support her pedagogic claims may not have been part of Willis's intended remit, the framework itself appears to have attracted relatively little empirical attention within the task research community. This means that a number of questions about how (to quote Willis as cited above) learners 'experience' the target language, 'examine' the language they use and – crucially – how and what they 'learn' from this are yet to be empirically addressed in the kinds of task-based context Willis advocates.

However, the perceived pedagogic relevance of the work is reflected in a growing number of teacher-initiated action research projects based on aspects of the task cycle. Edwards and Willis (2005) report a number of small-scale studies conducted by teachers, which explore pedagogically motivated questions emerging from task use in their own classroom across the world. Some of the issues that have been brought into focus through the use of tasks in Japan, Greece and Switzerland are summarised in Example 9.15.

Example 9.15   Some issues pursued in teacher action research projects

Predictability of language items in open tasks	(Cox, 2005)
Developing from PPP to TBL	(Loumpourdi, 2005)
Incorporating tasks in textbooks for beginning learners	(Muller, 2005)
Integrating task-based instruction into a business English programme	(Pullin Stark, 2005)
Learners' use of language at different stages of the task cycle	(Johnston, 2005)

As noted in Chapter 8, teacher-led research of this kind is a key element in building richer understandings of what happens when tasks are used in classrooms. However, much of the work reported in Edwards and Willis is not fully 'task-based' in the sense that we have been using the term here. In the classrooms studied, tasks were generally used in conjunction with other modes of instruction pre-set curricula, and thus more typical of what we would characterise as 'task-supported' contexts. This suggests that Willis's framework may be more influential in introducing the use of tasks to supplement and extend current practices than in promoting the fully-fledged *task-based* learning that Willis herself advocates – although the extent to which this represents a necessary 'halfway step' towards full implementation of TBLT, as suggested in Shehadeh (2005), is an interesting empirical question in its own right.

Looking back across the three examples – The Bangalore Project; Long and Crookes's proposals for task-based syllabus design and Willis's framework for task-based learning – it is clear that there are a number of distinctive differences in terms of context, scope and emphasis. However, a number of shared elements mark these as examples of 'task-based' learning and teaching in the sense that we are using the term:

- the curriculum is defined and driven by tasks;
- tasks are not pre-selected on the basis of form;
- the potential pedagogic focus of any given task emerges from sustained meaningful engagement with the demands of that task;
- engagement with meaning is the springboard for engagement with form;
- any engagement with form mediated by a teacher should be responsive to problems/needs that learners encounter in carrying out a task.

Importantly – and contrary to many common assumptions about TBLT – drawing attention to form is neither proscribed nor outlawed. Rather, as we saw in both the Long and Crookes and the Willis proposals, it is the *timing* of this focus – arising from task performance and not preceding it – that emerges as a key criterial element in 'task-based' learning. However, what is considerably less clear is how this works in practice. As we have seen here, apart from the now defunct Bangalore Project, to date there have been very few widely disseminated, fully documented examples of task-based programmes of instruction that have been implemented over time. Two major pedagogic initiatives widely described as 'task-based' are the Hong Kong Target-Oriented Curriculum (TOC), implemented by the Education Department of the Hong Kong/Special Administrative Region Government in 1999 and running in primary and secondary schools with various modifications since then, and a range of programmes introduced by the Flemish government in the 1990s for the teaching of Dutch to migrants to Flanders.

Hong Kong Target-Oriented Curriculum (TOC)

Strictly speaking, the Hong Kong/SAR TOC curriculum is not task-based. As its name implies, the curriculum is specified in terms of 'targets' – specific curricular goals that pupils are expected to reach, and the competencies, strategies and skills that they are expected to develop in pursuit of those targets, rather than tasks. Tasks, however, play a prominent role as carriers of curriculum content.

Example 9.16   Hong Kong/SAR Target-Oriented Curriculum: sample strands and objectives: KS1– KS4

Strands/dimensions
Language learning for the purposes of developing the ability to:

- establish and maintain relationships; to exchange ideas and information; to get things done *(Interpersonal)*
- provide or find out, interpret and use information; to explore, express and apply ideas; and to solve problems *(Knowledge)*
- respond and give expression to real and imaginative experience *(Experience)*

Learning objectives

Forms and functions (vocabulary, text, types, grammar items and structures, and communicative functions)
Language skills (listening, speaking, reading, writing)
Language development strategies (thinking skills, information skills, skills of planning, managing and evaluating one's learning)
Attitudes (e.g. confidence in using English, sensitivity towards language use in the process of communication, respect for different cultures)
(Curriculum Development Council, Hong Kong, 2002)

Tasks are seen as one of the means by which curricular targets like the ones exemplified above may be reached, and through which the desired competencies, strategies and skills may be developed. In practice, the prominence of the task element within the TOC may vary; for example, in recent years there has been a move towards 'school-based' materials development in Hong Kong and so the degree of emphasis given to task work might depend on teachers' assessment of local needs or their own attitudes towards task use later revisions to the TOC, and have tended to de-emphasise tasks (e.g. Curriculum Development Council, Hong Kong, 2002, compared with earlier versions). That there have been problems in implementing the TOC is widely acknowledged (Biggs and Lam, 1997; Tinker-Sachs et al., 2000; Candlin, 2001; Carless, 2004; Littlewood, 2007), and the demands placed on teachers and the expectations made are considerable, as suggested in the Curriculum Development Council document in Quote 9.1:

Quote 9.1   Teacher roles in planning, developing and implementing classroom tasks

Teachers should plan and organise tasks or activities with the aim of maximising learners' exposure to English both inside and outside the classroom ...
When designing tasks, teachers are encouraged to consider and apply what follows:

Learner-centred instruction
... Learner-centred instruction may be provided through:
- designing learning tasks or activities that cater for learners' ages, needs, interests, abilities, experiences and learning styles;
- engaging learners in group work or pair work for genuine communication;
- applying suitable questioning techniques to stimulate thinking, encourage experimentation and facilitate knowledge construction; and
- encouraging learners to contribute to the learning process by
  - sharing their views and learning experiences,
  - playing an active role in consulting the teacher, and
  - negotiating with the teacher on learning objectives, helping to select learning materials and choosing appropriate activities such as role-plays, games, debates and projects.

(Key Learning Area Curriculum Guide (Primary 1–Secondary 3) for English Language Education, 2002: 95–6)

This is a daunting brief. It assumes that teachers have a solid grasp of the possibilities and limitations of 'task' as have a pedagogic construct, and principled understandings of the ways that the pedagogic focus of tasks may be interpreted and managed. However, there appears to be a mismatch between what is expected and what teachers feel they can do. Although different kinds of support for implementing TOC are made available, including supplementary materials (for example, Mok, 2003), on-line resources (for example, TeleNex, which provides task banks, lesson plans, samples of student work, multi-media links, responses to teacher queries) and in-service workshops on pedagogic procedures (e.g. cooperative learning; Tinker-Sachs et al., 2000), a persistent problem reported by teachers is lack of preparation in how to respond to the demands of the TOC and how to handle it on an everyday basis.

Flanders task-based programmes for the teaching of Dutch as a second language

Task-based programmes for the teaching of Dutch in primary and secondary schools and in adult education have been offered to migrants to Flanders and subsidised by the Flemish government as part of its policy for social inclusion since the early 1990s. As reported by Kris Van den Branden and colleagues from the Centre for Language and Education at the Katholieke Universiteit, Leuven, who have been involved in developing and implementing these programmes since their inception, this work allies itself with 'task-based' learning as characterised above. The Flanders programmes provide a window on TBLT in action in different contexts and age ranges, and crucially, over time. Van den Branden (2006a), a collection of reports based on different aspects of the programmes, describes how tasks were derived from needs analyses, principles underlying curriculum development, assessment instruments and procedures for preparing teachers to introduce task-based innovations. This provides a close account of programme development within a particular SL setting, and Van den Branden is cautious about claims for generalisability to other types of learning situation. Nevertheless, there are many lessons to be learned, particularly with regard to the preparation of teachers, where a gradualist, bottom-up approach to the introduction of TBLT has been developed. Highly sensitive to teacher needs and perceptions, Van den Branden makes extensive use of school-based, practice-oriented coaching (Van den Branden, 2006b and c; Van Avermaet et al., 2006), with teachers involved as active agents in managing change. Ways of working with the new syllabuses were explored collaboratively in on-site coaching sessions; task-based syllabuses did not automatically replace older materials; and teachers had considerable freedom as to how much/how little of the new syllabuses they wished to adopt and how they made use of them. The highly intensive nature of this approach underscores the need for long-term investment of time and resources in teacher preparation and support if TBLT is to be introduced on a large scale; and the emphasis on gradual teacher ownership of tasks is an interesting point of comparison with the more top-down orientation of the Hong Kong TOC.

There are, however, a number of intriguing questions about the Flanders programmes, for example, Van den Branden (2006a), the most widely disseminated documentation to date, has relatively little about the impact of TBLT on language development over time. And although the process of curriculum development is described in considerable detail, there are limited examples of what the finished product looks like. Nevertheless, the Flanders programmes offer important insights into what is required for the large-scale implementation of TBLT, and considerable potential for further exploration of its impact on learning.

TBLT: Problems and Issues

We began by noting that 'task-based' has been loosely applied, and so we have tried here to unpick what could be considered criterial characteristics of TBLT. Our examples have been drawn from a limited range, largely because, as we have seen, there are to date relatively few situations in which TBLT as characterised here has been put into practice. Critics (e.g. Swan, 2005) have consistently argued that there is insufficient evidence on how TBLT works in real classroom contexts, particularly in the teaching of foreign languages in state schools, to warrant the current advocacy for task-based programme development. The critics are right to highlight the lack of such evidence – although this presents a classic chicken-and-egg situation: how can one systematically study TBLT in action over time in the absence of fully developed TBLT programmes to study? For some, the answer is to focus on task-supported contexts.

9.2.2   Task-supported language learning and teaching (TSLT)

In Chapter 4 we characterised 'task-supported' teaching and learning as involving the use of tasks:

- as one element in an overall programme of instruction within a range of syllabus types, and/or to realise a range of curricular objectives;
- in conjunction with different types of pedagogic activity (exercises, rule explanation, focused practice, etc.);
- in different ways to serve different types of pedagogic purposes.

In Example 9.17, we illustrate how these characteristics are reflected in pedagogic practice by listing some ways that tasks are commonly used in task-supported contexts:

Example 9.17   Using a task in a task-supported context: some pedagogic examples

1   To enact content-based/theme-based syllabuses (e.g. Leaver and Kaplan, 2004, language training programmes in Czech, Ukrainian and Russian).
2   To integrate diverse elements taught separately within a programme of instruction and to sustain motivation over a course of study (e.g. Fried-Booth, 1986, development of a full-scale project, e.g. making a class newspaper, alongside regular programme of instruction).

---

3   To diagnose students' strengths and weaknesses at the beginning of a unit of instruction to inform and shape subsequent pedagogic focus, and provide summative feedback at the end (e.g. Larsen-Freeman, 2000).

4   To create a platform for the negotiation of course/class content/modes of learning/forms of assessment (Kohnonen et al., 2001).

5   To contextualise/raise interest/activate prior knowledge of theme/topic of a unit of instruction (Nunan, 2004).

6   To raise awareness of specific lexico-grammatical features (Lee, 2000).

7   To activate previously introduced language features in the final phase of a pedagogic sequence (ESA, Harmer, 2001).

8   To mobilise and stretch students' existing knowledge and resources and develop fluency in light of real time processing demands (Johnson, 1996).

9   To create a learning space for the introduction of 'new' language (as used by the teacher in Samuda, 2001).

10   To give rein to individual self expression/creativity (Rinvolucri, 2002).

11   To raise awareness of different modes of learning (Legutke and Thomas, 1991).

12   To provide a tool for self-assessment/self-reflection (Finch et al., 2003).

13   To create a 'rehearsal rationale' for real life language demands (Nunan, 1991; Hutchinson and Waters, 1987).

14   To vary pace, to make a change, to provide a break from usual classroom work, to fill a hole in a lesson plan (Ur and Wright, 1992).

As can be seen, 'task-supported' appears to encompass a very broad range of ways of using tasks for a very broad range of purposes – to diagnose, to provide practice, to develop fluency, to raise awareness of specific language features, to assess progress, and so on – but tasks themselves are not the central unit of activity within the overall programme of instruction, nor are they associated with a particular syllabus type: any one of our examples could be used in a pre-set syllabus, defined in various ways – structurally, functionally, lexically, topically, textually, etc. – but not necessarily in terms of 'task'. We explore this further in the following examples of TSLT at three different levels of practice: 1) within a syllabus; 2) within an instructional sequence; and 3) within an individual task.

TSLT within a syllabus

A very common way of working tasks into a syllabus is shown in Example 9.18, where tasks are specified as a separate 'strand' within the overall scope and sequence of a theme-based course-book . This extract from the table of contents of a course aimed at young adults gives an overview of a unit of work called 'Around the World':

Example 9.18   Task-supported learning: tasks as a strand within a textbook scope and sequence: Cunningham and Moor, 2005

Module	Language Focus	Vocabulary as writing	Reading	Task	Further skills	Study Practise Remember
Around the world	Comparatives and superlatives Phrases for comparing *Pronunciation: stress and /∂/ sounds*	Describing towns and cities	Reading: *The top 100 places to see before you die*	Preparation: Listening: *A tour of Australia* Task: *Design a tour* (Speaking) Follow-up:	Real life: Booking a flight	Study tips: Keeping notes *Pronunciation: spot: the sounds /ı/ and /iː/*

Since 'task' is specified as a strand in its own right in Example 9.18, it is clearly considered a significant element within the overall syllabus.

TSLT at the level of an instructional sequence

The position of the task towards the end of the module suggests that its intended role here is to support linguistic content previously highlighted in other strands. The task itself is further preceded by several phases of pre-task 'preparation' based on a tour of Australia; these involve activating background knowledge, listening to recommendations about places to visit and drawing attention to useful language, so that by the time the students finally encounter the task, they will have been extensively primed to engage with both the topic and the language that it seeks to activate. This way of using a task will be very familiar to many teachers, since its position in the overall sequence of instruction and the role that it plays there correspond to well-established classroom procedures, such as the 'Production' phase in PPP, or the 'Activate' phase of an ESA (Engage, Study, Activate) cycle (Harmer, 2001). As we saw earlier, the 'supporting' role that tasks play there are in direct contrast with the catalysing role they are intended to play at the beginning of a pedagogic cycle, as in Willis's and Long and Crookes's approaches to TBLT.

TSLT at the level of task

The position of a task in a teaching sequence and the role that it plays there are thus two areas where we can detect differences between 'task-based' and 'task-supported' orientations to their use. How far do these play out when we look at the task itself?

Example 9.19   Task: Design a tour

A

1   Either in pairs or individually, you are going to design a tour similar to the one you heard described. Choose one of the options below.

• Design a tour of your country for one of the following groups. (You will be the guide!)
    – other students in your class;
    – a group of students on a budget holiday;
    – a foreign film star, singer, sports personality, etc.

• Design a tour of either California or Scotland using the information supplied.

• Design a tour of an interesting country you have visited for other students in your class.

• Design a 'fantasy tour' of a region/country/continent that you would like to visit (for example, 'Great Cities of Europe', 'Highlights of the USA', etc.).

B

Decide on the following:

• How long each tour will be, and how many days will be spent in each place.
• The best way to travel from one place to another.
• The main things to see in each place and why they are interesting.

2   Spend 10–15 minutes planning how to describe your tour. Ask your teacher for any words or phrases you need. If possible, draw a rough map to help explain your tour.

3   Work in pairs with a student who has planned a different tour. Explain your tours to each other. Answer your partner's questions.

Follow-up: writing

Write an itinerary for your tour describing what will happen on each day: Day one ..., day two ... Read each other's tours. Whose sounds the most interesting? (Adapted from Cunningham and Moor, 2005)

Interestingly, there doesn't appear to be anything specific in the design of the task in itself that would mark it out as either 'task-supported' or 'task-based'. The task seeks to engage holistic language use; there is a goal and an outcome, and the design offers flexibility over choice of topic, ways of working, resource material to be consulted and intended audience, all of which leave space for individual creativity and an element of learner control. But none of these characteristics in themselves mark the task as inherently 'task-based' or 'task-supported'. It is possible, for example, to envisage this task initiating a TBLT sequence within Willis's framework (with a language focus coming out of the work that learners engage in), as well as in the position illustrated in Example 9.18. Looking at a task like this outside its pedagogic context does not tell us anything about TSLT or TBLT. This suggests that the TBLT/TSLT distinction is not a property of 'task' in itself, but a function of the ways that tasks are used. This is important because somewhere along the way 'task' has become narrowly associated with assumptions about particular sets of pedagogic practices, and it is these assumptions that have made it hard for teachers to appraise the pedagogic potential of tasks in other contexts of use.

TSLT: Pedagogic roles for tasks within a sequence of instruction

In the next sections, we explore some of the different pedagogic roles that tasks commonly play within the instructional contexts that they are used and the different types of pedagogic focus that these can give rise to.

The task in Example 9.20 could be used in numerous ways at the beginning, middle or end of an instructional sequence, and depending on when and how it is used, it could play a number of different roles: for example at the beginning of a sequence, an *initiating* role, a more *reactive* role if used in the middle and an *integrative* role if used at the end, as illustrated in Example 9.21.

Example 9.20   What do you do to help yourself learn English?

Step 1: Working by yourself, read each statement about learning English. Circle the number that describes you best.
1 = never 2 = rarely 3 = sometimes 4 = often 5 = sometimes

1. I study textbooks and memorise examples and rules.	1 2 3 4 5
2. I read newspapers and magazines, watch films, and listen to songs	1 2 3 4 5
3. I use English as much as possible to practice what I know.	1 2 3 4 5
4. When I meet a new word, I look it up in my dictionary.	1 2 3 4 5
5. I keep a notebook with examples of the new words I come across.	1 2 3 4 5
6. I talk to myself in English.	1 2 3 4 5
7. I do exercises and check my answers with an answer key.	1 2 3 4 5
8. I use English to follow topics of interest to me on the internet.	1 2 3 4 5

9. I imagine situations where I will have to use English and practise
   what I would say.   1 2 3 4 5
10. If I don't know a word, I find another way of communicating
    what I want to say.   1 2 3 4 5

Step 2: Compare your answers with another student. Do you do many of the same things to help you learn? Note similarities and differences in the chart below:

SIMILARITIES	DIFFERENCES

Step 3: Are there things that you and your partner do that aren't on the list above? Add anything you do that is not on that list.

Step 4: Get together with some other students in the class and compare your lists. What do you find the most useful and what do you find the least useful in helping you learn English? Be ready to report back to the rest of the class.

Example 9.21   Some pedagogic roles the task 'What do you do to help yourself learn English' (Example 9.20) could play in a sequence of instruction

Point within sequence	Principal pedagogic role here	Some pedagogic purposes for using this task here
Beginning	Initiating	• to raise awareness of different learning styles and preferences at the beginning of a course, *or* ... • to act as a catalyst for a more extensive project, *or* . . . • to introduce a new topic/theme within a topic/theme-based syllabus *or*.. • to stimulate discussion on a topic of interest *or* • to provide a stimulus for written work *or* .. • to create an opening for exploring modes of learning/ areas of content in a process syllabus *or* • to act as a springboard for highlighting ways of expressing preference and/or comparison in a pre-set syllabus *or* ... • to diagnose/highlight uses of the simple present and adverbs of frequency at the beginning of a unit within a structural syllabus *(and so on)*

Example 9.21   (Continued)

Middle	Reactive	• to focus (or re-focus) learner attention on specific elements of form noted as problematic at a previous point in the sequence or on previous task performance *or* ... to follow up a reading text on the same topic *(and so on)*
End	Integrative	• to draw together and activate use of language features previously targeted in the sequence as separate items (e.g. simple present/ adverbs of frequency; comparisons; expressing preference) *or* ... • to create a context for free discussion at the end of a lesson/unit on this theme *or* ... • to provide summative feedback at end of unit *(and so on)*

Although there are undoubtedly many other ways of using this task, these illustrate the potential scope and versatility that a single task can offer. They also help pinpoint differences in the use of tasks on task-based and task-supported contexts. For example, a criterial feature of TBLT is the use of a task in an initiating role at the beginning of a sequence. But as is clear from Example 9.21, not all uses of a task in this role and position would be compatible with task-based principles: using it to launch a unit on the simple present in a pre-set structural syllabus would obviously not meet Willis's or Long's criteria. Nevertheless it is commonly assumed by teachers new to working with tasks that using a task at or near the beginning of a lesson is in itself synonymous with 'doing TBLT'. What the examples in 9.21 highlight is that the interrelationships between a task, its position in a teaching sequence, the pedagogic role it plays within that sequence, and the purpose motivating its use are complex, and that from a pedagogic perspective it is necessary to focus on understanding tasks in light of those relationships.

We are not making a case for 'task-based' or 'task-supported' as one form of pedagogy over another. But we are suggesting that each warrants understanding in its own right, and that making a distinction between the two can shift the focus of debate away from whether 'TBLT' works towards a more careful scrutiny of the range of roles that *tasks* play. If we unhook 'task' from 'TBLT' it becomes easier to distinguish between practitioner concerns about the feasibility/cultural appropriacy of TBLT for certain classroom contexts, and concerns about the feasibility/cultural appropriacy of the use of tasks more generally. Since these kinds of distinctions are not always consistently made in critiques of TBLT (see for example Swan, 2005), it has come to be assumed among practitioners that rebuttals of TBLT also imply a backlash against tasks themselves. Differentiating between 'task-supported' and 'task-based' orientations towards the use of tasks thus offers a way of re-focusing attention on *tasks* themselves and on the pedagogic purposes that they serve in different contexts of use; this in our view provides a more constructive basis for addressing some of the practitioner concerns voiced at the beginning of the chapter.

TSLT: Problems and issues

However, there are some problems with taking the broader perspective on tasks implied by TSLT. One is with the breadth of scope of TSLT itself; the other is with the way that the term 'task-supported' has come to be interpreted and applied in recent years.

In comparison with the distinct set of theoretical motivations and pedagogic practices associated with TBLT, TSLT may be perceived as lacking a firm theoretical base and endorsing an 'anything goes' approach to pedagogy. From this perspective, TSLT can appear atheoretical *vis-à-vis* language and *vis-à-vis* learning, and thus less worthy of empirical attention in its own right. This means that the ways tasks are most widely used (see Example 9.17) have not necessarily been widely researched. There has also been a tendency to characterise 'task-supported' as a weak form of task-based learning (Ellis, 2003), and/or as a transitional stepping-stone towards TBLT proper (Shehadeh, 2005). Paradoxically, rather than shifting attention *away* from TBLT as originally intended (see Bygate, 2000), this way of referring to 'task-supported' appears to have had the opposite effect. It implies a deficit relationship which characterises TSLT in terms of what it is not *vis a vis* TBLT: an incomplete version of the real thing, or a kind of TBLT 'lite'. This is unfortunate since it suggests a two-tier approach that devalues any use of tasks that falls outside the purview of TBLT, and one that risks obscuring 'task' as a pedagogic construct in its own right. Although it may be the case that TSLT plays a necessary transitional role in the implementation of fully-fledged TBLT syllabuses and practices (as reflected, for example, in Van den Branden's gradualist approach to teacher development, Van den Branden, 2006c.), this is a distinct line of inquiry in its own right. Broader understandings of the ways that tasks can contribute to language learning and teaching – whether in task-supported or in task-based contexts – must be grounded in understandings of 'task' as a pedagogic tool in different contexts of use, and in the next section we explore some of the insights to be gained from taking this perspective.

9.3   'Task' as a pedagogic tool

The effectiveness of any tool of course relates to its fitness for an intended purpose. Imagine you want to hang a picture on your wall. While it might be technically possible to use a screwdriver to bang a nail into the wall, how successful you will be depends – among other things – on the size and heaviness of the screwdriver at your disposal, the nail involved, the texture and condition of the wall, your own skills in appraising the situation, and your ingenuity in adapting the tool at hand. A well-chosen hammer brought to bear on an appropriately angled nail at exactly the right point on the wall is likely to have better results, but even so, there is still some leeway for misfire: misjudging the angle of the nail, or the strength of the hammer blow best suited to the texture of the wall, for example. Similarly with tasks: appraising fitness for purpose involves decisions about whether to use a task over an exercise at a particular point in a lesson, the selection of one task or type of over another, adapting or varying a task to respond to local needs, ways of implementing it with a particular group of individuals and ways of enabling connections with previous work. Such decisions come into play regardless of whether the teacher is 'doing TBLT' or using tasks on an occasional basis, but the outcomes of those decisions will be shaped by how the potential of the 'tool' is understood and how it is actually used. Recalling Dewey, 1910, (see Quote 2.21) this view of task-as-tool implies that tasks don't work by themselves by 'magic', but involve thought and planning, and through which they become open to systematic use. If a task is to be an effective and appropriate pedagogic tool, its selection and the way it is used needs to be motivated by principled understandings of how it might work.

Focusing attention on 'task' as a pedagogic tool could be seen as an element of the post-method perspective proposed in Kumaravadivelu, 2001, as we suggested earlier, since what it does is essentially detach tasks from an association with any one methodological approach, any one curriculum or syllabus type, and from a number of general assumptions with which tasks have come to be linked over recent years, including the view that tasks are incompatible with language play, creative expression of self, individual agency on the one hand (Cook, 2000; Mori, 2002; Kramsch, 2005 *inter alia*), and the view that they are incompatible with explicit instruction on the other (Swan, 2005). Similarly, focusing on 'task' as a pedagogic tool opens up broader perspectives for exploring learning: the roles that tasks might play in proceduralisation, for example, or the development of discourse routines or the acquisition of formulaic chunks. Focusing on task-as-tool enables us to re-situate tasks within the broader educational perspective that we sketched at the beginning of this book in relation to Dewey, Freinet, Bruner, Barnes and others. This in turn opens up broader perspectives for exploring the use of tasks in language teaching initiatives which do not ally themselves with 'TBLT', but within which tasks play a significant role. We focus on some examples below.

9.3.1   Exploring the potential of task as a pedagogic tool

Some of the key themes that we highlighted at the beginning of this book were personal relevance and learners' own experience as catalysts for learning, and the pedagogic challenges involved in harnessing these in classroom settings. These issues are not always made prominent in the literature on task-based learning or in task research, but they do emerge as powerful themes in a number of pedagogic initiatives. One of these is Dogme ELT.

Dogme ELT (Thornbury, 2000, 2005)

Dogme ELT, pioneered by Scott Thornbury and colleagues, was initially inspired by the Dogme 95 group of film makers, whose rejection of the slick production values of mainstream Hollywood films led them to create a set of guiding principles for themselves that eschewed technical gimmicks and special effects in favour of simple sets, natural lighting and an approach to cinema that focused on the inner life of the characters. Thornbury draws analogies between the commercialism of mainstream movie-making and its dependence on technical effect and recent developments in language teaching, which he argues, are marked by an over-reliance on pre-packaged formats, and complex technologies. Calling for a rejection of 'technicist' pedagogies, Thornbury argues for the adoption of a simpler, more pared-down way of teaching, and in the sprit of the Dogme 95 group of film makers, proposes a similar set of principles for language teachers. These include the following:

Example 9.22   Dogme ELT

- Teaching should be done using only the resources that teachers and students bring to the classroom – i.e. themselves – and whatever happens to be in the classroom. If a particular piece of material is necessary for the lesson, a location must be chosen where that material is to be found (e.g. library, resource centre, bar, students' club ...)
- Learning ... takes place in the here-and-now. What is learned is what matters. Teaching – like talk – should centre on the local and relevant concerns of the people in the room

(Thornbury, 2000: 4–5)

Although modified slightly in Thornbury (2005), which explores how materials based on Dogme principles would look, Dogme ELT is very much in line with the experienced pedagogies envisaged by Freinet and others. In workshops for teachers, for example, Thornbury invites participants to choose something from their bags/backpacks and talk about it the person sitting next to them. Drawing on the conversations that ensue, Thornbury and participants ('the people in the room') jointly construct a descriptive frame for key language features brought into play, which in a language classroom would be subsequently exploited for learning purposes. This frame is an interplay between general features of language use predicted by the nature of the 'task' initially set, and particularised elements of content arising from individual conversations, with the teacher working as a bridge between the two. We saw something similar in the teacher's use of the TIP task in Samuda (2001), although in the Thornbury example, there are no initial materials on paper, so the pedagogic focus emerges solely from what is jointly constructed among the 'people in the room'. Without invoking 'task-based learning', Thornbury's work is an example of the use of a task (as we would characterise it, following our definition earlier in the book) as a pedagogic tool.

Example 9.23 gives some other examples of tasks being used as a tool in teaching initiatives that do not usually define themselves in terms of task-based learning:

Example 9.23 Language teaching initiatives in which tasks play a significant role as a pedagogic tool

Learners as discourse analysts (Riggenbach, 1999)	The 'task' is for learners to design, set up and carry out discourse analysis activities on features of language use of interest to them following a 5-phase process: *predict* (make predictions about the target feature they want to focus on); *plan* (set up a research plan to elicit samples of the target feature; *collect data* (observe/record the feature in its discourse environment); *analyse* (data analysis/draw conclusions); *generate* (samples of their own); *review* (summarise and reflect on findings and their own learning)
Ready for a story (Artigal, 1991; 2005)	Involves young learners in bilingual and tri-lingual immersion contexts in Catalunya, Basque Autonomous Community, Germany, Italy, Finland, France and elsewhere. The 'task' is for children to narrate and act out a story to parents/family: a real-world outcome that the story building process works towards.

	Making special use of classroom space, the teacher works with the children to build a story through movement, mime, artefacts and text; the story is extended and enriched over time, with a number of elements repeated in its re-telling, culminating in the child's independent narration outside the classroom
Writing for Webheads (Stevens, 2004)	A virtual community, initially bringing together native and non-native speakers of all ages and backgrounds interested in exploring on-line CMC tools. Sustaining the community are purposeful, spontaneously arising, self-motivated 'tasks' that members bring forward for joint resolution, with successful outcomes documented on web pages. Community members experiment with technology, pool knowledge and resources while helping each other figure out ways of exploiting available tools for their personal or professional needs. Through this, the need for linguistic resources to support ways of using and giving directions and explaining processes are brought into focus.

Other related examples include Elsa Auerbach and Nina Wallerstein's use of problem-posing activities within a Freirean participatory framework (Wallerstein, 1983; Auerbach and Wallerstein, 1987), Alma Flor Ada's work with community literacy (Ada and Campoy, 2003), Leni Dam's work on autonomy (Dam, 1995) and Susan Feez's work on text-based syllabus design (Feez, 1998). Many others could be added – the general point that we are making here is that 'task' is a pervasive pedagogic construct that is present, albeit in different ways, in a more diverse array of teaching contexts than is generally acknowledged in the literature on tasks, and that exploring the role of tasks in such contexts could be a useful direction for broadening the scope of task research.

9.3.2   Exploring the potential of tasks as a pedagogic tool sequences of instruction

We turn now to examples of well-established pedagogic frameworks that make use of tasks as tools within sequences of work: Legutke and Thomas (1991), Ribé and Vidal (1993) and Estaire and Zanón (1994). Each has grown out of extensive work with language learners and teachers primarily across Europe, and particularly state school systems in FL settings, but none has received a great deal of empirical attention from task researchers.

Legutke and Thomas

Legutke and Thomas have a long-standing association with project work: a 'project' is seen as an extended piece of work (typically spanning weeks or months) with a non-linguistic outcome: designing and selling a T-shirt to raise money for charity; making a class magazine; designing and producing a brochure for overseas visitors. See Legutke and Thomas (1991), Fried Booth (1986), Finch et al. (2003), Beckett and Miller (2006), for example. A project involves holistic language use and typically draws on a broad range of morpho-syntactic, lexical, discourse and pragmatic resources and engages a broad range of language processing and procedural skills. A project opens with teacher and students jointly exploring what it is that they want to pursue and establishing the steps they will need to take in order to carry it through; this forms the basis for initial and subsequent planning, and steps are collaboratively refined over time as the project takes shape. Since projects are sometimes characterised as examples of 'mega-tasks', project work is of considerable potential interest as a site for researching task-based learning (as advocated in Skehan, 1998), but to date has received relatively little empirical attention (although see contributions to Beckett and Miller, 2006).

Legutke and Thomas make careful distinctions between 'task' and 'project', and the way that they situate tasks in relation to projects is central to their work. They view projects as a 'collection of a large variety of tasks . . . how these tasks are sequenced and relate to one another depends on the main objective of the project' (1991: 167). Since carrying out a project is a lengthy and demanding process, tasks are seen as useful building blocks for sustaining that process, with different types of task having distinct roles to play in supporting the way a project develops; these are shown in Example 9.24:

Example 9.24   Different task types within a project: Legutke and Thomas, 1991

Type of task	Purpose for use
Language learning tasks	To develop discrete language skills through controlled and guided practice and to focus attention on necessary or problematic language features. Can appear at any point in the process, and do not have to precede other forms of activity.

Pre-communicative tasks	To enable learners to react and deal with different types of input data, mainly in the form of texts. To engage learners in controlled and guided practice, and through sequences of such tasks, aim to enable them to gradually express their own views and meanings. Aim to replicate important aspects of real-life language use in the classroom
Communicative tasks	To act as a catalyst through which discourse emerges from genuine communicative needs and interaction.
Instrumental and management tasks	To enhance learners' managerial and procedural capacities through controlled and guided practice

For Legutke and Thomas, tasks provide a means of narrowing focus within the big picture of a project creating contexts in which the linguistic and process skills that will be needed at different phases of the project can be practised and developed. Tasks also provide a means of managing movement through a project, for example they can be used to maintain interest and revive motivation and to 'bridge' different phases of activity. They also provide a means for raising awareness and reflection on what has been achieved and for mapping subsequent steps. The rationale for task sequencing is thus motivated by how a given task relates to the needs of an overall project, and how it links with what has come before and what will follow. This is important, and Legutke and Thomas explicitly distinguish between the use of tasks within the framework of a project, and the use of tasks for their own sake as short term teaching gimmicks 'without reference to the thematic context or broader educational aims' in which they are used (1991: 155), arguing that the latter (which they see reflected in some forms of 'task-based learning') is to seriously undermine the pedagogic worth of tasks.

Ribé and Vidal

Ribé and Vidal (1993) offer a different take on relationships between 'project' and 'task'. Emphasising the role of tasks in 'creating new language needs and in providing students with the means for meeting them' (p.5), they differentiate among tasks in terms of duration, degree of elaboration and the different kinds of pedagogic purpose that teachers might want to use them for. They categorise tasks into three broad types: 'first generation', 'second generation' and 'third generation', as we see in Example 9.25:

Example 9.25　Different types of task: Ribé and Vidal, 1993

Type of task	Purpose for use
First generation tasks	Basic tasks designed to target specific structures/functions and to develop communicative ability in a specific area being taught. Widely and successfully used in private language schools where motivation is not an issue, and may be used in school systems to supplement more traditional work *EXAMPLES: Information gap activities like: Spot the Difference tasks; Map tasks; Describe and Draw tasks; controlled role plays*
Second generation tasks	Focus primarily on content, procedure and language in order to develop language skills as well as strategies for handling and processing information. Learners and teachers collectively decide on information needed, procedures for collecting, synthesizing and analyzing it and ways of representing findings and results. Language is seen as a vehicle for doing a 'real' piece of work and is approached globally, not incrementally. *EXAMPLES: Survey tasks involving collection and analysis of information from sources outside the classroom: What tourists of different nationalities think of students' country/town/city*
Third generation tasks	Involve all language and cognitive strategies associated with second generation tasks, but also aim for 'global personality development'. They seek to fulfil wider educational objectives (attitudinal change; learner awareness; motivation), and are open and flexible, emphasising imagination, creativity and affectivity Language is approached globally through the needs of the task. *EXAMPLES: Full scale projects: Designing an alternative world; A trip to an unknown planet*

Projects are presented here as a distinctive task type, although all three different tasks types complement and build on each other: basic 'first generation' tasks, for example can play an important role in creating a good class atmosphere, which in turn enables the introduction of more elaborated, larger scale, second- and third-generation tasks. Task types are thus characterised not only in terms of the roles they play in themselves, but also in relation to each other across a broader span of activity. Ribé and Vidal note that in the content in which they work, second- and third-generation tasks (but especially the latter) are better suited to state school systems where learner motivation is a problem, and first-generation tasks are more successful in private language schools where students are more likely to be motivated to participate. Interestingly, what Ribé and Vidal categorise as 'first-generation' are precisely the types of task that have been most extensively studied in the research literature – 'spot the difference', 'describe and draw', 'map tasks', and so on – and this again raises awkward questions about the gap between the kinds of task apparently of interest to researchers and those apparently of interest to practitioners, as well as suggesting a direction for exploring relationships between task type and learner motivation.

Estaire and Zanón

Estaire and Zanón (1994) focus on lesson planning. They present a framework for planning teaching sequences that culminate in a 'final task', and that can be applied to planning a lesson, a unit of work or an extended project. The process begins with specifying a final task and works backwards from there, and so it is the needs and demands of the 'final task' in a teaching sequence that determine the plan, not pre-determined items of language. Learners are involved as fully as possible throughout the planning process so that when they begin a sequence of work, they know what the final task will be and how they will work towards it. Estaire and Zanón identify three different tasks types as coming into play in planning as shown in Example 9.26.

Example 9.26   Types of task in planning a unit of work: Estaire and Zanón, 1994

Type of task	Purpose for use
Final task	Culmination of a unit of work, specified before any other aspect of the unit is planned (apart from overall theme), with unit objectives, content, processes and evaluation derived from the final task: everything within the unit builds towards it, and it is made clear to students at the beginning of the unit what it is that they are working towards. ***EXAMPLE:*** *Putting together a class magazine*
Communication tasks	Smaller scale tasks in the thematic area of the final task that may prepare students for an aspect of the

---

Example 9.26   (Continued)

	final task; these are focused on meaning rather than form, and are aimed at reproducing processes of everyday communication. **EXAMPLE:** *Horoscopes: Classify predictions given in the horoscope section of a magazine; Write predictions for classmates' star signs.*
Enabling tasks	These support communication tasks and the final task by providing necessary linguistic tools, raising consciousness about form and allowing for systematisation of linguistic knowledge. They include any kind of activity or exercise that will be necessary or useful for the final task: conventional exercises, small-scale tasks, structure tasks focused on a specific area of form, controlled pre-communication practice and awareness-raising tasks **EXAMPLE:** *Horoscopes: Identify star signs from their symbols, with correct pronunciation and spelling; Teacher-led focus on the use of* will *in making predictions based on magazine horoscopes.*

Planning backwards from a final task can create a thematic thread for a sequence of work, with 'communication' and 'enabling' tasks as the building blocks that provide direction and support along the way. An underlying pedagogic assumption here appears to be that learners (and teachers) are less likely to perceive tasks as random pieces of classroom work if they encounter them as part of a unified whole, although this has not been widely explored empirically.

These brief examples cannot do justice to the body of practical work built up by Legutke and Thomas, Ribé and Vidal and Estaire and Zanón and colleagues, but they do open up an interesting perspective on task use, selection and sequencing. All three distinguish task types on the basis of the different pedagogic roles they play within a sequence of instruction. Task selection is thus determined not just by the properties of individual tasks, but crucially here by sequential relationships among them across a span of work. A potential problem however is that it is not always clear what criteria teachers should draw on to make those selections, and choices of this kind presumably depend on having a solid grasp of the pedagogic potential of different kinds of task, both in themselves and in relation to each other and this brings us back to the kinds of concerns raised earlier in the chapter. Issues of sequencing in the research literature (e.g. Robinson, 2001, 2006) have focused on relationships among tasks primarily in terms of cognitive demand, and are not necessarily framed in the same terms of pedagogic reference as the examples from practice illustrated here. This seems to be an area where insights from task pedagogy and insights from task research could be usefully brought together, and existing pedagogic frameworks that have grown out of sustained task use in real classrooms over time, such as those highlighted above, offer a promising context for developing pedagogically-oriented research shaped by and responsive to the kinds of practitioner concern voiced at the beginning of this chapter.

In this chapter we have focused on ambiguities surrounding pedagogic interpretations of task-based learning; we have made a case for unhooking 'task' from its recent associations with TBLT, and re-situating it as a flexible pedagogic tool, open to systematic use in various ways for different purposes. We have argued that understanding the resources and limitations of task-as-tool also entails empirical understandings of its use in pedagogic contexts, and in the next chapter we explore ways in which these could be developed.

Part 3
Exploring Tasks

10
Research Directions

This chapter outlines potential directions for research that could be undertaken in pedagogical contexts under of the five themes discussed in Chapter 7:

1. tasks and language;
2. tasks and process;
3. tasks and development;
4. tasks and teachers and learners;
5. tasks and their ecological context.

Each section identifies a series of research topics, sometimes grouped by sub-theme, and ends with some comments on aspects of research methods.

Ways of approaching task research

Research in this domain can involve the collection and analysis of different types of data, including:

- oral recordings;
- written discourse;
- oral or written responses to comprehension tasks;
- self-report data:
  - questionnaire responses
  - interview responses
  - think-aloud responses
  - stimulated recall responses
  - diary/journal responses
- classroom observation fieldnotes.

Research can be based entirely on self-report data, entirely on languag data, or on a combination of the two.

Participants in this research are likely to be:

- language learners;
- language teachers;
- materials designers;
- testers.

In gathering the data, some kind of 'design' is needed – we must decid whether we wish to work with detailed case study data or group data and in what ways. The main design parameters are: i) participants; ii participant grouping; iii) time; iv) data transformation.

- *Participants*: People work with group data when they particularly wish to find out what typical responses are like. It is hard to know what i 'typical' unless we sample a range of participants. In contrast, case study data are preferable where we are trying to explore the details o a person's actions and perceptions in undertaking an activity. Both case studies and group studies offer choices in terms of grouping time and data transformation.
- *Grouping*: Case studies are typically thought of as involving single case (e.g. Samuda, 2001). However, several projects have employed a case study approach with 3–5 participants (e.g. Arndt, 1987; Lynch and Maclean, 2000, 2001; Mangubhai, 1991), in which part of the purpose is to study differences among the individuals. On the other hand group studies tend to be thought of as involving more than one group but here too researchers have a choice: it is possible to carry out a single large group study – for example around a whole lesson (Slimani, 1992) – or the parallel enactment of the same task by a number of pairs Group studies often use a 'cross-group' design in order to contrast groups from some perspective, such as in terms of differences in the level of proficiency (e.g. Yule and Macdonald, 1990), or differences in treatment (e.g. with different preparatory phases of the task as in Skehan and Foster, 1997). As with contrasting case studies, the purpose in using contrasting groups is to explore the possibility that the differences between the groups impacts on how they carry out the task.
- *Time*: The 'time' parameter simply refers to whether or not the data have been gathered at a series of time points, to create a 'longitudinal' sequence capable of showing change over time, or whether it is essentially one-off.

- *Data transformation*: Once collected, data need some kind of transformation during analysis. Typical transformations are *transcription, coding*, and *quantification*. Transcription immediately transforms the shape of oral data into a two-dimensional array. Much of the phonological and paralinguistic information can be lost at this point, reducing the richness of the original event. Data will also be coded, whether by tagging the language data, tagging interview, diary or open question responses, or by transforming the language data into statistical shape.

In what follows we focus in more detail on how these elements can come into play.

10.1   Researching tasks and language

Tasks can provide a workspace to focus on different aspects of language, and here we identify research projects in each of three main sub-areas:

- tasks and grammar;
- tasks and vocabulary;
- tasks and discourse.

10.1.1   Tasks and grammar

A functional approach to language (e.g. Halliday, 1994) and to the learning of language (e.g. Tomasello, 2003) implies that grammar cannot be properly learnt outside contexts of use. Tasks offer one such context. As we have seen (cf. Chapter 7) the relationship between oral tasks and particular grammar features is controversial and cannot be taken for granted. Yet Samuda (2001), Mackey (1999; cf. Chapter 8), McDonough (2006, on prepositional datives) and Izumi and Izumi (2004, on relative clauses) have shown that tasks can be used effectively to target specific grammatical fields. This suggests that tasks can be designed and used to activate particular areas of grammar. A first research challenge, then, is to explore how far tasks can be used to target particular grammatical domains. The questions here are:

- Can tasks be designed to engage learners in using and developing their ability to communicate reference, or to exploit the use of noun post-modification?
- Can tasks be used to lead learners to work with comparison, or verb aspect, such as the perfect?

This area of investigation highlights the relationship between task design, task use and lexico-grammatical domains of meaning. Some ways of researching these relationships via sample topics are illustrated in Examples 10.1–10.3.

Example 10.1   Researching task design, task use, and lexico-grammatical domains of meaning. Sample topic: *Comparatives*

Research question What expressions of comparison are elicited by a task selected to activate this area of language? What are the pedagogical implications for task design and implementation?

The problem Languages have a range of expressions of comparison for learners to explore. Plenty of tasks are available to generate descriptive or expository language. However the question arises how to design and implement a task so as to lead learners into reporting and commenting on similarities and differences between referents.

Some procedures

i)   Identify some tasks that can involve the language of comparison, and select one for investigation.
ii) Use the material with two different classes.
iii) Transcribe the talk.
iv) Analyse the transcription to identify the expressions of comparison that are elicited? How far is their language common across the two classes?
v)   Try to redesign the task to alter the aspects of the language of comparison that are used.
vi) Use the revised material with one of the classes.
vii) Transcribe and analyse to discover how far are those aspects are in fact activated.

Example 10.2   Researching task design, task use and lexico-grammatical domains of meaning. Sample topic: *Tasks and the future*

Research question What kinds of task are suited to engaging learners in the use of future forms (going to, will)?

The problem Expressions of futurity are used in relation to the time of speech. Typically, however, tasks engage talk about fictitious or factual material that generally derives from the past or is time-neutral. Students are not normally led into predicting future events, or the kinds of talk involved in planning future activities which they will themselves be involved in. The problem therefore is to identify or generate tasks which will engage this area of meaning in classroom contexts.

Procedure

i) Select or adapt a task likely to involve students in referring to future events or actions, or in planning their own actions.

ii) Gather the students' oral or written language, and analyse a) the extent to which students refer to future time, and b) the extent to which this is expressed through the choice of verb form.

iii) Consider the implications for the selection and development of tasks for focusing students on expressing future time.

Example 10.3   Researching task design, task use and lexico-grammatical domains of meaning. Sample topic: *Tasks and relative clauses*

Research question What kinds of task can elicit the use of relative clauses, and why?

   The problem: Relative clauses are typically used to help clarify reference, where a simple adjective, prepositional or participial phrase is not available or sufficient. Relevant contexts include those where the aspect, modality or tense, and possibly the agent of the activity, need to be specified; or where the use of a relative clause creates thinking time for the speakers. The question then is what kinds of tasks can generate use of this domain of grammar.

   Procedure As for the previous topics.

10.1.2   Tasks and vocabulary

A further question is whether tasks can be used to promote vocabulary development, and if so, how. This is an interesting but relatively unresearched direction. Classroom survey tasks (say, of people's views about travel, food, careers) might be expected to lead learners to use families of related vocabulary items, as would tasks centred on topics from a given subject area, such as geography, history or economics. Given coherent content, students are likely to be led into using a range of related vocabulary items. Research here could lead into studies of communication and negotiation strategies, and on students' use and re-use of target lexical items during task work.

Example 10.4   Researching tasks and vocabulary. Sample topic: *Tasks and the vocabulary of food*

Research question What tasks could be used to engage learners in the exploration and use of food vocabulary? What vocabulary is generated, and how does this occur as the task unfolds?

   The problem The teaching/learning of vocabulary is not generally associated with the use of tasks. Yet many tasks will typically activate particular lexico-semantic

---

Example 10.4   (Continued)

domains. The problem is how far the different participants in tasks use vocabulary from a particular domain, how far they borrow from each other, and how far this can be affected by the choice of task.

Procedure

i)   Gather oral or written data produced by students working on a task.
ii) Identify and mark all lexical items (lexical verbs, nouns, adjectives, adverbs).
iii) Code those which are semantically related to the topic of food.
iv) Analyse the frequency of each item, the proportions of each and, in the case of oral data, the extent to which each is used by the different students.
v)   How might the task be adjusted to change the frequency and distribution of vocabulary items?

10.1.3   Tasks and discourse

By requiring language use, tasks generate discourse. Depending on its function, discourse – both oral and written – varies in shape and in the 'constellation' of features (Schleppergell, 2004) it mobilises. The shape of different types of discourse may be something that teachers would wish students to experience (Carter and McCarthy, 1997), and tasks could be a useful means of doing this. To explore this theme, we distinguish between 'ideational' and 'interactional' discourse patterns. (A similar distinction is made by Brown and Yule, 1983; Eggins, 1990; and see Burns, Joyce and Gollin, 1996, for a summary.)

Ideational discourse patterns

'Ideational discourse patterns' occur where discourse is organised as a function of its information content. For instance, in describing a route or a procedure, a chronological sequence is likely to be used. Definitions are likely to involve some classification, a description of qualities and exemplification. In making comparisons, we have to refer serially to the things being compared as well as the relevant criteria. Using more than one criterion or comparing more than two things can be expected to result in greater complexity in the organisation of the information. Examples of ideational discourse structures include instruction, narration, description, explanation, prediction, planning and argumentation. Carter and McCarthy (1997) give examples of some of these categories. Each is characterised in terms of a small number of features – the presence or absence of temporal sequencing; consistency of reference of participants and location; causality; reference to physical, behavioural or other characteristics – and each tends to lead to some preferred patterns of sequencing. Tasks involving discourse with these functions will inevitably involve some form of ideational structure. The main research issue is how far tasks can do this and in what ways. Some directions for exploring them are suggested in Example 10.5.

Example 10.5   Researching discourse patterns. Sample topic: *The discourse of narration:*

Research question How can the language of oral and/or written narration be activated through tasks, and with what effect?
   The problem Materials for generating narratives are widely available (notably picture stories, but also sentence sequencing activities, and other kinds of oral or visual prompts). However, a sequencing task does not of itself necessarily lead to narration. So the problem is to design or develop tasks which will generate narrative talk or writing.

Some procedures

i)   Identify tasks that can activate the discourse of narration. Care is needed here because picture sequencing does not of itself necessarily give rise to narration, since students are likely to feel they have completed the task once the sequencing is completed. Hence some further demand is likely to be needed to motivate the production of a narrative.
ii) Select one and implement it with a class, working in groups, both orally and in writing.
iii) To enable analysis, for oral tasks, transcribe the talk; for written tasks photocopy the students' writing.
iv) Analyse the language of narration in both the oral and written data.

Interactional discourse patterns

It can be useful to distinguish ideational structures from interactional structures, since discourse is shaped not only by the ideational content but also by the interactional roles of the speakers. Take, for example, a comparison between two towns. At a simple level, the discourse would be partly shaped by whether this is being done in monologue or through some kind of dialogue. More importantly the shape of the discourse will also be affected by whether the speakers all share the information, or whether there is any asymmetry in their roles (such as some being only ones to lack information held by others, so that some adopting a questioning and others a helping role rather than all having the same role).

   Drawing on Burns, Joyce and Gollin (1996) and Carter and McCarthy (1997), one approach would explore interactional discourse patterns in terms of the discourse roles of the participants, their relative status, and their collaborative orientation. For instance, some tasks are described as one-way, with the speaker holding all the information needed by their partner. Discourse roles include informing, directing, enquiring. Yet in spite of the intentions behind the design and use of a task, the speaker without the information could easily take control. Why might this happen? And what happens to the discourse when it does? How far might it matter for the students' learning, and could it be avoided? If so, how?

Status varies between 'symmetrical' and 'asymmetrical' relations: in symmetrical relations all have equal status in the interaction; in asymmetrical relations at least one of the participants has lower status. But is 'symmetry' important in learner talk, and if so, why, and how can it be encouraged? What discourse features reflect a collaborative or divergent orientation? Once again, what importance might this have for learning? If it is important, what can be done via task design or implementation to foster it? (see Slade and Thornbury 2006). Finally, collaborative orientation is also relevant: convergent interactants will be mutually supportive, whereas divergent participants will not prioritise mutual support. How can these possibilities be exploited, and with what language implications? Some sample topics on this theme are outlined in Example 10.6.

Example 10.6   Researching discourse patterns. Sample topic: *Tasks and the discourse of instructional dialogue*

Research question What types of task can be used in which one or more students instruct other students in an activity, and what kinds of talk does this set up?

The problem Teachers and students may think that interaction patterns are less important than getting the task done. Group dynamics can then be left to shape the talk (cf. Cameron et al., 1997, who report a group behaving directively when the intention had been to promote joint decision-making). It could be useful to explore how far tasks can generate different kinds of talk, such as directive talk, joint decision-making, collaborative information-sharing, reciprocal questioning or argumentation.

Procedure

i) Select or adapt a task which deliberately targets instructional talk, such as a 'describe and draw' task, a 'describe and do' task, or a task in which one students instructs another in a skill they know.

ii) Introduce the task.

iii) Record the groups doing the task.

iv) Explore the data for similarities and differences in the interaction across the groups. For instance, what linguistic features are used by the 'instructors' and the 'tutees'? How is the discourse shaped?

v) Consider the pedagogical and design implications, for instance: how do the students perceive the task? What did they think their interaction was like? What did they learn, or think could be learnt, through such as task?

Example 10.7   Researching discourse patterns. Sample topic: *Tasks and collaborative talk*

Research question What interaction patterns do students use to explore a shared problem-solution task (such as a TIP task, or a task in which students work from a map to decide the best siting of a factory, housing, roads, railway and bridges in a valley)? What other features characterise their talk?

The problem Research suggests that all interpersonal discourse is collaborative (e.g. Wilkes-Gibbes, 1997; Yule and Tarone, 1991). However, some forms of talk may be more collaborative than others, engaging speaker and hearer in closer attention to meaning and in a wider range of collaborative moves. What then is the relationship between task design and interactive talk?

Procedure

i)   As with topic 10.6: Note: if keeping group personality factors constant would be an advantage, it could be valuable to do this with the same class as topic 10.6.
ii) After following the procedures for topic 10.6, compare the discourse gathered from the two tasks.
iii) Consider the overall pedagogical and design implications: might the way the task is implemented affect students' orientation and discourse? Could this be affected by the design of the task?

Tasks and language: research methods

Research in the domain of 'task and language' focuses on the analysis of language data. This requires the gathering of appropriate data-sets under the conditions that are of interest (e.g. in terms of timing, task type, lesson type, or the pre-task, on-task or feedback conditions). The design could involve case studies, as in the Lynch and Maclean, Donato, and Samuda studies, or cross-group comparative studies, as in Yule and Macdonald or Yuan and Ellis (see Chapter 8). Key steps are listed in Concept 10.1.

Concept 10.1   Steps in structuring a study

1. Choose a task and conditions relevant to the topic.
2. Decide the participants (classes or groups or individuals) to be involved.
3. Obtain permission to gather and analyse data (spiel out more the ethics here and the procedures).
4. Gather the data (via audio/visual recordings or via written materials).
5. Adjust the data into an analysable format:
   i) written data will need to be photocopied and possibly re-typed;
   ii) oral data need transcribing. Simple transcription conventions are suggested by Thornbury and Slade (2006: 3–4).

> ### Concept 10.1   (Continued)
>
> 6. Analyse the data: select and use appropriate categories of analysis. The most central ones here will focus on the broader discourse patterns, the lexico-grammatical patterns or the phonological patterns. Other categories, such as markers of fluency, indicators of accuracy or of complexity, may also be useful.

Step 6, is a particularly interesting part of the research process. This is partly because what happens in a given data-set may not meet the teacher's or researcher's expectations, which is one of the prime reasons for carrying out such studies. But it is partly also because the choice of a category is often not straightforward. There can be at least four reasons for this.

> ### Concept 10.2   Problems in selecting categories of analysis
>
> 1. Finding a category which reflects reasonably well the focus of interest.
> 2. Finding a category which occurs sufficiently frequently.
> 3. Finding a category which occurs sufficiently frequently with the intended function.
> 4. Finding a category which can be defined reasonably unambiguously.

Perhaps the major problem is finding a category which reflects reasonably well the focus of interest. Narrative discourse, for example, involves the use of different features, some of them grammatical (verb tense, referential markers of identity of participants, adverbial markers of time and markers of sequencing), and some of them more purely discoursal (setting, development, coda, along with personal comment). Hence the researcher needs to decide how to represent students' narrations through the analysis. Should it all be represented? Or is it possible that an inclusive analysis is less effective than focusing on one or two other the key features?

To give another example: research into lexico-grammatical patterning involves deciding whether to focus purely on analysing the occurrence of specific overt markers (such as the simple past, as in Ellis, 1987; or the article, as reported in Ortega, 2005), or whether to use broader functional categories. The occurrence of features within a given task cannot be taken for granted. Sien (2005) found that in writing tasks which were expected to elicit simple past forms, students responded to tabulated information about historical changes in transport patterns by quite acceptably reporting and discussing the contents of the tables through the use of the simple present. As a result he sometimes found it extremely difficult to analyse accuracy in past time use because it was hard to distinguish between obligatory and optional contexts. Three further issues include:

1. Checking that the feature occurs sufficiently frequently. Note how Samuda's study focused on the semantic category of modality, allowing her to include a range of different expressions and not depend on the frequency of occurrence of a single modal verb such as 'must' or 'might', or indeed on the occurrence of modal verbs at all (the study also allowed the inclusion of the use of modal adverbs, such as 'possibly', 'probably'); that is, expressions of probability as a whole would be needed constantly, whereas a single modal, or even all modals taken together, may have been too infrequent for their analysis to have been informative.
2. Ensuring that categories are not too multifunctional to interpret clearly. An example is article use. Articles have several distinct functions, so that a study of the use of all articles could generate a mixed bag, with no particular types of use sufficiently frequent for the results to be informative.
3. Ensuring categories are clearly defined. Formulaic chunks are a notorious example – see Foster (2001) for a discussion of this difficulty and for a way of resolving it. But most features (e.g. articles, comparisons, modals, or discourse categories such as initiations and responses) pose similar problems of definition.

10.2   Researching tasks and process

This has two sub-themes:

1. the contribution to language learning of the interactive processes that students adopt in carrying out tasks;
2. the extent to which tasks can lead students to attend differentially to the fluency, accuracy or complexity of their language.

The interactive processes are seen in terms of students negotiating for meaning or scaffolding each others' attempts to communicate. In contrast, variations in attention focus are seen as responses to the *processing demands* of the task. It is broadly accepted that the design of tasks can influence students' processing in these two ways. But despite the quite significant research already undertaken on these themes (for discussion, see Chapter 7), there are a number of ways in which these issues can be explored in more detail.

10.2.1 Task and negotiation processes

Little is known about how negotiation or scaffolding relate to issues such as learner awareness, learning style, age and level of proficiency, size of group and aspects of learning. Aspects of the topic that could be explored are set out in Examples 10.8–10.11.

Example 10.8 Researching negotiation and scaffolding (1)

Question How are students' scaffolding and negotiation behaviours affected by being told that this is one of the rationales for using tasks?

Problem Research into scaffolding and negotiation processes have so far been limited to seeing whether students use these processes simply as a result of the design of the task. Yet, in classrooms students can be made aware of these as potential learning processes. So the question is whether this affects how they do the tasks.

Procedure
i) Explain and illustrate to a class the concept of scaffolding (examples can be found in Barnes, 1976; Nassaji and Wells, 2000).
ii) Get initial feedback from them on how they perceive scaffolding themselves.
iii) Provide them with a task to do which offers them opportunities to use scaffolding moves in their talk.
iv) Record and then transcribe the talk.
v) After the task, debrief the students about their use of scaffolding during the task.
vi) Analyse the use of scaffolding in the transcript, and relate the analysis to students' perceptions of its use.

Example 10.9 Researching negotiation and scaffolding (2)

Question How far are students' scaffolding and negotiation behaviours influenced by the use of scaffolding and negotiation strategies by teachers?

Problem Scaffolding and negotiation processes have so far been researched without reference to the kinds of talk students experience when interacting with the teacher. But teachers' practices may be expected to influence how students talk with each other. Is this the case?

Procedure
i) Over a period of 3–4 weeks, develop the use of scaffolding and/or negotiation procedures in your own talk as a teacher.
ii) With the collaboration of a teacher who has not been using scaffolding features in their talk, record students in your respective classes doing the same task.
iii) Transcribe and analyse sample recordings.
iv) Conduct post-task feedback sessions with the two classes, exploring students' perceptions of scaffolding in their teachers' talk, and in their own talk.

Example 10.10   Researching negotiation and scaffolding (3)

Question Over time, do students change in the way they scaffold and negotiate, and if so, how?

Problem Research to date has mainly studied learner-learner talk in single sample data sets, without reference to learners' experience of the interaction type. Yet we can expect that regular use of scaffolding and/or negotiation would affect how learners do it. How does experience of this over time affect their talk?

Procedure

i) For this study you will need a longitudinal design, in which you collect recordings of students in the same class over a 6–9-month period, to observe whether there are changes in their use of scaffolding over time

ii) Select a series of 3–4 tasks of roughly comparable content and complexity which can be used over the 6–9-month period.

iii) Record students doing one of the tasks every three months.

iv) Transcribe.

v) Analyse and study any changes in the use of scaffolding across the 3–4 tasks over time.

Example 10.11   Researching negotiation and scaffolding. Further questions for investigation

1. Do different students negotiate and/or scaffold talk, and how far (and in what ways) is this a function of learner characteristics, such as peer status, pair/group affiliation, age, learning attitude, communication style (e.g. extroversion) or proficiency?

2. How far do scaffolding and negotiation behaviours help/fail to help language learning?

3. Is there a significant pedagogical difference between scaffolding and negotiation for meaning, and if so, what is it?

4. How far and in what ways are scaffolding and negotiation influenced i) by different conditions of implementation of a task; and/or ii) by the level of task demand?

10.2.2   Attention capacity and task demand

This sub-theme concerns the nature and impact of task demand on learners' attention or processing capacity, and in particular to its relation to a person's L2 fluency, accuracy and complexity. In principle it allows for the possibility that a task may be seen as varying in its demand for accuracy, fluency or complexity. The kinds of research questions that suggest themselves in this domain tend to concern the relationship between a) the design or implementation of tasks and b) the fluency, accuracy, complexity or learning represented in students use of language.

Example 10.12   Researching attention capacity and task demand (1)

Research question How consistently does a given task lead to a focus on fluency, accuracy or complexity 1) with the same students; 2) with different students?

Problem Much of the research to date has involved one-off (or single-shot) studies of learners' language on tasks. The statistics have on the whole shown interesting patterns, yet it is possible that a second encounter with the same task or with a very similar version of a given task could generate different patterns of response. This question then is very much a replication question: following the studies reported in Chapters 7 and 8, do other groups of students respond to similar tasks in the same ways?

Procedure

i) Select two or three task types which have been shown to differ in the fluency, accuracy or complexity of students' language.
ii) Choose two or three tasks for each type.
iii) Organise the students so that the same students do each of the tasks 6–9 times.
iv) Collect samples of the students' language.
v) Transcribe and analyse the data, to investigate the similarities and differences of the language on the tasks of each type.

Example 10.13   Researching attention capacity and task demand (2)

Research question How far is language learning affected by a learner's orientation to accuracy, fluency or complexity?

Problem Previous studies (e.g. Skehan and Foster, 1997, 1999, 2005) have found evidence that the fluency, accuracy and complexity of a students' language is related to the type of task they are working on. However, it is possible that behind this general pattern some students tend to prioritise fluency, accuracy or complexity differentially, as a result of their own personal orientation. Hence the question arises whether some students tend to prioritise fluency, others accuracy, while a third subgroup aim more to generate complex talk.

Procedure

i) As above, gather data from students doing three types of task that differ in the extent to which students' language tends to be fluent, accurate and complex.
ii) This time explore the differences between individual students in terms of fluency, accuracy and complexity : is the language of some students more consistently fluent, that of others more consistently accurate or complex?

Example 10.14   Researching attention capacity and task demand (3)

Research question Is there a difference in the impact on the learning of vocabulary, or of different aspects of grammar?

   Problem Studies of task-based talk have not paid much attention to the impact of the activity on students' learning. This study raises the issue of whether tasks affect the development of students' vocabulary or of their grammar.

Procedure

i)   Select a task which introduces students to new vocabulary and grammar which they need to use in the course of the task.
ii)   Gather written or recorded samples of students' language.
iii) Analyse it in terms of the occurrence of the target language features.

Carry out a short written test focusing on students' production, recall and interpretation of the targeted features, both post-task and delayed post-task.

Example 10.15   Researching attention capacity and task demand (4)

Research question What is the contribution to learning of attention to each of fluency, accuracy or complexity respectively?

   Problem So far studies have mainly explored the relationship between task, implementation and talk, in terms of fluency, accuracy and complexity. But the key question is what impact does attention to fluency, accuracy and complexity have on learners' language over time? Skehan (1998) suggests that complex language is 'cutting-edge' language, and that it may be more important for language development than increases in accuracy or fluency. So the question is, if students are given tasks which favour fluency, accuracy or complexity, does this affect their development differentially?

Procedure

i)   Select a task type which is thought to privilege accuracy, or fluency, or complexity.
ii)   Provide students with exposure on several occasions to one task type.
iii) Collect written or oral samples of their language.
iv)   Analyse the data to explore how far repeated exposure to one task type consistently results in increases in the target aspect of language processing, or whether the other aspects are also affected.

Example 10.16   Researching attention capacity and task demand (5)

Research question How does a learner's fluency, accuracy and complexity change over time and at what rate?

Example 10.16   (Continued)

Problem Although teachers are constantly confronted by learners' language, for various reasons it is not usually easy to assess their speed of development. This raises the longitudinal issue of the rhythm of development that we can find in terms of learners' fluency, accuracy and complexity. Towell et al. (1996) have shown fluency development over 12 -month periods, but what kinds of change occur over periods 3, 6 or 9 months?

Procedure:

i)   Select a balanced range of tasks for a group of students to use regularly, preferably weekly, over a period of 3, 6 or 9 months.
ii) Gather samples of their language on a three-monthly basis.
iii) Analyse samples of the language at three-month intervals to explore the extent to which their oral or written language changes in terms of fluency, accuracy or complexity.

Example 10.17   Researching attention capacity and task demand (6)

Research question How do fluency, accuracy and complexity on a given task differ at different levels of proficiency?

Problem It can be surprisingly difficult to infer a students' level of proficiency from a transcript of their performance. This may be due to a lack of experience in relating different levels of proficiency to performance on particular tasks. This question seeks to understand how learners' levels of proficiency are reflected in their oral performance of particular tasks. That is, the task is taken as a constant, with differences in patterns of performance taken as a reflection of students level of proficiency.

Procedure

i)   Select 1–3 sample tasks which are all feasible for classes of two or three different levels.
ii) Implement the tasks with each of the classes, gathering samples of their language.
iii) Analyse their oral or written language exploring the similarities and differences in fluency, accuracy and complexity by level.

Example 10.18   Researching attention capacity and task demand (7)

Research question How far does task repetition affect learning or performance in different lexical or grammatical domains?

Problem Task repetition has been studied in terms of global measures of fluency, accuracy and complexity. However, there has been no attempt to explore the possibility that it may affect certain aspects of language use more than others. This question then raises the issue of whether repetition might have a stronger impact on some aspects of language than on others.

Procedure

i) Select a task for individual, pair or group use, which could be repeated in similar form while retaining participants' interest (e.g. repeating the task with a different interlocutor; or repeating it with a slightly different purpose; or with a slightly different arrangement of the same information content).
ii) Get the students to do the task in two or more repetitions.
iii) Gather language data.

Analyse the data to explore possible changes in the language, studying changes in a) vocabulary; b) grammar.

Example 10.19   Researching attention capacity and task demand (8)

Research question How far does learners' awareness of the purpose of task repetition affect their performance?

Problem Rather like the questions raised about scaffolding in the previous section (see section 10.2.1 above), this seeks to explore the issue of whether learners' awareness of the rationale behind a particular pedagogical procedure affects their performance.

Procedure

i) Follow the same steps as in Example 18, but this time brief some of the students and discuss with them the possible value for learners of repeating the same activity.
ii) Explore whether knowledge about the reasons for task repetition affects the impact of repetition on students' language.

Example 10.20   Researching attention capacity and task demand (9)

Research question How far and in what ways does learners' focus of attention vary on successive repetitions of a task? For example, do learners attend serially to complexity, accuracy and fluency through the cycles of repetition (or quasi-repetition) of a given task? If so, are there common ways in which this happens, or do learners differ in this regard?

Problem Previous studies on task repetition have shown various types of impact on performance. However, it is possible that task repetition is exploited by learners in different ways, with learners attending variously to accuracy, complexity or fluency according to inclination. Subsequent enactments of the task, however, could see learners shifting their attention from one facet (e.g. fluency) to another (e.g. complexity or accuracy). If so, this would shed an interesting light on the

---

Example 10.20   (Continued)

ways in which learners attend to different aspects of their performance in turn, gradually integrating them together cyclically as they go.

Procedure
Follow the same procedure as in Example 10.18, but this time work through at least three repetitions, exploring the possibility that learners attend differentially to fluency, accuracy and complexity on each repetition cycle.

10.3   Researching tasks and development

As we saw in Chapter 7, relatively little attention has been paid to language learning in relation to the use of tasks. Samuda's (2001) study showed how tasks can be used to promote learning at various levels in terms of: experiencing an initial need for expressions to represent the target grammatical field; being aware of a lack of relevant lexico-grammatical forms; explicit awareness of new relevant forms; and experiencing the opportunity to use those forms to complete the task in hand. A post-test showed very significant gains in students' knowledge of relevant forms. Mackey's study worked slightly differently, since it relied exclusively on the indirect, non-explicit use of tasks to activate target features of grammar. Results showed that active participation in the tasks led to significantly increased frequency of use of the target forms, although the net increase was modest compared with those obtained by Samuda. Various questions arise, of which samples are given in Examples 10.21–24.

Example 10.21   Researching tasks and development (1)

Research question How far can development through work on tasks be enhanced by using tasks to draw students' attention explicitly to the relevant grammatical field, and to specific target forms?
   Problem The problem focused on here is that few studies (such as Samuda, 2001) have explored the processes whereby tasks can engage different phases of learning. Researching this question would shed light on the potential that tasks have for promoting different phases of learning around a particular language feature.

Procedure
i)   Select a task to target a specific lexico-grammatical domain (such as modality, face, location, time sequence, comparison).
ii) After beginning the task, interrupt the students to obtain an interim report on their progress on the task.

---

iii) Discuss explicitly with only some of the students the linguistic focus of the task.
iv) Compare the performance of those students who had been told explicitly the focus, with the performance of those who weren't briefed.
v) Use the performance data to study patterns of learning of the students.

Example 10.22   Researching tasks and development (2)

Research question Are different teaching strategies needed for different types of grammatical feature?

Problem DeKeyser (2005) argues that there is plenty of evidence for thinking that different aspects of grammar need different learning and teaching procedures. To explore this question, it would be useful to contrast the learning of two or three distinct types of feature, for example, formally and semantically simple (such as the simple past), formally simple and semantically complex (such as the third-person –s), formally simple but semantically complex (such as modal verbs), and formally and semantically complex (such as the present perfect).

Procedure

i)   Select two grammatical features which contrast in terms of their formal and semantic complexity. Select a different task to practice each feature, in different lessons.
ii) With a split design – class A working with task 1, class B working with task 2 – get the students to carry out the tasks.
iii) Gather the students' language data and compare their performances for differences in accuracy and fluency.
iv) Discuss the activities and language with the students, to explore similarities and differences in the learning problems, and the relationship between the use of the features and the tasks.
v)   Consider the roles of explicit and implicit modes of instruction for the two features.
vi) Repeat the use of the tasks, reversing the groups (class A now works with task 2, and class B with task 1) use the tasks, adding in a teaching procedure identified in step v).
vii) Collect samples of the students' language, and debrief the students after completion of the tasks.

Compare the language and students' views at steps vii) and iv).

Example 10.23   Researching tasks and development (3)

Research question What patterns of learning typically arise around the use of tasks through a lesson; within a scheme of work; or through the extent of a course of study (say, one to three terms)?

Problem So far, apart from Samuda (2001), little has been done to track learning through the different phases of a lesson structured around a task. It would be valuable

---

Example 10.23 (Continued)

to have a picture of how learners' understandings change through the pre-, on and post-task phases of a lesson; through a series of lessons; and across a term of work.

Procedure
i) Select a task which can play a constructive role in the teaching of a lesson or unit.
ii) Identify at least three ways in which the task can be used during the lesson or unit.
iii) Teach the lesson/unit, gathering samples of the learners' and teachers' language through the phases.

Analyse the data in order to track the ways in which the learners' language use changes, in ways that might reflect learning across the phases.

Example 10.24 Researching tasks and development (4)

Research question How far does the engagement of strategies (negotiation for meaning or scaffolding) or responses to different task demands (focusing on fluency, accuracy or complexity), or the use of task repetition, impact on short to medium term development?

Problem With some exceptions, little research into negotiation for meaning and scaffolding, or into task demand or task repetition has tracked learning processes through time. Without a more broadly researched landscape, what we know will remain relatively fragile.

Procedure (scaffolding)
i) Select a language domain for attention.
ii) Identify a task which you expect will engage learners in the chosen language domain.
iii) Get groups to undertake the task, gathering language data while they perform it.
iv) Analyse the data studying the ways in which students help each other to manage the language in general, and the chosen domain in particular.

Research methods

Research into learners' language development necessitates either close analysis of learner language (written or transcript data) across the duration of a task (e.g. Lynch and Maclean, 2001), or the use of pre- and post-tests (see the studies by Mackey and Samuda). As in the previous types of study, the researcher needs to make key decisions about the optimal categories of analysis, which here needs to be made in the light of the kinds of development that it is reasonable to anticipate over the time period of the study. For instance, over a three-week period, changes in proficiency may be more apparent in some grammatical domains than in others; over the same time-scale changes in fluency or complexity may be harder to detect.

10.4 Researching teachers' and learners' views of tasks

One of the most important areas of task research is how teachers and learners construe tasks: how do they interpret them, how do they experience them and how do they evaluate them? In spite of its importance, this has only rarely been attended to (exceptions are Murphy, 1993; Garret and Shortall, 2002; Carless, 2004; Lam, 2004; Ortega, 2005 – all, except Carless, focus on learners' perspectives). Here then there is substantial scope for what may turn out to be highly informative research. There is no argument about the need for expert opinion to take full account of teachers' and learners' construals of tasks: their perceptions are bound to be determinant. Various aspects of this theme need attention, which can be divided into the perspectives of teachers, and those of learners.

10.4.1 Teachers' views of tasks

Teachers' construals can be approached from at least three main perspectives. One is in terms of how teachers interpret the *design of tasks*; another is from the perspective of how teachers construe the *use of tasks in the context of particular lessons*, and why; and, more generally, there is the issue of how teachers *evaluate tasks*. Some sample research topics are sketched below.

Example 10.25 Researching teachers' interpretations of the design of tasks (1)

Research question How do teachers differ in their perceptions of the key functions of one or more given tasks?

  Problem A task is designed and used for a purpose, but it is an open question whether designs are interpreted in the same way by teachers as by materials designers. Use of specific tasks to elicit teachers' perceptions would provide better grounding for the data than relying on the use of simple open questions without specific tasks to refer to. Such data would also help us understand how teachers relate task designs to tasks in action.

Procedure

i) Using a case study design, select three simple tasks which you are familiar with.
ii) Invite three teachers to agree to be interviewed individually about the tasks.

Example 10.25   (Continued)

iii) Prepare a series of interview questions focusing on the following points: a) Ask the teacher to describe each of the tasks. b) what main differences does the teacher see between the three tasks? c) focusing on one selected task, what language is the task likely to activate? d) how are the learners likely to carry it out? e) what strengths and weaknesses does the teacher see in the task?

iv) Carry out the same interview with the other two teachers.

v) Analyse the interview, looking for similarities and differences in their 'reading' of the tasks.

vi) Compare teachers' accounts with the comments of the materials designers.

Example 10.26   Researching teachers' interpretations of the design of tasks (2)

Research question How does the extent of a teachers' professional experience relate to the way they interpret the design of a task?

Problem Samuda (2006) reported striking differences in the ways in which more and less experienced teachers used the same task during similar lessons. It would be useful to understand how far teachers' experience helps to mediate the relationship between design and interpretation.

Procedure

i) Follow the same case design and procedures as for Example 10.25, but selecting as participants teachers with different numbers of years' teaching experience. To ensure a reasonable difference of perspective, try to find three participants, one with 1–3 years' experience, one with 6–9 years' experience, and one with 12–15 years' experience.

ii) Analyse the data, and compare and contrast the perspectives of the three participants.

iii) To cross-check the reliability of the study, gradually extend it by additional sets of three participants, one from each of the experience bands.

Example 10.27   Researching teachers' views on the use of tasks within lessons (1)

Research question How do teachers envisage introducing, implementing, monitoring and concluding the use of a given task a) within a lesson; b) within a scheme of work?

Problem Understanding teacher thinking about tasks would be deepened by getting a picture of how they conceptualise the procedures they would use in handling tasks. Note that this issue would be usefully complemented by a cycle of in-class observation and post-observation discussion.

Procedure

i) Once again, use a case study design. This study is likely to be relatively labour-intensive, so it would be sensible to work with one teacher at a time.
ii) Select three tasks and invite a teacher to choose one to work with.
iii) As a warm-up phase, ask the teacher first to describe the task.
iv) Next explore how the teacher might introduce the task, what the teacher might do next, and how the teacher might use the task through a lesson.
v) If possible, observe the teacher working with this or similar task in a lesson, making an audio recording to complement fieldnotes.
vi) Shortly after the lesson, negotiate a time to discuss what students and teacher did through the lesson.
vii) Analyse the preliminary interview, the observation and the post-lesson interview, tracking similarities and differences between intension, action, and post-lesson comments.

Example 10.28   Researching teachers' views on the use of tasks within lessons (2)

Research question What roles do teachers see for the use of tasks within lessons?
   Problem Tasks can be used for awareness-raising, as a context for teaching (both as in Samuda, 2001), or as a context for practice (as in Samuda, 2001) and extension (as in Lynch and Maclean, 2001). Insights into these possibilities might be significantly enhanced through the study of teachers' perspectives.

Procedure

i) Once again, a case study approach is likely to be the most productive procedure for this kind of investigation.
ii) Invite the teacher to select a task they would be likely to use.
iii) Using an interview procedure, explore how and why they would use it, enquiring particularly into the various alternative uses the teacher could envisage for the task; if the teacher does not volunteer alternative uses, suggest some yourself for the teacher's consideration.

Example 10.29   Researching teachers' evaluation of tasks

Research question What are teachers' evaluations of the role and use of tasks in general within the language curriculum?
   Problem Tasks have tended to be seen in isolation from other aspects of the curriculum. This research question seeks to investigate how teachers contextualise their perspectives on tasks as one pedagogical resource within the overall context of a teaching programme.

Procedure

i) Could be conducted as a case study or a group design, using interview or questionnaire procedures.

Example 10.29   (Continued)

ii) Working with a range of titles and samples of tasks, first of all ensure the teachers are familiar with them all, by inviting them to group the tasks according to whatever criteria they choose, to consider the purposes each might be used for, and the levels of proficiency they might be most useful for.

iii) Then move into a phase where you elicit from the teachers their views of the strengths and weaknesses of each, moving into a rating or ranking activity, in which they rate each on a Likert-type scale from 1 to 5, or rank them in order of preference; invite them to comment orally or in writing on their ratings/rankings.

iv) This investigation could conclude by exploring teachers' perceptions of the teaching/learning potential of each task.

10.4.2   Learners' views of tasks

As Breen (1987) and van Lier (1996) among others have pointed out, learners are a particularly crucial source of information and insights into the project of using tasks within the language classroom: what happens to tasks-in-action depends ultimately on how learners understand them, use them, and evaluate them. Students' views may well provide insights into how their design might be improved, into alternative ways of using them and into ways of briefing future students. This suggests various potential research topics and questions, as mapped out in Examples 10.30 and 10.31.

Example 10.30   Researching tasks in action: learners' perceptions of tasks

Research question a) Are there differences in what students perceive to be happening across different types of tasks-in-action, and what reasons do they see for the way they handle the different tasks?

   Problem In exploring the relationship between task-as-workplan and task-in-action, it is important to understand how students themselves view the tasks. This should shed some light on how they use the tasks in practice, and could open the way to altering the ways tasks are used.

Procedure

i)   Work with a group of students who have used a small range of specific tasks.

ii) Through questionnaires and/or interviews, explore their perceptions of what happens on the different tasks, and why.

Research question b) How do students perceive the pedagogical *use* of one or more given tasks within a lesson, including the pre-task introduction, and any post-task follow-up? In their view, what do the tasks contribute to the lesson, and to their learning within the lesson?

Problem This is an extension of the previous question, moving into the issue of how students perceive the teachers' use of tasks, and how they see the tasks as contributing to the lesson as a whole.

i) Work with a group of students who have used a particular task.
ii) Through questionnaires and/or interviews, explore their perceptions and understandings of how the teacher uses the task, whether they view this positively or negatively, what alternatives they suggest and why.

Research question c) How do students construe the interaction patterns on different types of task?

Problem The question here addresses the problem of how aware students are of the processes by which tasks are completed. As with the preceding questions, this could inform teachers' selection and use of tasks.

i) Work with a group of students who have used one or more particular tasks.
ii) Through questionnaire, interview, or perhaps best a stimulated recall procedure, explore with them what they perceive and understand of the ways in which they carried out a particular task.

Example 10.31   Researching tasks in action: Tasks and learner differences

Research question: Do students have different focuses, styles and strategies in their use of tasks? Why, and what are the implications?

Problem Education must allow for the fact that whatever pedagogical procedures are developed, students differ in the ways in which they perceive them and in the ways they work. Given that uniformity of response is impossible, it becomes essential to find out and attempt to understand the perceptions and responses of different students.

Procedure

i) Design a questionnaire with closed and open questions, aimed at exploring the students' own individual perceptions and evaluations of different tasks.
ii) Design a follow-up interview to carry out with a small group of students selected for their variety of response.

Research question: What if any differences are there in students' perceptions of tasks at different levels of proficiency and language learning experience?

Problem Proficiency may make a difference to students' perceptions and responses.

Procedure

i) Follow similar questionnaire and interview procedures as in the preceding projects in this section, but this time ensuring roughly equal sized samples of students at different levels of proficiency.
ii) Compare the responses across proficiency levels.

Research methods

To gather data on the perspectives of teachers and learners, some kind of self-report procedures are needed (see Robson, 2002; Cohen, Manion and Morrison, 2000, for introductory accounts). These might involve the use of questionnaires (Dörnyei, 2003), individual or group interviews, personal construct repertory grids (Roberts, 1999) or stimulated recall procedures (Gass and Mackey, 2000). As with the other kinds of study discussed in this chapter, a key issue once again is the focus and categories of the analysis.

Categories can be derived from the data themselves. Personal construct techniques are the archetype of this approach to the identification of data categories, but an exploratory approach to data can also be used in the analysis of open questions within questionnaires, to the analysis of interview data and in the analysis of stimulated recall data. However as we noted above, as with other types of research, where theoretically and pedagogically interesting categories can be found in previous research or in theoretical reflection, it is legitimate to use these with a view to deepening our understanding of their legitimacy and applicability.

10.5　Researching tasks in their ecological context

The final but in many ways the most crucial area for us to consider is that of the contexts in which the tasks are studied. Throughout this volume we have been studying research into pedagogical tasks. Our approach has been to see tasks as phenomena that can only be understood in action, that is, as events determined and interpreted by participants. Pedagogical tasks need to be studied within pedagogical contexts. This is because, as Bruner noted (see Part 1), action on tasks is heavily influenced by the context, since it is the context that provides the primary grounds for the participants' interpretations of what they are doing and why they are doing it. This is bound to affect the kinds and qualities of action they engage in. Participants will respond differently to a task being used for testing purposes, compared with a task being used for a specified pedagogic purpose or to one being used with purposes unspecified. In other words, if we are interested in researching tasks for pedagogic purposes, it is essential that research focuses precisely on the use of for pedagogic purposes.

In terms of research topics, all those outlined in the previous sections of this chapter deserve study within classroom contexts. However, some particular themes deserve mention here, notably those concerned with the contribution of tasks to classroom learning, and a sample is given in Example 10.32.

Example 10.32   Researching tasks in classroom contexts: some topics for investigation

a) Teachers' strategic uses (including adaptations) of tasks within lessons

Problem In the context of lessons, teachers use tasks for particular purposes. At different points in the lesson these may differ in many ways from those for which the tasks were originally designed: what purposes, and why? Understanding this could contribute to an understanding of the pedagogical uses of tasks.

Procedure

i)   Identify a teacher who would be interested in getting observation and feedback on their use of a task during a lesson.
ii)   Invite the teacher to identify aspects of their use of the task which they would like to focus on. Note any aspects you would be interested in observing.
iii) Observe, take fieldnotes and record the lesson.
iv) Copy your notes and the recording of the lesson, providing a copy of each to the teacher.
v)   Both you and the teacher read the notes and view the recording separately. Note as you go anything relating to the pre-selected aspects. Note down anything else that strikes you.
vi) Meet the teacher and, with their permission, record the meeting.
vii) Invite them to take you through the things they noticed, describing and commenting. Do the same yourself.
viii) Write up a report of the findings, relating the recorded data, the observations and comments.

b) The relationship between task-based work and teacher talk (particularly in terms of plenary input and feedback)

Problem The discourse of a task needs to be related to the use of language in the classroom immediately before, during and after the task. What is the relationship, why and what is its pedagogical importance?

Procedure

Following steps i) and ii) in the procedure above, record a lesson and analyse the teacher's discourse in relation to the phases of task activity.

c) The contribution of tasks to learning within a lesson and/or within a scheme of work

Problem Within the classroom context tasks play a role over time: how do they contribute to learning within a scheme of work running over several lessons?

Procedure

i)   Following steps i) and ii) above, carry out a series of recordings following a scheme of work across a sequence of lessons.

Example 10.32   (Continued)

ii) Analyse the use of similar or related tasks across the lessons.

d) The nature of the selection, and the types of implementation, of tasks throughout a syllabus/curriculum

Problem Studying the use of a single task at a given point in time may not reveal the range of types of task or of the variety of ways they are used throughout a course or programme of studies. Studying the use of tasks over a broader time frame would provide a fuller picture of their ranges of use.

Procedure

Using your own class, or with the help of colleagues' classes within a year-round syllabus, carry out a questionnaire and/or interview survey focusing on the range, interest, implementation type, and learning value, of tasks used during the year.

e) The relationship between tasks and end-of-year assessment/examinations

Problem So far, tasks have been studied without reference to the overall assessment criteria used on a programme of studies. It would help to inform pedagogy to understand the roles tasks can play in preparing students for end-of-course assessment.

Procedure

i)   Select one more end-of-year exams and collect sample tasks from the relevant year's programme.
ii) Compare and contrast the design of the tasks and the language used on the exam tasks and the coursework tasks.

f) The evaluation of task design and pedagogical value of tasks by teachers, materials and task designers, and testers

Problem For a fuller understanding of the design and pedagogical value of tasks these need to be set within the broader context of the perceptions of teachers, materials designers, and testers.

Procedure

i)   Invite a small sample of two examiners, two test task designers, two materials designers and two experienced teachers to participate in the study.
ii) Select three representative tasks.
iii) Conduct and record an interview with each, asking them to describe each task, concentrate on describing how they think one of the tasks could be used, what language activity it would be likely to give rise to, how it might contribute to learning, how the teacher might use it, and what its key design features are.
iv) Analyse the interviews, and compare and contrast the perspectives of the different interviewees.

The final topic of this set – topic f – connects the classroom-based research to outside expertise. Topic f opens the channel between the design of tasks and task designers – who may or may not have adequate experience of the pedagogical use of their tasks – and researchers also and explicitly explores the relationship between classroom-based data and the views of language teaching professionals on tasks in language learning. As we said at the outset, the use of tasks in language pedagogy is a hypothesis. However practically and theoretically well informed, our disciplinary commitment is above all to the use of empirical data as a basis for developing pedagogical programmes: if the data suggest that tasks can at best have a limited role in classroom language learning, then to the extent that the data is robust, language pedagogy will be strengthened.

Research methods

It is clear that the area of pedagogical tasks is in urgent need of research contextualised within teaching programmes. Reliance on research gathered from non-pedagogical context runs the risk of lacking relevance and validity. For instance, a laboratory study may well show that fluency can be promoted by task repetition (e.g. Bygate, 2001), but this result could be an artefact of the fact that students were repeating the task for no obvious purpose, and as a result simply wished to complete it as quickly as possible. Furthermore, laboratory studies omit all kinds of contextual factors which could contribute very significantly to the impact of the task. This applies also to studies conducted within classroom contexts, where the activities are not part of a normal teaching plan: the lack of pedagogical motivation is bound to leave a question mark over how the participants construed and engaged in the task. In contrast, within a teaching plan, the teacher's explanation of the rationale behind the use of repetition could well enhance its impact on students' fluency; but equally possible, the classroom context could serve to draw students' attention to other aspects of their performance, such as their lexico-grammatical formulation or their accuracy. Laboratory-type research clearly has a role to play in initial investigations of the impact of different types of design and implementation. However ultimately what matters most is the nature of tasks-in-action in classroom contexts, in interaction with other pedagogical phenomena. For this to be possible, it is important for research to be able to access pedagogical processes within classroom contexts.

Yet, in Chapters 8 and 9 we noted the occupational paradox (see also Edwards, 2006), that while on their own full-time researchers are generally not best situated to investigate what teachers see as most needing investigation, in turn teachers are generally not best placed in terms of workloads to carry out the research themselves. As an alternative we propose the development of collaborative projects focusing on teacher-driven and research-supported enquiry. In this model, teachers play a central role in determining the context and focus of the research and in providing the participants and data, while researchers carry out an enabling role in providing the terms for focusing the research, in shaping the content and design, and in carrying out the analysis. Defined and implemented in this way, research projects can be optimally grounded in the perspectives of teachers and learners, appropriate data can be made accessible, and at the same time, the additional workload of the research is lifted off the shoulders of the full-time teacher. In other words, this kind of model is most likely to avoid the twin dangers of teacher overload on the one hand, and loss of pedagogical focus on the other. Examples of research designed in this way are the Birkdale project funded at Leeds (see Cameron et al., 1996), and the task-based teaching project funded at the Institute of Education in Hong Kong (see Lam et al., 2005). The model resembles in many ways that of the 'Design Experiment' (Gorard et al., 2004).

In education, the design experiment typically involves the systematic longitudinal study of a pedagogical practice *in situ*, through the collaborative involvement of one or more teachers and researchers. This hinges on the agreement of teachers and researchers on the value of carefully documenting the systematic use of some pedagogical innovation. Hence, at the outset, the focus of the research has to be carefully negotiated between teachers and researchers. If agreed, the pay-off for the researcher is the potential for direct contribution of teaching expertise into the design and evaluation of the project, and the generation of significant amounts of ecologically valid data. For the teacher, it is direct involvement in and feedback from an exploratory project.

In research into the use of pedagogical tasks, this structure could enable a focus on the pedagogically motivated involvement of teacher and students in activities they see as relevant. This could includes matters such as the selection of tasks which the teacher is willing to use to teach with; the embedding of the task within a lesson (and preferably within a scheme of work) focusing on material on which the students will expect to be assessed; the participation of intact classes; the accessibility of the lesson for the collection of oral and/or written language data; the possibility of gathering pre- and post-test data from the participating students; and the availability of teacher and students to generate introspective report data.

An issue related to that of ecological context in contemporary research concerns the derivation of categories of analysis (such as definitions of

linguistic features, interaction features (such as scaffolding or negotiation for meaning), or learning strategies of processes. Some argue that
categories of analysis should be derived afresh from each data sample, so
as to respect the uniqueness of the participants and the event being
researched and avoid distorting the data by importing pre-established
assumptions; while others tend to adopt an approach in which new data
is used to investigate and if appropriate develop pre-existing categories.
Clearly both approaches are justified (we noted in Chapter 8 that
Ortega, 2005, adopted a similar stance). Our field is young, much of the
research undertaken so far has been groundbreaking, and as a result the
selection or identification of categories of analysis (as much as the choice
of the data) has generally been a matter of trial and error. So for some
time to come it will be necessary to explore new data samples in their
own terms: it would be a mistake to assume that we know enough about
any of the potential categories of analysis to be confident of their relevance in the handling of any research question, and by implication in
the definition of those questions. So we should not be limited by our
available terminology.

Nonetheless re-application of previously used or theoretically derived
categories is also important. That is because new research projects shed
light not only on the nature of the data, but also on the categories we use
to describe it. So as a field we also need to be searching for replicability,
commonalities, generic differences, that is, for the emergence through
empirical research of categories of analysis which we understand in terms
of what they mean in relation to other categories and in relation to language use, language proficiency, language development, and language pedagogy. In other words, new studies should also help to clarify the categories
used to analyse the phenomena (whether of formulaic sequences, of discourse patterns, of fluency, accuracy or complexity), rather than ignoring the tools used in previous studies. Every new analysis of data need
not then aim to generate new categories of analysis: some can, but what
is needed is an interplay between exploring familiar categories and testing them against potential new categories derived from appropriate
informants, notably from teachers and learners, but also from relevant
others, such as materials designers, teacher educators, and researchers.

Part 4
Resources

11
Further Resources

11.1   Books

Throughout this book, we have referred to a range of multidisciplinary influences on tasks in second language research and pedagogy. For ease of reference we bring together here a list of books that specifically focus on tasks in second language pedagogy/task-based learning theory and practice that we would consider essential readings on the topic.

Books primarily focused on theoretical/empirical perspectives on tasks

Bygate, M., Skehan. P. and Swain, M. (eds.) 2001. *Researching pedagogic tasks: second language learning, teaching and testing.* Harlow: Pearson Education.

Candlin, C. N. and Murphy, D. F. (eds.) 1987. *Language learning tasks.* Lancaster Practical Papers in English Language Education, Vol. 7. Lancaster and London: Lancaster University Institute for English Language Education, also published by Pergamon Press.

Crookes, G. and Gass, S. (eds.) 1993a. *Tasks in a pedagogical context: integrating theory and practice.* Clevedon: Multilingual Matters.

Crookes, G. and Gass, S. (eds.) 1993b. *Tasks and language learning: integrating theory and practice.* Clevedon: Multilingual Matters.

Ellis, R. 2003. *Task-based language learning and teaching.* Oxford: Oxford University Press.

Johnson, K. 2003. *Designing language teaching tasks.* Basingstoke: Palgrave Macmillan.

Skehan, P. 1998. *A cognitive approach to language learning.* Oxford: Oxford University Press.

Yule, G. 1997. *Referential communication tasks.* Mahwah, NJ: Lawrence Erlbaum.

Other key publications have appeared as articles in refereed journals, as noted below in section 11.4.

Books primarily focused on the use of tasks in pedagogic contexts

Edwards, C. and Willis, J. (eds.) 2005. *Teachers exploring tasks.* Basingstoke: Palgrave Macmillan.
Estaire, S. and Zanón, J. 1994. *Planning classwork: a task based approach.* Oxford: Macmillan Heinemann.
Leaver, B. L. and Willis, J. (eds.) 2004. *Task-based instruction in foreign language education.* Washington, DC: Georgetown University Press.
Lee, J. F. 2000. *Tasks and communicating in language classrooms.* Boston, MA: McGraw-Hill.
Legutke, M. and Thomas, H. 1991. *Process and experience in the language classroom.* Harlow: Longman.
Nunan, D. 1989. *Designing tasks for the communicative classroom.* Cambridge: Cambridge University Press.
Nunan, D. 2004. *Task-based language teaching.* Cambridge: Cambridge University Press.
Prabhu, N. S. 1987. *Second language pedagogy.* Oxford: Oxford University Press.
Ribé, R. and Vidal, N. 1993. *Project work step by step.* Oxford: Macmillan Heinemann.
Van den Branden, K. 2006. *Task-based language education: from theory to practice* Cambridge: Cambridge University Press.
Willis, J. 1996. *A framework for task-based learning.* Harlow: Addison Wesley Longman.
Willis, D. and Willis, J. 2007 *Doing task-based teaching.* Oxford: Oxford University Press.

To these we would add the following as key influences in shaping the perspective on tasks and second language learning explored in this book:

Barnes, D. 1976. *From communication to curriculum.* Harmondsworth: Penguin Books.
Brumfit, C. J. 1984. *Communicative methodology in language teaching.* Cambridge: Cambridge University Press.
Bruner, J. S. 1960 (2nd edn. 1977). *The process of education.* Cambridge, MA: Harvard University Press.
Dewey, J. 1910/1991. *How we think.* Amherst: Prometheus.
Dewey, J. 1938/1963. *Experience and education: The Kappa Delta Phi lecture series..* Toronto: Collier Books.
Freinet, E. 1971. *Naissance d'une pedagogie populaire.* Paris: Maspéro.

Freire, P. 1970. *Pedagogy of the oppressed*. Harmondsworth: Penguin Books.

Kilpatrick, W. H. 1918/1922. *The project method: the use of the purposeful act in the educative process*. New York: Teachers College, Columbia University. 3–18. Reprinted from *Teachers College Record* XIX.4. September 1918.

Kolb, D. 1984. *Experiential learning: experience as the source of learning and development*. Englewood Cliffs, NJ: Prentice-Hall.

Mohan, B. 1985. *Language and content*. Reading, MA: Addison-Wesley.

Swales, J. 1990. *Genre analysis: English in academic and research settings*. Cambridge: Cambridge University Press.

Van Lier, L. 1996. *Interaction in the language curriculum: awareness, autonomy, and authenticity*. London: Longman.

Widdowson, H. G. 1978. *Teaching language as communication*. Oxford: Oxford University Press.

11.2   Professional associations/dedicated websites/specialist conferences TBLT

Organises biennial international conferences bringing together practitioners and researchers to reflect on the potential of task-based language teaching for promoting first, second, and foreign language acquisition.

First annual TBLT conference: 'From Theory to Practice' September 2005, Leuven, Belgium. This conference focused on the implementation of TBLT in the classroom, exploring the theoretical rationale behind task-based language teaching and what needs to be done (in terms of teacher training, syllabus and curriculum development, development of assessment tools, etc.) to make TBLT 'work' in the real world.

Second annual TBLT conference: 'TBLT: Putting Principles to Work', September 2007, University of Hawai'I, Manoa, Honolulu. The conference aims to provide al forum for the dissemination of original, unpublished, or in-press work on empirical, theoretical, and educational dimensions of TBLT.

TBLT webpages, with links of interest to task researchers and practitioners: www.tblt2007.org

11.3   Related professional associations and conferences

Issues relating to theoretical and applied aspects of tasks in second language learning are also regularly addressed at major international conferences. These include:

AAAL (American Association of Applied Linguistics)
www.aaal.org/

BAAL (British Association of Applied Linguistics)
www.baal.org.uk/

AILA (Association Internationale de Linguistique Appliquée: http://
www.aila.soton.ac.uk/aila_news01.html)

EuroSLA (European Second Language Association)
http://www.swan.ac.uk/cals/eurosla/index.htm

SLRF (Second Language Research Forum)
slrf@u.washington.edu

PacSLRF (Pacific Second Language Research Forum)
http://www.uq.edu.au/slccs/AppliedLing/pacslrf/

EUROCALL (European Association for Computer Assisted Language
Learning)
http://www.eurocall-languages.org/

TESOL (Teachers of English to Speakers of Other Languages)
http://www.tesol.org/s_tesol/index.asp

IATEFL (International Association of Teachers of English as a Foreign
Language)
http://www.iatefl.org/

RELC (Regional Language Centre)
http://www.relc.org.sg/

JALT (Japan Association for Language Teaching)
http://www.jalt.org/

11.4   Journals

At the time of writing, there are no journals exclusively dedicated to task
research/pedagogy. However, theoretical, empirical and applied perspectives on tasks and task-based learning are represented in the major journals in the field.

Applied Linguistics
http://www3.oup.co.applij

Language Learning
http://www.blackwellpublishing.com/journal.asp?ref=0023-8333

Language Teaching Research
http://www.arnoldpublishers.com/JOURNALS/pages/lan_tea/13621688.htm

Studies in Second Language Acquisition
http://journals.cambridge.org/action/displayAbstract?fromPage=online&aid=36405

TESOL Quarterly
http://www.tesol.edu/pubs/amrz/tq.html

System
http://www.elsevier.nl/inca/publications/store/3/3/5

Modern Language Journal
http://polyglot.lss.wisc.edu/mlj

International Journal of Applied Linguistics
http://www.blackwellpublishing.com/journal.asp?ref=0802-6106

English Language Teaching Journal
eltj.oxfordjournals.org

Journal of Applied Linguistics
http://www.equinoxpub.com

11.5   Further useful associations and websites

Here we include associations and websites relating to work not directly associated with tasks, but which have been influential on aspects of the thinking represented in this book.

Current work following Freinet's pedagogy:
Fédération Internationale des Mouvements d'Ecole Moderne
www.freinet.org
Pédagogie Freinet
www.pemf.fr

Current work in the Freirean tradition:
Instituto Paulo Freire
www.paulofreire.org
www.pucsp.br/paulofreire

Experiential education
Association for Experiential Education (AEE)
www.aee.org

Discussion list AEELIST: listserv@pucc.princeton.edu
Email: info@aee.org

Further resources for experientially-oriented work
Foxfire (magazine and books grounded in local community and culture
    written and published by high school students)
www.foxfire.org
foxfiremagazine@yahoo.com

'Learning how to learn' guide for students based on Kolb's experien
tial cycle
www.ic.polyu.edu.hk.posh97

Center for Business Simulations
www.towson.edu/~absel/
Discussion list ABSEL: mailserv@toe.towson.edu

Association for Business Simulation and Experiential Learning (ABSEL)
Discussion list ABSEL: mailserv@toe.towson.edu
Website: www.towson.edu/~absel/

Professional development through experiential learning
http://www.virtualteamworks.com/

Webheads
On-line communities of practice, including:

Webheads in Action brings together language teaching professionals and
language learners for collaborative projects; exploration of web-based
tools for personal and professional development; pooling of mutual
expertise on web technology; opportunities to experiment with emerg
ing technology, and much more (including open enrolment language
courses where these principles are put into practice).

Writing for Webheads: brings together native and non-speakers worldwide
to participate on writing projects, and to provide a supportive develop
ment for language development.
Webheads also host webcasts, sykpecasts and chatrooms.
http://webheadsinaction.org
http://webheads.info

Dogme ELT
Online discussion of issues relating to Dogme ELT principles and prac
tices, and links to teachers who have adopted Dogme principles in thei
teaching:
www.groups.yahoo.com/group/dogme

11.6   Design guides for the development of second language pedagogic tasks

In this section we note manuals offering practical guidance on aspects of second language pedagogic task design and development, specifically intended for language teachers unfamiliar with task design/novice task designers:

Mackey, A. and McDonough, K. 1998. *Tasks for communication and grammar: Thai and Japanese*. Center for Language Education and Development, Michigan State University Press.

Practical guide to the development of tasks for the teaching of Thai and Japanese, grounded in empirical studies of task interaction. Sample tasks, and guidance on how they could be adapted/modified.

Samuda, V., Johnson, K. and Ridgway, J. 2000. *Designing language learning tasks: a guide*. Vol. 1. Working Papers on Task Design, Department of Linguistics and Modern English Language. University of Lancaster.

Task-driven practical design guide for teachers, grounded in empirical studies of working practices of task designers and teachers, focuses on design procedures, design features and criteria for task evaluation. Glossary of design terminology and sample tasks.

Other task design issues are reflected in contributions to *Folio*, the journal of the Materials Development Association (MATSDA), who also run annual conferences on all aspects of materials design and development:
http://www.matsda.org.uk/
Guidance on aspects of task design can also be found in sections of a number of the books listed above in 11.1.

11.7   Databases: learner corpora

Current learner spoken and written and corpora have been for the most part compiled from academic essays, interviews, and academic speech events, with little attention specifically focused on learner performance on pedagogic tasks. However an interesting development is:

SULEC (Santiago University Learner English Corpus)
A corpus of oral and written learners' working with materials collected from learners of all levels (elementary, intermediate and advanced), including pedagogic tasks:
http://www.usc.es/ia303/SULEC/SULeC.htm

11.8 Resources for task design and development from other domains

Here we list a selection of resources for task design and development in other domains which we consider potentially relevant for aspects of the design and development of L2 pedagogic tasks. However, many of these frameworks/design criteria require considerable modification/adaptation to accommodate the needs of second language learners (although see 'TalenQuests' for one way of approaching this; Koenraad and Westhoff 2003), and so readers are invited to apply with caution and in light of issues raised throughout this book.

Webquests: Web-based tasks on a broad range of topics, widely used across the school curriculum.

For a taxonomy of task types (retelling, compilation, analytical, creative judgment, self-knowledge *inter alia*), criteria for developing well-designed tasks in each category and numerous exemplars: http://edweb.sdsu.edu/webquest/taskonomy.html

For a WebQuest design guide:
http://edweb.sdsu.edu/webquest/task-design-worksheet.html
TalenQuests: An adaptation of the WebQuest format to meet the needs of second language learners, incorporating scaffolding activities, form focus guides, text tools and strategy guidance. Examples:
http://www.talenquest.nl

Authentic Task Design: Interdisciplinary tasks for use in web-based learning environments. Key characteristics: real-world relevance, open to multiple interpretation, open to investigation over a period of time, collaborative, reflective, interdisciplinary, enable diverse roles and expertise, permit a diversity of outcomes, culminate in the creation of a whole product rather than a preparation for something else. Although developed for web-based content learning, also applicable to language learning tasks in blended and face-face-face environments.

For theoretical framework, examples and design criteria:
http://www.authentictasks.uow.edu.au/

PALS: Interactive resource bank for science performance and assessment tasks, indexed via the US National Science Education Standards.

Numerous examples of poorly/well-designed tasks; practical guidance on task design from scratch/adaptation of existing tasks, and design criteria potentially applicable to aspects of second language pedagogic task design: pals.sri.com/guide/tasksdetail.html

Problem-Based Learning: An active, collaborative approach to the development of problem-solving skills in tandem with the acquisition of basic knowledge based on case studies and problem scenarios; widely used in medical education, a range of other professional domains and also as a model for lifelong learning.

Examples on the application of PBL principles in different domains and approaches to task design and materials development potentially applicable to L2 task contexts:

http://www.materials.ac.uk/guides/pbl.asp
http://www.pbli.org/
www.economicsnetwork.ac.uk/handbook/pbl/31.htm
http://lifelonglearning.cqu.edu.au

MARS (Mathematics Assessment Resource Service): Tasks for mathematics teaching: focuses on the use of 'rich, substantial' tasks close to those that students need to be able to tackle to be effective in everyday life and work.

Design guidelines, wide range of tasks, examples of how students work on them and how they are assessed. Potentially of interest for aspects of the development of L2 pedagogic tasks:

http://www.nottingham.ac.uk/education/MARS/tasks/

11.9 Potential material for task development

We list here a small selection of sites and corpora that could be used as resources for task content material.

Directories of links to earth science resources:
http://www.met.fsu.edu/explores/explores.html
http://www.energyquest.ca.gov/links/index.php?pagetype=energyed
Links to international news media, archived by theme/topic:
http://www.currentaffairs.com/

Space for artists to share work + links to related arts/media sites:
http://www.art.net/

Anti-racist, inter-cultural websites, seen through the eyes of young people from Spain, Sweden, Britain and Holland:
http://www.britkid.org http://www.eurokid.org
Also see the WebQuest and TalenQuest links above for numerous other resources

Corpora
MICASE: approximately 1.7 million words; academic speech events:
www.hti.umich.edu/m/micase

Corpus of Spoken Professional American English: interactions in professional settings
http://www.athel.com/cpsa.html

CANCODE: corpus of spoken English
http://www.cambridge.org/elt/corpus/cancode.htm

BNC: 100 million words: written and spoken language from a wide range of sources:
http://www.natcorp.ox.ac.uk/

References

Ada, A. F. 2003 (2nd edition). *A magical encounter: Latino children's literature in the classroom*. Harlow: Allyn & Bacon

Ada, A. F. and Campoy, I. 2003. *Authors in the classroom: a transformative education process*. Harlow: Allyn & Bacon

Aljaafreh, A. and Lantolf, J. P. 1998. Negative feedback as regulation and second language learning in the zone of proximal development. *The modern language journal* 78: 465–83

Allwright, R. L. 1984. The importance of interaction in classroom language learning. *Applied linguistics* 5: 156–71

Anderson and Lynch, T. 1988. *Listening*. Oxford: Oxford University Press.

Arndt, V. 1987. Six writers in search of texts. *ELTJ* 41: 257–67

Artigal, J. M. 1991. The Catalan immersion program: the joint creation of shared indexical territory. *Journal of multilingual and multicultural development* 12/1&2 *Infantil*. Infancia y Aprendizaje. N 86

Artigal, J. M. 2005. *Ready for a story*. Barcelona: Josep Maria Editor

Aston, G. 1986. Trouble-shooting interaction with learners: the more the merrier? *Applied linguistics* 7: 128–43

Auerbach, E. R. 1992. *Making meaning, making change: participatory curriculum development for adult ESL literacy*. McHenry, IL: Center for Applied Linguistics/Delta Systems

Auerbach, E. and Wallerstein, N. 1987. *ESL for action: problem-posing at work*. Reading, MA: Addison-Wesley

Baddeley, A. 1991. *Human memory*. Mahwah, NJ: Lawrence Erlbaum.

Barnes, D. 1976. *From communication to curriculum*. Harmondsworth: Penguin Books

Barnes, D. and Todd, F. 1977. *Communicating and learning in small groups*. London: Routledge & Kegan Paul

Barnes, D. and Todd, F. 1995. *Communication and learning revisited: making meaning through talk*. Portsmouth, NH: Boynton/Cook, Heinemann

Beckett, G.H. and Miller, P.C. (eds) 2006. *Project-based second and foreign language education*. Charlotte, N.C: Information Age Publishing

Bereiter, C. and Scardamalia, M. 1993. *Surpassing ourselves: an inquiry into the nature and implications of expertise*. Chicago and La Salle, IL: Open Court

Beretta, A. 1990. Implementation of the Bangalore Project. *Applied Linguistics* 11.4: 321–37

Beretta, A. and Davies, A. 1985. 'Evaluation of the Bangalore Project'. *ELT journal* 39.2: 121–7

Bialystok, E. 1990. *Communication strategies: a psychological analysis of second-language use*. Oxford: Basil Blackwell

Biggs, J. and Lam, R. 1997. Teaching through Action Learning: helping innovation in Hong Kong. *New horizons in education* 38: 76–84

Blake, R. J. and Zyzik, E. C. 2003. Who's helping whom? Learner/heritage-speakers' networked discussions in Spanish. *Applied linguistics* 24/4: 519–44

Bongaerts, T. and Poulisse, N. 1989. Communication strategies in L1 and L2: same or different? *Applied linguistics* 10: 253–68

Breen, M. P. 1987. Learner contributions to task design. In Candlin, C. N. and Murphy, D. F. (eds.) *Language learning tasks*. Lancaster Practical Papers in English Language Education, Vol. 7. Lancaster and London: Lancaster University

Breen, M. P. (ed.) 2001. *Learner contributions to language learning: new directions in research*. Harlow: Pearson Education

Breen, M. P. and Candlin, C. N. 1980. The essentials of a communicative curriculum in language teaching. *Applied linguistics* 1/2: 89–112

Breen, M. P. and Littlejohn, A. 2000. The significance of negotiation. In Breen, M. P. and Littlejohn, A. (eds.) *Classroom decision-making: negotiation and process syllabuses in practice*. Cambridge: Cambridge University Press: 5–38

Brindley, G. and Slatyer, H. 2002. Exploring task difficulty in ESL listening assessment. *Language testing* 19.4: 369–94

Brinton, D., Snow, M. A. and Wesche, M. B. 1989. *Content-based second language instruction*. New York: Newbury House

Brown, G. and Yule, G. 1983. *Teaching the spoken language*. Cambridge: Cambridge University Press

Brown, G., Anderson, A., Shillcock, R. and Yule, G. 1984. *Teaching talk: strategies for production and assessment*. Cambridge: Cambridge University Press

Brumfit, C. J. 1978. 'Communicative' language teaching: an assessment. In Strevens, P. (ed.) *In honour of A. S. Hornby*. Oxford: Oxford University Press

Brumfit, C. J. 1980. Some experimental investigation into language teaching methodology, and some of their limitations. In Brumfit, C. J. (ed.) *Problems and principles in English teaching*. Oxford: Pergamon Press: 130–7

Brumfit, C. J. 1984a. *Communicative methodology in language teaching*. Cambridge: Cambridge University Press

Brumfit, C. J. 1984b. Bangalore procedural syllabus. *ELT Journal* 38,4: 233–41

Bruner, J. S. 1960/1977. *The process of education*. Cambridge, MA: Harvard University Press

Bruner, J. S. 1973. *Beyond the information given*. Selected, edited and introduced by J. M. Anglin. New York: W. W. Norton

Bruner, J. S. 1983. *Child's talk*. Cambridge: Cambridge University Press.

Bruner, J. S. 1986. *Actual minds, possible worlds*. Cambridge, MA: Harvard University Press

Bruner, J. S., Goodnow, J. J. and Austin, G. A. 1956/1973. The process of concept attainment. *In A study in thinking*. New York: Wiley. Reprinted in Bruner, J. S. *Beyond the information given*. New York: W. W. Norton: 131–57

Bruton, A. 2002a. From tasking purposes to purposing tasks. *ELT journal* 56/.3: 280–8

Bruton, A. 2002b. When and how the language development in TBI? *ELT journal* 56.3: 296–7

Bruton, A. 2005. Process writing and communicative task-based instruction: many common features, but more common limitations? *TESL-EJ* 9.3: 1–30

Burns, A., Joyce, H. and Gollin, S. 1996. *'I see what you mean'. Using spoken discourse in the classroom: a handbook for teachers*. Sydney: NCELTR, Macquarie University

Bygate, M. 1988. Linguistic and strategic features in the language of learners in oral communication exercises. Unpublished PhD thesis, Institute of Education, University of London

Bygate, M. 1996. Effects of task repetition: appraising the developing language of learners. In Willis, D. and Willis, J. *Challenge and change in language teaching*. London: Heinemann: 36–46

Bygate, M. 1999a. Task as the context for the framing, re-framing and unframing of language. *System* 27: 33–48

Bygate, M. 1999b. Quality of language and purpose of task: patterns of learners' language on two oral communication tasks. *Language teaching research* 3: 185–214

Bygate, M. 2000. Introduction to special issue: 'Tasks in language pedagogy'. *Language Teaching Research* 4.3: 185–92

Bygate, M. 2001. Effects of task repetition on the structure and control of oral language. In Bygate, M. et al. (eds) *Researching pedagogic tasks: second language learning, teaching and testing*. Harlow: Pearson Education

Bygate, M. 2005. Research on tasks for language pedagogy: the need for a pedagogical agenda. Plenary lecture to the BAAL Language Learning and Teaching SIG, York, April

Bygate, M. and Samuda, V. 2005. Integrative planning and the use of task repetition. In Ellis, R. (ed.) *Planning and task performance in a second language*. John Benjamins

Bygate, M., Skehan, P. and Swain, M. (eds.) 2001. *Researching pedagogic tasks: second language learning, teaching and testing*. Harlow: Pearson Education.

Cameron, L. J., Moon, J. and Bygate, M. 1996. Development of bilingual pupils in the mainstream. *Language and education* 10.4: 221–36

Candlin, C. N. 1987. Towards task-based language learning. In Candlin, C. N. and Murphy, D. F. (eds.) *Language learning tasks*. Lancaster Practical Papers in English. Lancaster and London: Lancaster University

Candlin, C. N. 2001. Afterword: taking the curriculum to task. In Bygate, M., Skehan, P. and Swain, M. (eds.) *Researching pedagogic tasks: second language learning, teaching and testing*. Harlow: Pearson Education: 229–43

Candlin, C. N. and Candlin, S. (eds.) 2003. *Research on Language and Social Interaction*. Special issue, 32/June

Candlin, C. N. and Murphy, D. F. (eds.) 1987. *Language learning tasks*. Lancaster Practical Papers in English Language Education, Vol. 7. Lancaster and London: Lancaster University

Carless, D. 2004. Issues in teachers' re-interpretation of a task-based innovation in primary schools. *TESOL quarterly* 38.4: 639–62

Carter, R. and McCarthy, M. 1997. *Exploring spoken English*. Cambridge: Cambridge University Press

Clarke, H. and Wilkes-Gibbes, D. 1986. Referring as a collaborative process. *Cognition* 22: 1–39

Chomsky, N. 1958. *Syntactic structures*. The Hague: Mouton

Cohen, L., Manion, L. and Morrison, K. 2000. *Research methods in education*. New York: Routledge

Coleman, H. 1987. 'Little tasks make large return': task-based language learning in large classes. In Candlin, C. N. and Murphy, D. (eds.): *Language learning tasks*. Lancaster Practical Papers in English Language Education, Vol. 7. Lancaster and London: Lancaster University: 121–46

Cook, G. 2000. *Language play and language learning*. Oxford: Oxford University Press

Coughlan, P. and Duff, P. 1994. Same task, different activities: analysis of SLA from an activity theory perspective. In Lantolf, J. and Appel, G. *Vygotskian approaches to second language research*. Oxford: Oxford University Press

Cox, D. 2005. Can we predict language items for open tasks? In Edwards, C. and Willis, J. *Teachers exploring tasks*. Basingstoke: Palgrave Macmillan: 171–86

Crookes, G. 1989. Planning and interlanguage variation. *Studies in Second Language Acquisition* 11: 367–83

Crookes, G. and Gass, S. (eds.) 1993a. *Tasks in a pedagogical context: integrating theory and practice*. Clevedon: Multilingual Matters

Crookes, G. and Gass, S. (eds.) 1993b. *Tasks and language learning: integrating theory and practice*. Clevedon: Multilingual Matters

Cunningham, S. and Moor, P. 2005. *New cutting edge intermediate*. Harlow: Longman

Curriculum Development Council, Hong Kong 1999. *Syllabuses for secondary schools English language, secondary 1–5*. Hong Kong: Education Department

Curriculum Development Council, Hong Kong 2002. *Key learning area curriculum guide (primary 1 – secondary 3) for English Language Education*. Hong Kong: Education Department

Curriculum Development Council, Hong Kong 2004. *English language curriculum guide (primary 1–6)*. Hong Kong: Education Department

Dam, L. 1995. *Learner autonomy 3: From theory to classroom practice*. Dublin: Authentik

Dam, L. and Gabrielsen, G. 1988. Developing learner autonomy in a school context a six-year experiment beginning in the learners' first year of English. In Holec, H (ed.) *Autonomy and self-directed learning: fields of application*. Strasbourg: Council of Europe: 19–30

de Groot, A. D. 1978. *Thought and choice in chess*. The Hague: Mouton

DeKeyser, R. 2005. What makes learning second language grammar difficult? A review of issues. *Language Learning*, Special issue 2: 1–25

Dewey, J. 1910/1991. *How we think*. Amherst: Prometheus

Dewey, J. 1913/1975. *Interest and effort in education*. Arcturus Books

Dewey, J. 1938/1963. *Experience and education: The Kappa Delta Phi lecture series*. Toronto: Collier Books

Di Pietro, R. 1987. *Strategic interaction: learning languages through scenarios*. Cambridge: Cambridge University Press.

Donato, R. 1994. Collective scaffolding in second language learning. In Lantolf, J. P and Appel, G. (eds.) *Vygotskyan approaches to second language research*. Norwood NJ: Ablex

Donato, R. 2000. Sociocultural contributions to understanding the foreign and second language classroom. In Lantolf, J. P. (ed.) *Sociocultural theory and second language learning*. Oxford: Oxford University Press: 27–50

Dörnyei, Z. 2003. *Questionnaires in second language research: construction, administration and processing*. Mahwah, NJ: Lawrence Erlbaum

Dörnyei, Z. and Kormos, J. 2000. The role of individual and social variables in oral task performance. *Language Teaching Research*. Special issue, *Tasks in language pedagogy* 4/3: 275–300

Doughty, C. and Pica, T. 1986. Information gap tasks: do they facilitate second language acquisition?' *TESOL Quarterly* 10.2: 305–25

Duff, P. 1993. Tasks and interlanguage performance: an SLA research perspective In Crookes, G. and Gass, S. M. (eds) *Tasks and language learning*, Clevedon Multilingual Matters: 57–95

Dufficy, P. 2004. Predisposition to choose: the language of an information gap task in a multilingual primary classroom. *Language Teaching Research*, 8.3: 241–62

Edwards, C. 2005. Epilogue: teachers exploring research. In Edwards, C. and Willis, J. (eds.) *Teachers exploring tasks*. Basingstoke: Palgrave Macmillan: 256–67

Edwards, C. and Willis, J. (eds) 2005. *Teachers exploring tasks*. Basingstoke: Palgrave Macmillan

Eggins, S. 1990. The analysis of spoken discourse. Paper given at NCELTR Spoken Discourse Project Workshop. Sydney: NCELTR, Macquarie University

Ellis, R. 1987. Interlanguage variability in narrative discourse: style-shifting in the use of the past tense. *Studies in second language acquisition*. 9: 12–20

Ellis, R. 1995. Modified input and the acquisition of word meanings. *Applied Linguistics* 16: 409–41

Ellis, R. 2000. Task-based research and language pedagogy. *Language teaching research*. Special issue, *Tasks in language pedagogy* 4.3: 193–220

Ellis, R. 2001. Non-reciprocal tasks, comprehension and second language acquisition. In Bygate, M., Skehan, P. and Swain, M. (eds.) *Researching pedagogic tasks: second language learning, teaching and testing*. Harlow: Pearson Education: 49–74

Ellis, R. 2003. *Task-based language learning and teaching*. Oxford: Oxford University Press

Ellis, R. 2005. *Planning and task performance in a second language*. Amsterdam: John Benjamins

Ellis, R. and He, X. 1999. The roles of modified input and output in the incidental acquisition of word meanings. *Studies in second language acquisition* 21: 319–33

Ellis, R. and Heimbach, R. 1997. Bugs and birds: children's acquisition of second language vocabulary through interaction. *System* 25: 247–59

Ellis, R., Tanaka, Y. and Yamakazi, A. 1994. Classroom interaction, comprehension and the acquisition of word meanings. *Language Learning* 44: 449–91

Ellis, S. and Siegler, R. S. 1994. Development of problem solving. In Sternberg, R. J. (ed.) *Thinking and problem solving*. San Diego: Academic Press: 334–68

Engestrom, Y. and Middleton, D. (eds.) 1998a. *Cognition and communication at work*. Cambridge: Cambridge University Press

Engestrom, Y. and Middleton, D. 1998b. Introduction: studying work as mindful practice. In Engestrom, Y. and Middleton, D. (eds), *Cognition and communication at work*. Cambridge: Cambridge University Press: 1–14

Ericsson, K. A. and Hastie, R. 1994. Contemporary approaches to the study of thinking and problem solving. In Sternberg, R. J. (ed.) *Thinking and problem solving*. San Diego: Academic Press: 37–82

Estaire, S. and Zanón, J. 1994. *Planning classwork: a task based approach*. Oxford: Macmillan Heinemann

Feez, S. 1998. *Text-based syllabus design*. Sydney: Ames/NCELTR, Macquarie University

Finch, A., Sampson, K. and Park-Finch, H. 2003. *It's up to you*. Seoul: Chonghab Publishing

Foster, P. 1998. A classroom perspective on the negotiation of meaning. *Applied Linguistics* 19: 1–23

Foster, P. 2001. Rules and routines: a consideration of their role in the task-based language production of native and non-native speakers. In Bygate, M. Skehan, P. and Swain, M. (eds.) *Researching pedagogic tasks: second language learning, teaching and testing*. Harlow: Pearson Education.

Foster, P. and Ohta, A. 2005. Negotiation for meaning and peer assistance in second language classrooms *Applied Linguistics* 26: 402–30

Foster, P. and Skehan, P. 1996. The influence of planning and task type on second language performance. *Studies in second language acquisition* 18: 299–323

Fotos, S. and Ellis, R. 1992. Communicating about grammar: a task-based approach. *TESOL Quarterly* 25: 605–28

Freinet, E. 1971. *Naissance d'une pédagogie populaire*. Paris: Maspéro.

Freire, P. 1970. *Pedagogy of the oppressed*. Harmondsworth: Penguin Books

Fried-Booth, D. 1986. *Project work*. Oxford: Oxford University Press

Garrett, P. and Shortall, T. 2002. Learners' evaluations of teacher-fronted and student-centred classroom activities. *Language Teaching Research* 6.1: 25–58

Gass, S. 1997. *Input, interaction and the second language learner*. Mahwah, NJ: Lawrence Erlbaum

Gass, S. and Mackey, A. 2000. *Stimulated recall methodology in second language research*. Mahwah, NJ: Lawrence Erlbaum.

Gass, S. and Madden, C. (eds.) 1985. *Input in second language acquisition*. Rowley MA: Newbury House

Gass, S. and Varonis, E. M. 1985. Task variation and native/non-native negotiation of meaning. In Gass, S. and Madden, C. (eds) *Input in second language acquisition* Rowley, MA: Newbury House

George, H. V. 1972. *Common errors in language learning*. Rowley, MA: Newbury House

Goodwin, C. and Goodwin, M. H. 1998. Seeing as situated activity: formulating planes. In Engestrom, Y. and Middleton, D. (eds) *Cognition and communication at work*. Cambridge: Cambridge University Press: 61–95

Gorard, S., Roberts, K. and Taylor, C. 2004. What kind of creature is a design experiment? *British educational research journal*, 30: 577–90

Greenaway, R. 1995. Powerful learning experiences in management learning and development. Unpublished PhD. Lancaster University: Centre for the Study of Management Learning

Greenwood, J. 1985. Bangalore revisited: a reluctant complaint. *ELT Journal*, 39.4 268–73

Griffin, P., Cole, M. and Newman, D. 1982. Locating tasks in psychology and education. *Discourse processes* 5: 111–25

Hackman, J. R. 1969. Toward understanding the role of tasks in behavioral research *Acta psychologica* 31: 97–128

Hall, D. and Kenny, B. 1988. An approach to a truly communicative methodology the AIT pre-sessional course. *ESPJ* 7.1: 19–32

Halliday, M. A. K. 1994. *An introduction to functional grammar*. 2nd edition. London Edward Arnold

Hampshire, S. and Aguarales Anoro, M. A. 2004. The siren call of the task. *English language teaching journal* 58.1: 71–4

Harmer, J. 2001. *The practice of English language teaching*. Harlow: Longman

Hutchins, E. 1995. *Cognition in the wild*. Cambridge, MA: MIT Press

Hutchinson, T. and Waters, A. 1987. *English for specific purposes: a learning-centred approach*. Cambridge: Cambridge University Press

Izumi, S. and Bigelow, M. 2000. Does output promote noticing and second language acquisition? *TESOL Quarterly*. 34/2: 239–278

Izumi, S. and Izumi, I. 2004. Investigating the effects of oral output on the learning of relative clauses in English: issues in the psycholinguistic requirements for effective output tasks. *Canadian Modern Language Review*

Johnson, K. 1979. Communicative approaches and communicative processes. In Brumfit, C. J. and Johnson, K. (eds) *The communicative approach to language teaching*. Oxford: Oxford University Press

Johnson, K. 1996. *Language teaching and skill learning*. Oxford: Blackwell

Johnson, K. 2000. What task designers do. *Language teaching research* 4.3: 301–21

Johnson, K. 2003. *Designing language teaching tasks*. Basingstoke: Palgrave Macmillan

Johnston, C. 2005. Fighting fossilization: language at the task versus report stages. In Edwards, C. and Willis, J. (eds.) *Teachers exploring tasks*. Basingstoke: Palgrave Macmillan: 191–200

Kahan, L. D. and Richards, D. D. 1986. The effects of context on referential communication strategies. *Child development* 57: 1130–41

Kasper, G. and Kellerman, E. (eds.) 1997. *Communication strategies. Psycholinguistics and sociolinguistic perspectives*. Harlow: Longman

Kellerman, E. and van Hoof, A. M. 2003. Manual accents. *IRAL* 41: 251–69

Kelly, G. A. 1955. *Theory of personality: The psychology of personal constructs*. New York: W. W. Norton

Kilpatrick, W. H. 1918/1922. The project method: the use of the purposeful act in the educative process. New York: Teachers College, Columbia University: 3–18. Reprinted from *Teachers college record* XIX.4: September 1918

Koenraad, T. and Westhoff, G. 2003. Can you tell a LanguageQuest when you see one? Design criteria for Talenquests. Paper presented at EUROCALL, Limerick, Ireland

Kohonen, V. 2001. Towards experiential foreign language education. In Kohonen, V., Jaatinen, R., Kaikkonen, P. and Lehtovaara, J. (eds.) *Experiential learning in foreign language education*. Harlow: Pearson Education: 8–60

Kohonen, V., R. Jaatinen, P. Kaikkonen and J. Lehtovaara (eds.) 2001. *Experiential learning in foreign language education*. Harlow: Pearson Education

Kolb, D. 1984. *Experiential learning: experience as the source of learning and development*. Englewood Cliffs, NJ: Prentice-Hall

Kramsch, C. 2005. Post 9/11: foreign languages between knowledge and power. *Applied Linguistics* 26/4: 545–67

Krauss, R. and Weinheimer, S. 1964. Changes in references as a function of frequency of usage in social interaction: a preliminary study. *Psychonomic Science* 1: 113–14

Kumaravadivelu, B. 1993. The name of a task and the task of naming: methodological aspects of task-based pedagogy. In Crookes, G. and Gass, S. (eds.) *Tasks in a pedagogical context: integrating theory and practice*. Clevedon: Multilingual Matters: 69–96

Kumaravadivelu, B. 1994. The postmethod condition: merging strategies for second/foreign language teaching. *TESOL quarterly* 28: 27–48

Kumaravadivelu, B. 2001. Towards a postmethod pedagogy. *TESOL quarterly* 35: 537–60

Labov, W. 1972. *Sociolinguistic patterns*. Oxford: Blackwell

Labov, W. and Waletzky, J. 1967. Narrative analysis. In Helm, J. (ed.) *Essays on the Verbal and Visual Arts*. Seattle: University of Washington Press: 12–44

Lam, W. Y. K. 2004. Teaching strategy use for oral communication tasks to ESL learners. Unpublished PhD thesis. School of Education: University of Leeds

Lam, W. Y. K., Littlewood, W., Luk, J. C. M., Ma, A., Pang, M. Y. M. and Wong, R. H. M. 2005. *Attention to language knowledge and attention to language use within the English language curriculum*. Funded project: Department of English, Hong Kong Institute of Education

Lantolf, J. P. 2000. Introducing sociocultural theory. In Lantolf, J. P. (ed.) *Sociocultural theory and second language learning*. Oxford: Oxford University Press: 1–26

Larsen-Freeman, D. (series director) 2000. *Grammar dimensions: form, meaning, use*. Books 1–4: Platinum Edition. Boston, MA: Heinle & Heinle

Laufer, E. A. and Glick, J. 1998. Expert and novice differences in cognition and activity: a practical work activity. In Engestrom, Y. and Middleton, D. (eds) *Cognition and communication at work*. Cambridge: Cambridge University Press: 177–98

Lave, J. 1990. The culture of acquisition and the practice of understanding. In Stigler, J. W., Shweder, R. A. and Herdt, G. (eds.), *Cultural psychology*. Cambridge: Cambridge University Press: 259–86

Lave, J. and Wenger, E. 1991. *Situated learning – legitimate peripheral participation*, Cambridge: Cambridge University Press

Leaver, B. L. and Kaplan, M.A. 2004. Task-based instruction in US government Slavic language programs. In Leaver, B. L. and Willis, J. (eds) *Task-based instruction in foreign language education*. Washington DC: Georgetown University Press: 47–66

Leaver, B. L. and Willis, J. (eds) 2004. *Task-based instruction in foreign language education*. Washington DC: Georgetown University Press

Lee, J. F. 2000. *Tasks and communicating in language classrooms*. Boston, MA: McGraw-Hill

Legutke, M. and Thomas, H. 1991. *Process and experience in the language classroom*. Harlow: Longman

Leung, C. 2001. Evaluation of content learning in the mainstream classroom. In Mohan, B., Leung, C. and Davison, C. (eds.) *English as a second language in the mainstream: teaching, learning and identity*. Harlow: Pearson Education

Levelt, W. M. 1978. Skill theory and language teaching. *Studies in second language acquisition*. 1/1:53–70

Levelt, W. J. M. 1989. *Speaking: from intention to articulation*. Cambridge, MA: MIT

Lewin, K. 1951. *Field theory in social science*. New York: HarperCollins

Linde, C. and Labov, W. 1975. Spatial networks as a site for the study of language and thought. *Language* 51: 924–39

Littlewood, W. 2004. The task-based approach: some questions and suggestions. *ELT Journal* 58.4: 319–26

Littlewood, W. 2007. Communicative and task-based learning in East Asian classrooms. *Language Teaching*. 40:243–249

Long, M. H. 1981. Input, interaction and second language acquisition. *Annals of New York Academy of Sciences:* 259–78

Long, M. H. 1985. A role for instruction in second language acquisition: task-based language training. In Hyltenstam, K. and Pienemann, M. *Modelling and assessing second language acquisition*. Clevedon: Multilingual Matters

Long, M. H. 1989. Task, group and task-group interactions. *University of Hawaii Working Papers in ESL* 8.2: 1–26

Long, M. 1996. The role of the linguistic environment in second language acquisition. In Ritchie, W. and Bhatia, T. (eds.) *Handbook of second language acquisition*. San Diego: Academic Press: 413–68

Long, M. H. 2005. TBLT: building the road as we travel. Plenary address, 1st International Conference on Task-based Language Teaching, University of Leuven

Long, M. H. 1997. Focus on form in task-based language teachin'. Fourth Annual McGraw-Hill Satellite Conference. http://www.mhhe.com/socscience/foreignlang/conf/task1.htm. Accessed September 2006

Long, M. H. and Crookes, G. 1992. Three approaches to task-based syllabus design. *TESOL quarterly* 26: 27–56

Long, M. and Crookes, G. 1993. Units of analysis in syllabus design: the case for task. In Crookes, G. and Gass, S. M. (eds.) *Tasks in a pedagogical context.* Clevedon, Avon: Multilingual Matters: 9–54

Long, M. H. and Robinson, P. 1998. Focus on form: theory, research, practice. In Doughty, C. and Williams, J. (eds) *Focus on form in second language acquisition.* Cambridge: Cambridge University Press: 15–41

Loschky, L. and Bley-Vroman, R. 1993. Grammar and task-based methodology. In Crookes, G. and Gass, S. M. (eds) *Tasks in language learning.* Clevedon: Multilingual Matters: 123–67

Loumpourdi, L. 2005. Developing from PPP to TBL: a focused grammar task. In Edwards, C. and Willis, J. *Teachers exploring tasks.* Basingstoke: Palgrave Macmillan: 33–9

Lynch, T. and Maclean, J. 2000. Exploring the benefits of task repetition and recycling for classroom language learning. *Language Teaching Research.* Special issue, *Tasks in language pedagogy* 4.3: 221–50

Lynch, T. and Maclean, J. 2001. A case of exercising: effects of immediate task repetition on learners' performance'. In Bygate, M., Skehan, P. and Swain, M. (eds.) *Researching pedagogic tasks: second language learning, teaching and testing.* Harlow: Pearson Education

Mackey, A. 1999. Input, interaction and second language development: an empirical study of question formation in ESL. *Studies in second language acquisition* 21.4: 557–89

Mackey, A. and McDonough, K. 1998. *Tasks for communication and grammar: Thai and Japanese.* Ann Arbor, MI: Center for Language Education and Development, Michigan State University Press

Mangubhai, F. 1991. The processing behaviours of adult second language learners and their relationships to second language proficiency. *Applied linguitics* 12.3: 268–98

McDonough, K. 2006. Interaction and syntactic priming. English L2 speakers' production of dative constructions. *Studies in second language acquisition* 28: 179–207

McDonough, K. and Mackey, A. 2000. Communicative tasks, conversational interaction and linguistic form: an empirical study of Thai. *Foreign language annals* 33: 82–92

McEldowney, P. 1982. *English in context. Learning materials.* Walton-on-Thames: Nelson

Mohan, B. 1986. *Language and content.* Reading, MA: Addison-Wesley

Mohan, M. and Marshall Smith, S. 1992. Context and cooperation in academic tasks. In Nunan, D. (ed.) *Collaborative language learning and teaching.* Cambridge: Cambridge University Press: 81–99

Mohan, B., Leung, C. and Davison, C. (eds.) 2000. *English as a second language in the mainstream: teaching, learning and identity.* London: Longman

Mok, A. (ed.) 2003. *Task-based English learning: interactive resource materials*. Hong Kong: Hong Kong Institute of Education

Moore, J. 1979. *Reading and thinking in English: discovering discourse*. Oxford: Oxford University Press.

Moore J. 1980. *Reading and thinking in English: discourse in action*. Oxford: Oxford University Press.

Mori, J. 2002. Task design, plan and development of talk-in-interaction: an analysis of a small group activity in a Japanese language classroom. *Applied Linguistics* 23.3.

Morrow, K. 1980. *Skills for reading: with extracts from New Scientist*. Oxford: Oxford University Press

Muller, T. 2005. Adding tasks to textbooks for beginner learners. In Edwards, C. and Willis, J. *Teachers exploring tasks*. Basingstoke: Palgrave Macmillan: 69–77

Munby, J. 1978. *Communicative syllabus design*. Cambridge: Cambridge University Press

Murphy, D. 1993. Evaluating language learning tasks in the classroom. In Crookes, G. and Gass, S. M. (eds) *Tasks and language learning: integrating theory and practice*. Clevedon: Multilingual Matters: 139–161

Nakahama, Y., Tyler, A. and van Lier, L. 2001. Negotiation of meaning in conversational and information gap activities. *TESOL quarterly* 35.3: 377–406

Newton, J. and Kennedy, G. 1996. Effects of communication tasks on the grammatical relations marked by second language learners. *System* 24.3: 309–322

Nunan, D. 1989. *Designing tasks for the communicative classroom*. Cambridge: Cambridge University Press

Nunan, D. 1991. Communicative tasks and the language curriculum. *TESOL quarterly* 25.2: 279–96

Nunan, D. 1995. *Atlas: learning-centred communication*. Boston, MA: Heinle & Heinle

Nunan, D. 2001. *Expressions*. Boston, MA: Heinle & Heinle

Nunan, D. 2004. *Task-based language teaching*. Cambridge: Cambridge University Press

Ohta, A. S. 2001. *Second language acquisition processes in the classroom: learning Japanese*. Mahwah, NJ: Lawrence Erlbaum

Oliver, R. 1999. Exploring strategies for on-line teaching and learning. *Distance Education* 20.2: 240–54

Oliver, R. and Herrington, J. 2001. *Teaching and learning online: a beginner's guide to e-learning and e-teacher in higher education*. Perth: Edith Cowan University

Ortega, L. 2005. What do learners plan? Learner-driven attention to form during pre-task planning. In R. Ellis (ed.), *Planning and task performance in a second language*. Amsterdam: John Benjamins: 77–110

Oxford, R., Cho, Y., Leung, S. and Kim, H.-J. 2004. Effect of the presence and difficulty of task on strategy use: and exploratory study. *IRAL* 42: 1–47

Pepinsky, H. B. and Pepinsky, P. N. 1961. Organization, management strategy, and team productivity. In L. Petrullo, L. and B. M. Bass (eds) *Leadership and interpersonal behavior*. New York: Holt. Cited in Hackman, J. R. 1969. Toward understanding the role of tasks in behavioral research. *Acta psychologica* 31: 97–128

Peters, A. 1983. *The units of language acquisition*. Cambridge: Cambridge University Press

Pfeiffer, W. and Jones, J. E. 1975. *A handbook of structured experiences for human relations training*. Vols 1–5. La Jolla, CA: University Associates

Piaget, J. and Inhelder, B. 1956. *The child's conception of space*. New York: W. W. Norton.

Pica, T. 2005. Classroom learning, teaching, and research: a task-based perspective. *Modern language journal*. 89/3: 339–52

Pica, T. and Doughty, C. 1985. Input and interaction in the communicative language classroom: a comparison of teacher-fronted and group activities. In Gass, S. and Madden, C. (eds.) *Input in second language acquisition*. Rowley, MA: Newbury House

Pica, T., Kanagy, R. and Falodun, J. 1993. Choosing and using communication tasks for second language instruction. In Crookes, G. and Gass, S. (eds.) *Tasks and language learning: integrating theory and practice*. Clevedon: Multilingual Matters

Plough, I. and Gass, S. 1993. Interlocutor and task familiarity: effects on interactional structure. In Crookes, G. and Gass, S. (eds.) *Tasks and language learning: integrating theory and practice*. Clevedon: Multilingual Matters: 35–56

Prabhu, N. S. 1987. *Second language pedagogy*. Oxford: Oxford University Press

Pullin Stark, P. 2005. Integrating task-based instruction into a business English programme. In Edwards, C. and Willis, J. *Teachers exploring tasks*. Basingstoke: Palgrave Macmillan: 40–9

Rampton, B. 1995. *Crossing: language and ethnicity among adolescents*. London: Longman

Ribé, R. and Vidal, N. 1993. *Project work step by step*. Oxford: Macmillan Heinemann

Richards, J. C. 2005. *Communicative language teaching today*. RELC Portfolio Series 13. Singapore: SEAMEO Regional Language Centre

Richards, J. C., Hull, J. and Proctor, S. 1997/2005. *New interchange: English for international communication*. Cambridge: Cambridge University Press

Riggenbach, H. 1999. *Discourse analysis in the language classroom: the spoken language*. Ann Arbor, MI: University of Michigan Press

Riggenbach, H. and Samuda, V. 2000. *Grammar dimensions: form, meaning, use*. Book 2. Boston, MA: Heinle & Heinle

Rinvolucri, M. 2002. *Humanising your coursebook*, Delta Books

Roberts, J. 1999. Personal construct psychology as a framework for research into teacher and learner thinking. *Language teaching research* 3.2: 117–44

Robinson, P. 1995. Task complexity and second language narrative discourse. *Language learning* 45.1: 99–140

Robinson, P. 2001. Task complexity, task difficulty, and task productions: exploring interactions in a componential framework. *Applied linguistics* 22: 27–57

Robinson, P. 2006. Second language speech production research: processing stages, task demands, individual differences and the assessment of proficiency. Paper presented in the colloquium 'Current issues in second language production research', at the annual conference of AAAL/CAAL, Montreal, June

Robson, C. 2002. *Real world research* 2/e. Oxford: Blackwell.

Rogers, Y. and Ellis, J. 1994. Distributed cognition: an alternative framework for analysing and explaining collaborative working. *Journal of information technology* 9 (2): 119–28

Rogoff, B. 1990. *Apprenticeship in thinking:* New York: Oxford University Press

Samuda, V. 2001. Guiding relationships between form and meaning during task performance: the role of the teacher. In Bygate, M., Skehan, P. and Swain, M. (eds.) *Researching pedagogic tasks: second language learning, teaching and testing*. Harlow: Pearson Education

Samuda, V. 2005. Expertise in second language pedagogic task design. In Johnson, K. *Expertise in language teaching*. Basingstoke: Palgrave Macmillan

Samuda, V. 2006. Teaching to the task: exploring the boundaries between task-as-workplan and task-in-process. Paper presented at AAAL, Montreal

Samuda, V., Johnson, K. and Ridgway, J. 2000. *Designing language learning tasks: a guide*. Vol. 1. Working Papers on Task Design. Lancaster: Department of Linguistics and English Language. Lancaster University

Schleppegrell, M. J. 2004. *The language of schooling*. Mahwah, NJ: Lawrence Erlbaum.

Scott, M. R. 1981. *Read in English*, London and New York: Longman

Seedhouse, P. 1999. Task-based interaction. *ELT journal* 53.3: 149–56

Seedhouse, P. 2005. 'Task' as research construct. *Language learning* 55.3: 533–70

Sheen, R. 1994. A critical analysis of the advocacy of the task-based syllabus. *TESOL quarterly* 28.1: 127–51

Shehadeh, A. 2005. Task-based language learning and teaching: theories and applications. In Edwards, C. and Willis, J. *Teachers exploring tasks*. Basingstoke: Palgrave Macmillan: 13–30

Sien, C.L. 2005. An investigation into the acquisition of simple past regular and irregular verb morphology produced by a group of L1 Chinese learners. Unpublished MA dissertation. Department of Linguistics and English Language: Lancaster University

Skehan, P. 1996. A framework for the implementation of task-based instruction. *Applied linguistics* 71.1: 38–62

Skehan, P. 1998. *A cognitive approach to language learning*. Oxford: Oxford University Press

Skehan, P. 2001. Tasks and language performance assessment. In Bygate, M., Skehan, P. and Swain, M. (eds.) *Researching pedagogic tasks: second language learning, teaching and testing*. Harlow: Pearson Education

Skehan, P. 2002. A non-marginal role for tasks. *ELT journal* 56.3: 289–95

Skehan, P. 2003. Review article: task-based learning. *Language teaching*

Skehan, P. and Foster, P. 1997. Task type and task processing conditions as influences on foreign language performance. *Language teaching research* 1.3: 185–211

Skehan, P. and Foster, P. 1999 The influence of task structure and processing conditions on narrative retellings. *Language Learning* 49.1: 93–120

Skehan, P. and Foster, P. 2005. Strategic and on-line planning: the influence of surprise information and task time on second language performance. In R. Ellis (ed.) *Planning and task performance in a second language*. John Benjamins: 193–216

Slade, D. and Thornbury, S. 2006. *Conversation: From description to pedagogy*. Cambridge: Cambridge University Press

Slimani, A. 1992. Evaluation of classroom interaction. In Alderson, J.C. and Beretta, A. *Evaluating second language education*. Cambridge: Cambridge University Press

Slimani-Rolls, A. 2005. Practitioner research: Rrethinking task-based language learning: what we can learn from the learners. *Language Teaching Research* 9.2: 195–218

Snow, C., Cancino, H., Gonazalez, P. and Shriberg, E. 1989. Second language learners' formal definitions: an oral language correlate of school literacy. In D. Bloome (ed.) *Literacy in functional settings*. Norwood, NJ: Ablex

Snow, M. A. and Brinton, D. (eds.) 1997. *The content-based classroom: perspectives on integrating language and content*. New York: Addison Wesley Longman ong, J-W. 2000. The effect of selected processing conditions on spoken language performance on a narrative task. Unpublished PhD thesis: School of Education, University of Leeds

Stevens, V. 2004. Webhead communities: writing tasks interleaved with synchronous online communication and web page development. In Leaver, B. J. and Willis, J. (eds.) *Task-based instruction in foreign language education*. Washington, DC: Georgetown University Press: 204–27

Swain, M. and Lapkin, S. 2000. Task-based second language learning: the uses of the first language. *Language teaching research*. Special issue, *Tasks in language pedagogy* 4.3: 251–74

Swain, M. and Lapkin, S. 2001. Focus on form through collaborative dialogue: exploring task effects. In Bygate, M., Skehan, P. and Swain, M. (eds.) *Researching pedagogic tasks: second language learning, teaching and testing*. Harlow: Pearson Education

Swales, J. 1990. *Genre analysis: English in academic and research settings*. Cambridge: Cambridge University Press

Swan, M. 2005. Legislation by hypothesis: the case of task-based instruction. *Applied linguistics* 26.3: 376–401

Tannen, D. 1980. A comparative analysis of oral narrative strategies. In W. L. Chafe (ed.) *The pear stories: Cognitive, cultural and linguistic aspects of narrative production*. Norwood, NJ: Ablex: 51–87

Tarone, E. 1988. *Variation in interlanguage*. London: Edward Arnold

TeleNex http://www.telenex.hku.hk/telec

Thornbury, S. 2005. Dogme: Dancing in the dark? *Folio* 9.2 Supplement

Thornbury, S. 2000. A dogma for EFL. *IATEFL Issues* 153, February/March

Tinker Sachs, G., Candlin, C., Rose, K. and Shum, S. 2000. Developing cooperative learning in the EFL/ESL secondary classroom. *Perspectives* 12.1: 178–231

Tomasello, M. 2003. *Constructing a language. A usage-based theory of language acquisition*. Cambridge, MA: Harvard University Press

Tsui, A. 2003. *Understanding expertise in teaching: case studies of ESL teachers*. Cambridge: Cambridge University Press

Ur, P. 1982. *Discussions that work*. Cambridge: Cambridge University Press

Ur, P. and Wright, A. 1992. *Five-minute activities: a resource book of short activities*. Cambridge: Cambridge University Press

Van Avermaet, P., Colpin, M., Van Gorp, K., Bogaert, N. and Van den Branden, K. 2006. The role of the teacher in TBLT. In Van den Branden, K. (ed.) *Task-based language teaching: from theory to practice*. Cambridge: Cambridge University Press

Van den Branden, K. (ed.) 2006a. *Task-based language teaching: from theory to practice*. Cambridge: Cambridge University Press

Van den Branden, K. 2006b. Introduction: Task-based language teaching in a nutshell. In Van den Branden, K (ed.) *Task-based language teaching: from theory to practice*. Cambridge: Cambridge University Press

Van den Branden, K. 2006c. Training teachers: task-based as well? In Van den Branden, K (ed.) *Task-based language teaching: from theory to practice*. Cambridge: Cambridge University Press

VanPatten, B. 1996. *Input processing and grammar instruction*. Norwood, NJ: Ablex

Van Lier, L. 1996. *Interaction in the language curriculum: awareness, autonomy, and authenticity*. London: Longman

Wallerstein, N. 1983. *Language and culture in conflict: problem-posing in the ESL classroom*. Reading, MA: Addison-Wesley

Wells, G. 1981. *Learning through interaction: the study of language development*. Cambridge: Cambridge University Press

Wells, G. 1985. *Language development in the pre-school years*. Cambridge: Cambridge University Press

Wertsch, J. V. 1985. *Culture, communication and cognition: Vygotskian perspectives*. Cambridge: Cambridge University Press

White, R. V. 1978. *Functional English 1*. Walton-on-Thames: Nelson

White, R. V. 1979. *Functional English 2*. Walton-on-Thames: Nelson

Widdowson, H. G. 1978. *Teaching language as communication*. Oxford: Oxford University Press

Widdowson, H. G. 1979–80. *Reading and thinking in English*. Oxford: Oxford University Press

Williams, J., Inscoe, R. and Tasker, T. 1997. Communication strategies in an interactional context: the mutual achievement of comprehension. In Kasper, G. and Kellerman E. (eds.) *Communication strategies. Psycholinguistics and sociolinguistic perspectives*. Harlow: Longman: 304–22

Willis, J. 1996. *A framework for task-based learning*. Harlow: Addison Wesley Longman

Willis, J. 2004. Perspectives on task-based instruction: understanding our practices, acknowledging different practitioners. In Leaver, J. and Willis J. *Task-based instruction in foreign language education*. Washington, DC: Georgetown University Press: 3–44

Willis, J. 2006. Adapt your textbook for task-based teaching. IATEFL conference, Harrogate

Willis, D. and Willis, J. 1988. *The Collins co-build English course*. London: Collins

Willis, D. and Willis, J. 2007. *Doing task-based teaching*. Oxford: Oxford University Press

Woods, D. 1996. *Teacher cognition in language teaching: beliefs, decision-making and classroom practice*. Cambridge: Cambridge University Press

Yuan, F. and Ellis, R. 2003. The effects of pre-task planning and on-line planning on fluency, complexity and accuracy in L2 monologic oral production. *Applied linguistics* 24/1: 1–27

Yule, G. 1997. *Referential communication tasks*. Mahwah, NJ: Lawrence Erlbaum

Yule, G. and MacDonald, D. 1990. Resolving referential conflicts in L2 interaction: the effect of proficiency and interactive role. *Language learning* 40.4: 539–56

Yule, G., Powers, M. and MacDonald, D. 1992. The variable effects of some task-based learning procedures on communicative effectiveness. *Language learning* 42: 249–77

Yule, G. and Tarone, E. 1991. The other side of the page: integrating communication strategies and negotiated input in SLA. In R. Phillipson, E. Kellerman, L. Selinker, M. Sharwood Smith and M. Swain (eds) *Foreign/Second Language Pedagogy Research*: 177–96. Clevedon, Avon: Multilingual Matters

Name Index

Ada, A. F.   28, 224, 277
Aguarales Anoro, M. A.   195, 283
Aljaafreh, A.   93, 277
Allwright, R. L.   52, 277
Anderson, A.   60, 277, 278
Appel, G.   280
Arndt, V.   234, 277
Artigal, J. M.   223, 277
Aston, G.   58, 151, 277
Auerbach, E. R.   27, 28, 224, 277
Austin, G. A.   43, 83, 85, 127, 278

Baddeley, A.   42, 277
Barnes, D.   18, 32, 33, 34, 102, 118,
    119, 222, 244, 269, 277
Beckett, G.H.   224, 225, 277
Bereiter, C.   67, 277
Beretta, A.   200, 277, 289
Bialystok, E.   44, 45, 277
Bigelow, M.   127, 283
Biggs, J 209, 278
Blake, R. J.   118, 127, 278
Bley-Vroman, R.   91, 99, 285
Bogaert, N.   54, 211, 290
Bongaerts, T.   45, 46, 278
Breen, M. P.   10, 49, 52, 57, 61, 65,
    257, 278
Brindley, G.   59, 278
Brinton, D.   54, 55, 278, 289
Brown, G.   104, 238, 279
Brumfit, C. J.   52, 59, 126, 200, 203,
    268, 278, 283
Bruner, J.S.   18, 29, 30ff, 42ff, 47,
    74ff, 79, 80, 83, 85, 114, 127, 149,
    221, 258, 268, 278, 291
Bruton, A.   58, 203, 278
Burns, A.   238, 239, 279
Bygate, M.   56, 59, 60, 61, 62, 64, 88,
    95, 99, 100, 101, 102, 114, 115,
    125, 126, 182, 183, 196, 219, 262,
    267, 279, 281, 282, 285, 288, 289

Cameron, L. J.   56, 240, 263, 279
Campoy, I.   28, 224, 277

Cancino, H.   46, 289
Candlin, C. N.   52, 57, 63, 64, 209,
    267, 278, 279, 280, 290
Carless, D.   195, 205, 254, 279
Carter, R.   238, 239, 289
Chomsky, N.   151, 289
Clarke, H.   45, 289
Cohen, L. 258, 289
Cole, M.   48, 49, 292
Coleman, H.   200, 280
Colpin, M.   54, 211, 290
Cook, G.   58, 221, 280
Coughlan, P.   49, 50, 93, 119, 280
Cox, D.   207, 280
Crookes, G.   58, 60, 113, 169, 196,
    200ff, 206, 207, 209, 214, 267,
    280, 285, 286, 287
Cunningham, S.   214, 215, 280
Curriculum Development Council,
    Hong Kong 57, 209, 280

Dam, L.   27, 224, 280
Davies, A.   200, 277
de Groot, A. D.   37, 290
DeKeyser, R.   251, 290
Dewey, J.   1, 18, 19, 20, 21, 25, 28,
    29, 32, 35, 36, 61, 71, 74, 75, 121,
    220, 221, 268, 280
DiPietro, R.J.   146, 280
Donato, R.   49, 88, 118, 127, 133,
    134, 136, 137, 138, 139, 145–51,
    152, 190, 241, 280
Dörnyei, Z.   127, 258, 280
Doughty, C.   58, 110, 116, 127, 280,
    287
Duff, P.   49, 50, 93, 119, 280
Dufficy, P.   54, 99, 101, 102, 281

Edwards, C.   207, 268, 280, 281, 283
Eggins, S.   238, 282
Ellis, J.   40, 288
Ellis, R.   59, 62, 64, 65, 66, 67, 68,
    69, 90, 92, 96, 113, 122, 123, 126,
    127, 133, 135, 137, 138, 139, 162,

Subject Index